MEASURING
ROI
IN LEARNING &
DEVELOPMENT

Case Studies from Global Organizations

Patricia Pulliam Phillips
and Jack J. Phillips, editors

ROI INSTITUTE™

ASTD Press is an internationally renowned source of insightful and practical information on workplace learning and performance topics, including training basics, evaluation and return on investment, instructional systems development, e-learning, leadership, and career development. Visit us at www.astd.org/astdpress.

Ordering information: Books published by ASTD Press can be purchased by visiting our website at store.astd.org or by calling 800.628.2783 or 703.683.8100.

Library of Congress Control Number: 2011943854
ISBN-10: 1-56286-799-7
ISBN-13: 978-1-56286-799-7

ASTD Press Editorial Staff:
Director: Anthony Allen
Senior Manager, Production & Editorial: Glenn Saltzman
Community of Practice Manager, Learning & Development: Juana Llorens
Associate Editor: Ashley McDonald
Associate Editor: Heidi Smith
Editorial Assistant: Stephanie Castellano

Editorial, Design, and Production: Abella Publishing Services, LLC
Cover Design: Mazin Abdelgader

Printed by Versa Press, Inc., East Peoria, IL, www.versapress.com

Contents

Preface

Since the publication of volume 1 of ASTD's *In Action* series, titled *Measuring Return on Investment,* the interest in measuring the return on investment (ROI) in training and performance improvement has grown exponentially. Volume 1 filled an important void in the training literature. Published in 1994, it remains one of ASTD's all-time bestsellers. This new publication places emphasis on the international arena with case studies from a dozen different countries.

In our visits to more than 25 countries each year, we have been impressed with the work with ROI outside the United States. We also have noticed that the issues involved in creating, developing, and sustaining a comprehensive evaluation system are similar from one country to another.

This publication includes global case studies that are at the forefront of measurement and evaluation. It introduces more examples of how ROI is being applied in a variety of settings and countries. The authors of these case studies are diligently pursuing accountability in learning and performance improvement programs. Through their writing, they share their experiences with a process that continues to be at the forefront of measurement and evaluation.

TARGET AUDIENCES

This book should interest anyone involved in learning and development, human resources (HR), and performance improvement. The primary audience is practitioners who are struggling to determine the value of programs and to show how programs contribute to the strategic goals of an organization. They are the ones who request more real-world examples around the globe. The same group also expresses concern that there are too many models, methods, strategies, and theories and too few examples to show whether any of them have really made a difference. This publication should satisfy practitioners' needs by providing successful examples of the implementation of comprehensive evaluation processes in a global setting.

The second audience consists of facilitators and professors. Whether they choose this book for university-level students who are pursuing degrees in human resources development (HRD), internal workshops for professional learning and development staff members, or public seminars on learning and development implementation, this casebook will be a valuable reference. It can be used as a supplement to a standard HRD, HR, or performance improvement textbook. In our workshops on ROI in learning and performance improvement, we use casebooks as supplements to other books supporting our ROI Methodology. This combination of text and casebook offers the technical details of the measurement and evaluation process along with examples of practical applications, which together show participants that the measurement and evaluation process makes a difference.

Our third audience is made up of the researchers and consultants who are seeking ways to document results from programs. This book provides additional insight into how to satisfy clients with impressive results. It shows the application of the leading process on ROI evaluation for learning and performance improvement—a process based on sound theory and logical assumptions. The methodology prescribed in these examples follows a set of standards that ensure reliable, valid results.

The last audience is the managers who must work with learning and development on a peripheral basis—managers who are participants in learning and development programs intended to develop their own management skills, managers who send other employees to participate in learning and development programs, and managers who occasionally lead or conduct sessions of learning and development programs. In these roles, managers must understand the process and appreciate the value of learning and development, HR, and performance improvement. This casebook should provide evidence of this value.

Each audience should find the casebook entertaining and engaging reading. Although in some cases the case study authors faced challenges with securing ideal response rates to follow-up, as well as achieving desired thresholds, in others, the studies show programs to be successful beyond expectations. In all cases, lessons were learned and improvements in the programs and the evaluation process were made. Discussion questions appear at the end of each case to stimulate additional thought and discussion. One of the most effective ways to maximize the usefulness of this book is through group discussions, using the questions to develop and dissect the issues, techniques, methodologies, and results.

THE CASES

The most difficult part of developing this book was to identify the "best" case studies—those that proved to be flawless. We did find that there were many willing authors with successful applications. We pared down our selection based on challenges faced and overcome, lessons learned, and the variety of programs, industries, and countries represented. Most selected case studies have adhered to the standards supporting the ROI Methodology. Some have attempted to adhere to the standards, noting lessons learned by not doing so. We are pleased with the studies presented in this volume and believe that those who have followed the progress with ROI use will find them a nice addition to the more than 100 ROI case studies published to date.

Although there was some attempt to structure cases similarly, they are not identical in style and content. It is important for the reader to experience the case studies as they were developed in order to identify the issues pertinent to each particular setting and situation. The result is a variety of presentations with a variety of styles. Some cases are brief and to the point, outlining precisely what happened and what was achieved. Others provide more detailed background information, including how the need for the program was determined, the personalities involved, and how their backgrounds and biases created a unique situation. In addition, while all case studies have been translated into English, we have tried to leave the nuances of the various languages and cultures intact. Where translation has not occurred, case study authors have attempted to describe the elements and issues in the text.

In some cases, the name of the organization is identified, as are the individuals who were involved. In others, the organization's name is disguised at the request of either the organization or the case study author. In today's competitive world and in situations where there is an attempt to explore new territory, it is understandable that an organization would choose not to be identified. Identification should not be a critical issue, however.

CASE AUTHORS

It would be difficult to find a more impressive group of contributors than those for this casebook. The authors presented in this book are experienced, professional, knowledgeable, and on the leading edge of learning and development and performance improvement. Collectively, they represent practitioners, consultants, researchers, and professors. Individually, they represent a cross section of the learning and development field. Some authors have a global presence, others are renowned within their own countries, and still others are making their mark quietly, achieving success within their organizations. All of them are or will be highly successful in their fields.

BEST PRACTICES?

In our search for cases, we contacted the most respected and well-known organizations in the world, leading experts in the field, chief learning officers, and prominent authors and researchers. We were seeking examples that represent best practices in measurement and evaluation. Have they been delivered? We will leave that up to you, the reader. What we do know is that if these are not best practices, no other publication can claim to have them either. These are excellent examples of real attempts to show value for the learning investment.

SUGGESTIONS

We welcome your input. If you have ideas or recommendations regarding presentation, case selection, or case quality, please send them to us at ROI Institute, Inc., P.O. Box 380637, Birmingham, AL 30543 or send them via email to patti@roiinstitute.net.

ACKNOWLEDGMENTS

Although this casebook is a collective work of many individuals, the first acknowledgment must go to all the case authors. They are appreciated not only for their commitment to developing their case studies, but also for their interest in furthering the development and implementation of ROI evaluation in their organizations. We also want to acknowledge the organizations that have allowed us to use their names and programs for publication. We realize this action is not without risk. We trust the final product has portrayed them as progressive organizations interested in results and willing to try new processes and techniques.

Many thanks go to the publishing team at ASTD for their willingness to publish our work. We are proud of our many publications with ASTD and look forward to continuing our partnership as we work together to develop new content for learning and development professionals worldwide.

We would also like to thank our team at the ROI Institute and their continued support and tireless effort to make all of our publications successful. Particular thanks go to the team for putting out fires and taking care of business as we embark on our many endeavors.

Patricia Pulliam Phillips
patti@roiinstitute.net

Jack J. Phillips
jack@roiinstitute.net

TABLE 1   Overview of Case Studies by Country, Industry, Program, and Target Audience

Case Study	Chapter Number	Country	Industry	Program	Target Audience
NSW Community Services	1	Australia	Federal government	Staff and management development	Underrepresented staff and their managers
Chemical Company	2	Germany	Chemicals	Value-based selling and negotiations	Sales managers Sales professionals
PolyWrighton	3	USA	Plastics	Management learning program	Managers
Nova Scotia Public Service Commission	4	Canada	Federal government	Management development	Managers with policy-related responsibilities
XYZ County	5	USA	Local government	Conflict management skills training	Supervisors
Aircraft Maintenance Company	6	Ireland	Aviation	Business processes training	Technicians Supervisors
HortResearch	7	New Zealand	Government-owned research institute	Leadership development and coaching	Team leaders Senior leaders
Home Town Care	8	USA	Healthcare	LEAN manufacturing training	Healthcare staff Project leads
Premier Retail	9	South Africa	Retail	Store operations development	Store managers
Garanti Bank	10	Turkey	Banking	Business performance management	Branch manager candidates
Wyeth Pharmaceuticals	11	USA	Pharmaceuticals	Online English as a second language	High potential employees
Telecommunications Company	12	Chile	Telecommunications	Consultative sales training	Account managers
Global Consulting, Inc.	13	USA	Consulting	Knowledge management	Staff Supervisors Managers
TataSky, Ltd	14	India	Satellite television	Sales skills	Retail operations managers Retail operations incharges
Brazilian Beverage Company	15	Brazil	Beverages	Sales force coaching	Team leaders

1

Building and Managing an Effective Indigenous Workforce

NSW Community Services
Australia

Sean O'Toole and Al Dawood

This case was prepared to serve as a basis for discussion rather than an illustration of either effective or ineffective administration and management practices. Names, dates, places, and data may have been disguised at the request of the author or organisation.

Abstract

This case study highlights the return on investment for a cohort of Aboriginal or Indigenous staff in an Australian government agency with its core business being the welfare and well-being of children and families. The agency's clients include children and families at risk of significant harm, 25 percent of whom are Aboriginal. In order to effectively meet the needs of these clients, the agency has over the past five years actively pursued a policy of recruiting and retaining a high percentage of Aboriginal staff and providing them with significant learning and development opportunities. Simultaneously, the agency has attempted to offer Aboriginal staff the opportunity to develop management skills in order to provide a viable career path for them. Ultimately, these strategies have been successful and are highlighted by a range of business and workforce outcomes and by the learning and career development of the individuals involved.

PROGRAM BACKGROUND

NSW Community Services (CS) is a midsized Australian government agency with more than 4,500 staff members. CS field, or frontline, staff number more than 2,500. These staff members support the safety and well-being of children and young people and work to build stronger families

1

and communities. CS provides child protection services, out-of-home care services, intensive family-based services, parenting support and early intervention, foster care, adoption services, and help for communities affected by disaster.

More than 25 percent of the client families and children with whom the agency works are Aboriginal or Indigenous Australians. Aboriginal staff represent 8 percent of the CS workforce, the majority in field-based roles. Over the past seven years, CS has been pursuing successive large-scale reforms, featuring the attraction, skill building, and retention of increased numbers of Aboriginal caseworkers as a key aspect of the reform strategy.

Upon commencing employment with CS, all casework staff must undertake a six-month Caseworker Development Program (CDP), which is a blended on-the-job learning experience, accomplished via distance learning and a series of one-week workshops. This program is particularly challenging for Aboriginal staff, many of whom are not degree-qualified and do not have the theoretical knowledge base or the levels of self-confidence and interpersonal skills of their colleagues.

PROGRAM OBJECTIVES

The agency is determined to demonstrate that it values the skills and experience that Aboriginal people bring to their roles. It is committed to ensuring that employees are valued and respected for their cultural expertise. For CS to achieve continued success in service delivery and staff retention, a comprehensive approach to the professional development of Aboriginal staff is required. While CS has endeavoured to actively recruit Aboriginal caseworkers, it is often difficult to retain these staff, particularly due to significant learning and development demands placed on new caseworkers.

In September 2006, a survey was distributed to Aboriginal staff and their managers throughout the agency. The purpose of the survey was twofold: to obtain views about the effectiveness of the CDP for Aboriginal staff; and to gain some general information about the collective longer-term career aspirations of Aboriginal staff. Appendix 1.A and Appendix 1.B present the 2006 survey. The findings of the survey were presented at the department's Aboriginal staff conference for further discussion and validation.

Ultimately, the research revealed that *new* Aboriginal casework staff needed particular and specific support. The help that would be made available to them could also be suitable for *existing* Aboriginal staff that had identified weaknesses in the following areas:

■ communication skills, both written and interpersonal

■ information technology skills

■ social welfare theory.

The targeted assistance might also provide access to a nationally recognised qualification at diploma level.

Consequently, a wide-ranging support strategy has been developed to provide Aboriginal staff with additional learning platforms before, during, and after participation in the CDP (Figure 1.1). The continuum of support spans three phases. Each of these stages is outlined in the following paragraphs.

FIGURE 1.1   Caseworker Development Program (CDP) for New Aboriginal Staff

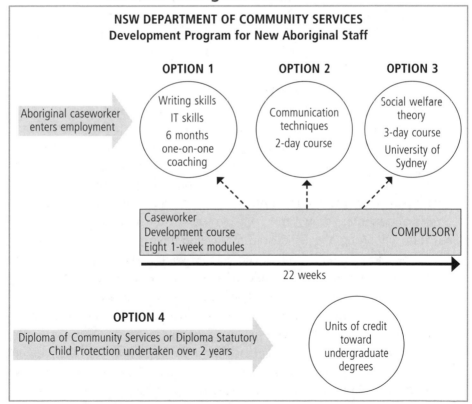

General Development Options for Aboriginal Staff

Parallel to the foundation program, a range of other learning and development initiatives have been introduced for existing Aboriginal staff and those aspiring to management roles. The agency has committed to a process where five Aboriginal staff will have the opportunity to assume three-month placements in different parts of the organisation. This program will enable them to gain workplace experience in roles in which they can build on their strengths and challenge themselves in an unfamiliar environment. The placement program is a form of immersion learning, which can be defined as a development activity with an experiential focus. These activities will be relevant to the staff member's work experience and based in a parallel working environment in order to obtain maximum benefits.

Through the placements, it is envisaged that a wide range of staff will be able to develop a more direct understanding of Aboriginal staff in regard to their culture and aspirations. As a result of the placements, Aboriginal staff will build on their existing strengths and gain experience in a setting that could greatly benefit their confidence and capacity in their substantive role, as well as influence their future development.

Mentoring for Managers

NSW government workforce analysis shows that it is five times more difficult for an Aboriginal staff member to attain a mainstream management role. In May 2007, a 12-month pilot mentoring program commenced, which was specifically designed to increase the representation of Aboriginal staff in mainstream management positions. The pilot involved 10 pairs, with participants drawn from Aboriginal staff who aspired to management roles and mentors drawn from eligible staff who had an interest or expertise in supporting Aboriginal staff to develop their management skills.

The pilot program commenced with a two-day training program for 10 pairs that established the context and guidelines for mentoring. At the conclusion of the training, the pairs had been selected and a plan constructed for the months ahead. The pairs were also given access to resources and to a consultant to provide advice and manage the mentoring process (Figure 1.2). All of the staff who participated are now in permanent management roles or have experienced long-term secondments in a management role. A total of 21 pairs have now completed this program.

FIGURE 1.2 Mentoring for Aboriginal Managers

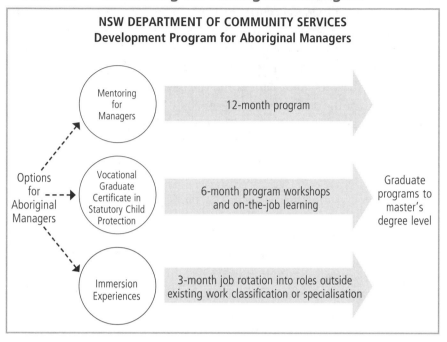

NSW DEPARTMENT OF COMMUNITY SERVICES
Development Program for Aboriginal Managers

Options for Aboriginal Managers

- Mentoring for Managers — 12-month program
- Vocational Graduate Certificate in Statutory Child Protection — 6-month program workshops and on-the-job learning
- Immersion Experiences — 3-month job rotation into roles outside existing work classification or specialisation

Graduate programs to master's degree level

Vocational Qualifications

During 2007, approximately 50 Aboriginal casework staff enrolled in the Diploma in Community Services (Protective Intervention). The program ran over the ensuing 18 months and involved on-the-job assessments and the gathering of the required portfolio of evidence. This is a way of providing a nationally recognised qualification to staff that may not have had formal qualifications when joining CS. Twenty-nine Aboriginal staff completed the program.

In 2010, the department increased the minimum education standard for all managers in the organisation to tertiary degree level. All managers in the organisation without tertiary qualifications were given the opportunity to earn a Vocational Graduate Certificate. In the first intake of that course, 30 staff enrolled and 29 completed the full qualification by the end of 2010. Thirteen Aboriginal staff in management roles began the course and all completed it successfully.

Why This Program Was Evaluated at the ROI Level

Evaluation of this program occurred because of its cost. In addition to cost, the scope of the program is quite large. CS wants to ensure that the program remains relevant for all stakeholders.

The impact of this initiative will continue to be directly measured by staff retention and the improvement in the quality of casework and levels of confidence of the staff involved. Over the past two years, CS has been able to attract and retain a higher percentage of Aboriginal field staff than at any time in the organisation's history. The agency now has more than 8 percent Aboriginal staff (compared to the NSW government target rate of 2 percent).

Evaluations of the program demonstrate significantly improved levels of self-confidence for those who have been involved. This has been validated in research with their respective managers. All of the available programs have been offered on a voluntary basis; however, to date the majority of Aboriginal casework staff has participated in all the available programs. These initiatives are now well established in CS and could be replicated in any human services organisation.

CS has articulation arrangements in place with several universities, with substantial credit available for the successful completion of the Caseworker Development Program and the Diploma of Community Services. Thus, Aboriginal staff members have the opportunity to complete an undergraduate degree or postgraduate certificate as part of a long-term career plan.

EVALUATION METHODOLOGY AND RESULTS

Participants in all programs are evaluated on all levels of the ROI scale except Level 2. Given the nature of the programs, we believe the transfer of learning is better measured by application of the learning in the workplace, perceived behaviour change among participants as recorded by managers, and business improvements and return on investment data. However, for future evaluations, we are evaluating at Level 2 using an online quiz. Appendix 1.C presents questions from the program's module 1 learning assessment.

For the evaluation described in this case study, Level 1 evaluation took place at the end of each program. Level 3 evaluation took place one month after the program. Level 4 outcome measures of employment, retention, and promotion are routinely monitored. For purposes of the evaluation, the improvement in these measures was collected five years after the program was launched. Given that length of time, it is sometimes difficult to attribute all improvement to the program. Feedback data from follow-up surveys and input at annual conferences provided evidence of the program's contribution to improvement in these measures.

Level 1 Reaction

Level 1 evaluations were undertaken for all programs using the same evaluation instruments, using what is termed a reactionnaire containing the critical identifying information for each participant and specific questions covering a score for the development activity, including learning objectives and the purpose of the course; course content; timing of the day; relevance of the training material; and delivery style of the trainer. Participants were asked to rate how the activity met their learning needs on a score of 1 to 5 using a Likert scale, where 1 is "strongly disagree" and 5 is "strongly agree." By averaging the scores on these measures, an overall Level 1 rating was developed for each of the programs. Table 1.1 represents these results.

Common notable comments communicated from the individual program components were that the programs highlighted strengths and areas for further development; helped participants learn about the motivations of others; improved relationships with their colleagues; encouraged

TABLE **1.1**   Level 1 Ratings

Program	Level 1 Rating
Caseworker development program	4.57
Social welfare short course	4.23
IT/writing skills	4.11
Diploma Community Services	4.15
Vocational Graduate certificate	4.69
Mentoring for management	4.51

self-reflection; and increased existing skills in the areas of communication, decision making, and problem solving.

Level 3 Transfer of Learning

The next evaluation phase followed one month after the participants returned to their respective workplaces. The electronic survey tool Survey-Monkey was used to produce the same Likert scale–based questionnaire via a centrally generated email to all participants and their managers. This tool asked participants to rate the transfer of learning about one month after having returned to their roles. Their managers were also asked to comment on their perceptions about transfer of learning among participants.

The SurveyMonkey process automatically tallies the results and provides a downloadable analysis. The results for participants and managers in relation to whether the learning outcomes of the course related to the subsequent work they were required to do or at least aided their understanding of that work was measured using a scale of 1 to 5, where 1 is "strongly disagree" and 5 is "strongly agree." Results are shown in Table 1.2. Responses to questions regarding the transfer of learning issues were averaged, and an index score was developed. Table 1.2 presents the transfer of learning score for each program from the participants' and the managers' perspectives.

In addition to these results, a range of questions were asked during all of the programs and again one month after they were completed to gauge whether the programs were successfully meeting the goals set by participants at the outset. These goals often varied according to the programs and

TABLE **1.2**   **One-Month Follow-up Scores on Transfer of Learning**

Course Participants		Participants' Managers	
Program	**Level 3 Rating**	**Program**	**Level 3 Rating**
Caseworker development program	4.16	Caseworker development program	4.17
Social welfare short course	4.07	Social welfare short course	4.08
IT/writing skills	4.23	IT/writing skills	4.21
Diploma Community Services	4.05	Diploma Community Services	4.02
Vocational Graduate certificate	4.55	Vocational Graduate certificate	4.56
Mentoring for management	4.62	Mentoring for management	4.20

included achieving greater work–life balance; career development; professional development; and personal development. Seventy-one percent of the participants in the programs reported that their goals changed over the life of the programs. Seventy-eight percent of the participants reported that the programs were highly valuable to them and assisted them in meeting the goals they had set.

Level 4 Outcomes for the Organisation

A range of data has also been collected that provides insights into the business impact variables that these programs have influenced. Improvement in the impact measures of retention of Aboriginal staff and promotion of Aboriginal staff to manager were the key measures. These measures were taken five years after the program began.

Retention of Aboriginal Staff

The NSW government sets a target of a minimum of 2 percent Aboriginality for the public sector workforce. Within the NSW Community Service agency, the rate of Aboriginal staff in 2005–2006 was 4.57 percent. By 2011, after the full effect of the development programs had been measured, that rate had increased to 8 percent. Additionally, in 2005–2006, 28 percent of Aboriginal staff had greater than five years experience in the organisation. In 2011, that figure had increased to 33 percent, demonstrating a significant increase in the experience levels of the workforce.

Attribution of this improvement is reliant upon feedback from Aboriginal staff and their managers provided in follow-up surveys and during annual conferences. Based on this feedback, it is evident that ongoing professional development opportunities serve to both attract staff and retain Aboriginal staff in the organisation. Professional and career development has been a major feature of the organisation's recruitment and advertising campaigns for the past five years.

Promotion of Aboriginal Staff into Management Roles

The NSW government does not set a rate or target for Aboriginal staff in management roles. In 2005–2006 with NSW Community Services, there were 29 Aboriginal managers, and the rate of Aboriginal managers represented 2.8 percent of the total number of managers. By 2011, there were 57 Aboriginal managers, and the percentage of Aboriginal managers had increased to 5.5 percent.

All of the participants in the Aboriginal Mentoring for Managers program have now achieved permanent management roles or have had opportunities to assume significant relieving roles in management positions. In follow-up surveys, these participants attribute what was learned from the program to that success. Table 1.3 shows the improvement in Aboriginal employment, retention, and promotion rates.

Level 5 ROI

Two ROI calculations were developed. One ROI was calculated for the staff training resulting in retention of staff; the second was calculated for the Mentoring for Managers program. This program resulted in increased promotions of staff into management roles.

Monetary Benefits and Program Costs of Staff Training

The average costs and benefits per participant are shown in Table 1.4 in Australian dollars. Please note that these costs are all-inclusive of venue hire, facilitator fees, meals, travel, and accommodations for participants, as well as course fees where the courses have been delivered by a third-party provider or institution.

Retaining staff members is a benefit for the organisation when the alternative is not having staff in the organisation to do the work.

TABLE 1.3   Improvement in Impact Measures

Employment		
Aboriginal staff in the NSW public sector 2%	Community services 2005–2006 4.57%	Community services 2010–2011 8%
Retention		
Aboriginal staff with more than 5 years experience NSW public sector No rate set	Community services 2005–2006 28%	Community services 2010–2011 33%
Promotion		
Aboriginal managers NSW public sector No rate set	Community services 2005–2006 2.8%	Community services 2010–2011 5.5%

Note: Aboriginal employment rates, NSW government and community services comparisons.

TABLE 1.4   Staff Training Program Costs

Cost Categories	Costs (AUD)
Casework training	$60,000.00
Caseworker development program	$897.04
Social welfare short course	$974.40
IT/writing skills	$1,237.30
Total costs	**$63,108.74**

Additionally, we need Aboriginal staff to work with Aboriginal families—which is proven to be more effective than having non-Aboriginal staff working with those families as they don't have the knowledge to deal with this population's unique problems. As the nature of the business is a government service industry, revenues are not collected and there are no other internal or external monetary benchmarks to consider. Given the provision of service and the standard of that service being the return on investment, this is achieved through individual staff and the cumulative effect of workforce capability. The benefit of staff is the work performed by the staff member and is valued based on what that staff member is paid in terms of salary. Therefore, improvement in this measure is converted to money using the annual salary of a staff member:

$$\text{Benefit} = \text{Annual salary of staff member} = \$58,249$$

Given the program costs of $63,108 and the program benefits of $58,249, the ROI for this program is as follows:

$$\frac{\text{Net benefits}}{\text{Costs}} \times 100$$

$$\frac{(\$58,249 - \$63,108)}{\$63,108 \times 100} = -7.7\%$$

While the resulting ROI was negative, our team felt comfortable that it was a conservative indicator of economic success of the program. In addition, the program has been reported to provide Aboriginal staff members greater confidence in their work along with other intangible benefits.

Monetary Benefits and Program Costs of Management Development

As in the case of the staff training, the management development costs represent the per person costs and are fully loaded. These costs are shown in Table 1.5.

TABLE **1.5**   **Management Development Costs**

Cost Categories	Costs (AUD)
Vocational graduate certificate	$8,601.56
Mentoring for management	$2,289.98
Three-month immersion experience	$46,176.60
Total costs	**$57,068.14**

There are many benefits of promoting staff to managers within the organisation. Avoiding the cost of recruiting new managers and acclimating those managers to the organisation are just two of the monetary benefits. However, it was decided that in order to standardize and simplify the data conversion process and to keep it consistent with the method used with the benefits of retaining staff, the average annual salary should be used as the data conversion technique:

Benefit = Annual salary of new manager = $89,076

Given program costs of $57,068 and program benefits of $89,076, the ROI for the management development program is as follows:

Net benefits/Costs × 100

$$\frac{(\$89,076 - \$57,068)}{\$57,068} \times 100 = 56.09\%$$

COMMUNICATION STRATEGY

The results of the various development activities were noted in the agency's annual reports and via a range of internal communication devices such as the organisation newsletter and the annual Aboriginal staff conference. The organisation executive team was also recruited to show its strong commitment to the program in meetings and briefings. This had a cascading effect throughout the organisation and builds commitment and awareness from managers at all levels.

The results have also been communicated externally via the organisation's external newsletter and via the publicity associated with the success of the initiative in the 2008 NSW Training Awards. Additionally, this project has often been cited in government cross-agency forums as the how-to model for developing Aboriginal staff within NSW government agencies.

Data that has been captured via the Level 1 to 4 evaluations has contributed to the continuation and expansion of the project and includes a range of initiatives for Aboriginal managers. We have learned, for example, the value of having Aboriginal people learn together as a group without non-Aboriginal colleagues. We have also learned that one-on-one coaching and mentoring yields superior results to classroom-based instructional techniques, and that the individual is more likely to be successful when a career goal can be matched to the development initiative.

LESSONS LEARNED

A variety of positive outcomes were evidenced from all of these programs:

- The opportunity for long-term retention of Aboriginal staff increased. This occurs as Aboriginal staff become more confident in their abilities and feel valued by the organisation.
- The programs established a model for cross-agency partnerships and for working successfully for flexible delivery and learning outcomes with external vocational training providers and the university sector.
- The programs demonstrated outcomes using the Australian National Training Framework for a government agency. CS could not have created such a successful result if it had attempted to design and run these programs internally. Partnership arrangements such as this have great credibility with participants and their managers. CS has been able to leverage the reputations of partner organisations to get participant involvement.
- A range of successful learning strategies were developed for Aboriginal people working in human services organisations. Most of these strategies involve getting away from the traditional classroom setting, encouraging individual learning based on workplace projects, and one-on-one coaching.
- Relevance increased. All of the component programs take into account the learning styles specifically suited to Aboriginal people.
- There were long-term benefits for Aboriginal people, such as being skilled for employment opportunities generally beyond their immediate career with CS.
- This program was developed initially for Aboriginal caseworkers who were new to the organisation. However, aspects of the program were

piloted with existing Aboriginal caseworkers. There is also scope to expand the program to include new staff from culturally and linguistically diverse (CALD) backgrounds that may benefit from additional development in the target areas.

CONCLUSION

Development programs for minority groups within an organisation can be extremely challenging. Such programs often attract a disproportionate amount of the resources available for general staff development programs. Consequently, a suitable ROI will only be achieved if the program can be linked directly to a broader organisational need or to a specific human resources target or strategy. The program must be multifaceted and capable of adapting to the particular learning needs of the individuals involved. In this case, the strategy employed was promoted to other NSW government organisations. However, it was not adopted elsewhere as it was deemed too expensive and did not meet the specific needs or targets of those organisations. The strategy is, however, seen as one of the benchmarks for developing and retaining Aboriginal people in the Australian public sector, and it received a NSW training award for innovation in 2008 and gold and platinum awards at the 2011 Asia-Pacific Learnx awards. While many of the staff who have benefited from these initiatives will move on in the years ahead, it is hoped they will not be lost to the broader public sector and will take on new roles with renewed self-esteem and the confidence to embrace future learning opportunities.

Questions for Discussion

1. If these programs were to be applied to other occupational groups, such as staff in rural and remote areas or staff from a multicultural background, what could we do differently?
2. How important is it that these programs result in outcomes aligned to business needs? Is it appropriate that they be shown to be successful for participants alone?
3. What specific development options or needs do indigenous people in other countries or occupations familiar to you have?

4. Should client Aboriginal families be consulted in time about perceived improvements in services as a measure of ROI?

5. What is the value of negative ROI? What are the intangible benefits of a program such as the CDP? Can these intangible benefits balance or even outweigh the negative ROI?

About the Authors

Sean O'Toole is the director of learning and development in the NSW department of Human Services–Community Services. Sean previously worked as director of the NSW Corrective Services Academy and also lectured at NSW TAFE and universities such as Sydney and Western Sydney. Sean is the author of five books, including *People Development* (Tilde University Press), and numerous articles on management and education. He recently completed postgraduate studies in organisational behaviour at Harvard University.

Al Dawood is the manager of professional development for Community Services, an agency of the NSW Department of Human Services. His role focuses on designing innovative professional development initiatives for staff in response to identified organisational priorities specialising in management development and Aboriginal staff development. Over the last 15 years, Al has worked in the field of learning and development for several Australian government departments. Al has a master's of adult education and a graduate certificate in business administration. His areas of professional interest include organisational development, evaluation, and change management. He is a member of the Australian Institute of Management and the American Society of Training & Development.

Appendix 1.A

Aboriginal Staff Survey
Caseworker Training & Career Development
June 2006

PART ONE: About You

Providing the following information about yourself is voluntary. All information you provide on this survey will remain anonymous and is confidential.

This section is for all staff to complete.

Your Age: **Your Gender:** SELECT   **Your Region:**

How long have you worked for DoCS?   **Your Postcode:**

Is there anything else you think we should know about you?

PART TWO: Caseworker Development Course

If you have completed the CDC training in the last two years, please answer the following questions. If not please go directly to Part Three.

Thinking about the training you received in the Caseworker Development Course (CDC), please answer the following questions by selecting your answer from the drop-down menu. If you have further comments, please provide them in the space below each statement. The more information you provide, the more improvements we can make.

1. **Has attending CDC training helped you to do your job?**   SELECT

2. **Was the training delivered at a suitable level for you?**   SELECT

3. **Were there things that made learning difficult for you?**   SELECT
   If YES, what were they?

4. **Were there things that made learning easier for you?**   SELECT
   If YES, what were they?

5. **Are there things that could have happened before the training started that might have made**   SELECT
   completing the course easier?
   If YES, what are your suggestions?

6. **Have you been able to complete all of the assessment tasks?**   SELECT

7. **Do you think that the assessment tasks equipped you to do your job?**   SELECT

8. **Were there things that would have made the assessment tasks easier to complete?**   SELECT
   If YES, what are they?

9. **Which of these modules has been the *MOST* useful to you?**

☐ Introduction to CDC	☐ Alcohol and Other Drugs	☐ Cultural Awareness
☐ Legal Responsibilities	☐ Responding to Domestic Violence	☐ Case Management
☐ Dual Diagnosis	☐ Mental Health	☐ Child Protection Dynamics
☐ Legal Issues	☐ Out of Home Care	☐ KIDS Training
☐ Working with Aboriginal Children & Families	☐ Affidavit Writing & Recording Evidence	☐ Interviewing Children and Gathering Evidence
☐ Conducting Secondary Assessments	☐ Building Relationships with Children, Young People & Careers	☐ Working with Children and Young People

Please provide comments:

10. **Which of these modules has been the *LEAST* useful to you?**

☐ Introduction to CDC	☐ Alcohol and Other Drugs	☐ Cultural Awareness
☐ Legal Responsibilities	☐ Responding to Domestic Violence	☐ Case Management
☐ Dual Diagnosis	☐ Mental Health	☐ Child Protection Dynamics
☐ Legal Issues	☐ Out of Home Care	☐ KIDS Training
☐ Working with Aboriginal Children & Families	☐ Affidavit Writing & Recording Evidence	☐ Interviewing Children and Gathering Evidence
☐ Conducting Secondary Assessments	☐ Building Relationships with Children, Young People & Careers	☐ Working with Children and Young People

Please provide comments:

Aboriginal Staff Survey
Caseworker Training & Career Development
June 2006

11. How has CDC training assisted you in your work environment?

PART THREE: Career Development

Thinking about your job and your current skills and qualifications, please tell us about any further training, aspirations, and/or development you would like.

12. Are there any additional skills or knowledge you feel you need to do your job?   SELECT

If YES, please provide further details below:

What is the skill/knowledge you would like to learn?	Why would you like to learn it?	What training or development do you need to be able to develop/learn this skill?	What are you current skills, qualifications, and/or experience in this area?
1.			
2.			
3.			
4.			

Please provide comments:

13. What do you find hard in your job?

14. What has been good in your job?

15. What type of support would help you to do your job?

16. Would you be interested in participating in a mentoring program?   SELECT

17. The ASB and L&D currently provide opportunities to enroll in the Diploma of Community Services (Protective Interventions). Would you be interested in enrolling in this course to be completed on the job?   SELECT

Thank you for your participation!

Your time and effort is greatly appreciated, and your answers will help us to develop a better, more useful online HR resource for all DoCS staff. You should now **SAVE** this document and forward it as an email attachment to **leanne.boyd@community.nsw.gov.au** in the **Aboriginal Services Branch.**

Appendix 1.B

Managers' Survey
Supervision of Aboriginal Staff
June 2006

Are you: ☐ Aboriginal ☐ Non-Aboriginal

Instructions: Thinking about the Aboriginal Caseworkers you supervise, please answer the following questions by selecting your answer from the drop-down menu and/or providing details as required in the space below each statement. The more information you provide, the more improvements we can make.

1. **How long have you been supervising Aboriginal Caseworker/s?** SELECT

2. **Do you feel confident providing supervision and support to Aboriginal Caseworkers?** SELECT
   Please comment:
   If NO, can you identify any gaps/barriers?

3. **Can you identify any gaps or barriers that may impact negatively on the experience of Aboriginal Caseworkers in their roles?** SELECT
   If YES, please provide details:

4. **Can you identify any gaps or barriers that limit the support you can provide to Aboriginal Caseworkers?** SELECT
   If YES, please provide details:

5. **What things help you to provide good support and supervision to Aboriginal Caseworkers?**
   Please provide details:

6. **Are there things that would help you provide better support and supervision to Aboriginal Caseworkers?** SELECT
   If YES, what were they?

7. **Are there things that DoCS can do to better support Aboriginal Caseworkers and their managers to get the most out of attending the Caseworker Development Course (CDC)?** SELECT
   If YES, please provide details:

8. **Apart from the CDC, can you identify any additional training that would assist Aboriginal Caseworkers?** SELECT
   If YES, please provide details:

9. **Apart from training, what else would assist new Aboriginal Caseworkers?**
   Please provide details:

10. **What career and development needs have you identified for your staff?**
    Please provide details:

11. **Please provide any further comments you would like to make.**

12. **Would you be interested in participating in a mentoring program?** SELECT

13. **The ASB and L&D currently provide opportunities to enroll in the Diploma of Community Services (Protective Interventions). Would you be interested in enrolling in this course to be completed on the job?** SELECT

Thank you for your participation!
Your time and effort is greatly appreciated, and your answers will help us to develop a better, more useful online HR resource for all DoCS staff. You should now **SAVE** this document and send it as an email *attachment* to **sean.o'toole@community.nsw.gov.au** in the **Aboriginal Services Branch.**

Appendix 1.C
Quiz Questions for Module 1

1. In Secondary Assessment (SAS2), the purpose of the Pre-Assessment Consultation (PAC) is to:
   a) Discuss key issues prior to conducting an assessment interview
   b) Identify key information to gather in the assessment interview
   c) Develop an assessment case plan
   d) All of the above
   (Refer to SECONDARY ASSESSMENT for further information or to reconsider your answer.)

2. The Case Management process has how many elements?
   a) 4
   b) 7
   c) 8
   d) 3
   (Refer to CASE MANAGEMENT for further information or to reconsider your answer.)

3. Two crucial phases of case management in the early stages are:
   a) Screening and assessment and case planning
   b) Case planning and implementation
   c) Screening and assessment and monitor/review
   (Refer to CASE MANAGEMENT for further information or to reconsider your answer.)

4. Professional judgment plays an important role in risk assessment?
   True
   False
   (Refer to PROFESSIONAL JUDGEMENT for further information or to reconsider your answer.)

5. Which Section of the Children and Young Persons Care and Protection Act 1998 refers to children and young people at risk of significant harm?

   a) S.24

   b) S.34

   c) S.23

   (Refer to ASSESSING RISK OF HARM or the Children and Young Persons Care and Protection Act 1998 for further information or to reconsider your answer.)

6. The process of case planning ensures intervention and support is planned, purposeful, and **responsive** to the specific needs of the child, young person, or family.

   (Refer to CASE PLANNING for further information or to reconsider your answer.)

7. A case plan record is updated in KiDS when:

   a) A family moves to a different area

   b) Further action is required and decisions are made

   c) When the case is closed

   d) When all case plan goals are achieved

   (Refer to CASE PLANNING for further information or to reconsider your answer.)

8. The major purpose of case planning in child protection is to:

   a) Outline the actions FaCS will take to address the needs of a child or young person through assessment

   b) Increase safety and decrease risk through identifying strategies to meet the needs of clients

   c) Provide clarity to all parties about the goals and objectives of FaCS involvement

   d) All of the above

   (Refer to CASE PLANNING for further information or to reconsider your answer.)

9. The Helpline has received a report of a 3-year-old boy with concerns about bruising and other non-accidental injuries. They have completed an Initial Assessment and are transferring the case to CSC Intake for further response. Select the most appropriate case plan goal from one of the following options in KiDS.

	Adoption of child/young person
	Permanent care (court order)
	Supported care (no Children's Court order)
✔	**Assessment**
	Magellan – Community Services / Family Court of Australia Protocol
	Independent living
	Maintain child/young person with parents
	Provision of assistance
	Restoration
	Information forwarded to Community Services unit
	Community Services – DADHC Protocol Assessment
	CIS goal / objective – see description

(Refer to CASE PLANNING for further information or to reconsider your answer.)

10. A **strengths-based** approach is effective in building relationships.
(Refer to STRENGTHS-BASED PRACTICE for further information or to reconsider your answer.)

11. Name the fourth key function of professional supervision:
a) Developmental / educative function
b) Support function
c) Administrative / managerial function
d) Mediative function
(Refer to SUPERVISION for further information or to reconsider your answer.)

12. Successful professional supervision is the responsibility of:
a) The manager (supervisor)
b) Caseworker (supervisee)
c) Caseworker and Manager
(Refer to SUPERVISION for further information or to reconsider your answer.)

13. The timeframe for decisions about restoration for a child under 6 months of age need to be made within what period following removal:

    a) 30 days

    b) 2 months

    c) 6 months

    d) 12 months

    (Refer to PERMANENCY PLANNING for further information or to reconsider your answer.)

14. What does s.13 of the Children and Young Persons Care and Protection Act 1998 refer to?

    a) Aboriginal and Torres Strait Islander Child and Young Person Placement Principles

    b) Aboriginal and Torres Strait Islander participation in decision making

    c) Permanency planning principles

    d) All of the above

    (Refer to PERMANENCY PLANNING or the Children and Young Persons Care and Protection Act 1998 for further information or to reconsider your answer.)

15. The objectives of permanency planning are to: (there may be more than one correct answer)

    a) Make early and informed decisions about permanent placement options

    b) Provide for continuity and stability in the child/young person's life

    c) Make decisions that are cost effective

    d) Obtain permanent placements that will support early case closure

    (Refer to PERMANENCY PLANNING for further information or to reconsider your answer.)

Evaluating a Global Sales Training Program

Industrial Company
Germany

Frank C. Schirmer

This case was prepared to serve as a basis for discussion rather than an illustration of either effective or ineffective administrative and management practices. Names, dates, places, and data may have been disguised at the request of the author or organization.

Abstract

This chapter describes the evaluation of a global sales training initiative. This initiative, Value-Based Selling and Negotiation (VBS), was intended to help a global leader in its field improve margin in comparison to its key competitor. The whole implementation with training and evaluation was conducted by German-based LearnVision. The primary focus of the evaluation was to determine the impact of the initiative on margin.

BACKGROUND

The company is a global leader in its field. Strong business relationships, a commitment to outstanding service, and wide-ranging application know-how make it a preferred partner to its customers. The company, which is located on five continents, employs more than 20,000 people and generated sales of more than 5 billion euros.

The company's innovative products play a key role in its customers' manufacturing and treatment processes and add value to their end products. The company's success is based on the know-how of its employees and their ability to identify new customer needs at an early stage and to work together with customers to develop innovative, efficient solutions.

The margin of this company in their industry fell dramatically in the last quarters of 2005–2006. Analysis showed that many of their customers had merged and achieved higher purchasing power (more volume for lower prices). However, this reflected the whole industry. A margin benchmark in the industry showed a clear weakness in achieving the right margin in comparison to its key competitor. Therefore, the company launched a program to turn around its margin erosion. The program included two key elements:

1. Global pricing software to reflect the cost to serve in the pricing as well as to react to raw material increases more effectively.

2. A new academy with skill development for Value-Based Selling and Negotiations by involving all levels (from CEO to all sales professionals) in all countries.

The training and evaluation was conducted by a German-based consulting organization, LearnVision. The evaluation was conducted to control and manage the global development program. It was designed to develop all necessary skills and tools for all levels as well as to identify barriers and enablers and to demonstrate the success and necessity of a sales effectiveness program. The main focus was on finding out whether the program had a positive effect on the organizational margin.

PROGRAM DESCRIPTION

This training initiative was developed to establish skills and tools in the work field to link performance improvements with business measures (margin). "Value-Based Selling and Negotiation (VBS)" was the initial program launched for the newly created academy. Overall, more than 2.000 participants were trained in modular training sessions—across all regions, all divisions, and all sales levels. Roughly 450 sales managers were trained in "Sales Coaching I" (three-day program) and "Sales Coaching II" (two-day program), and about 1.700 sales professionals (marketing and sales) were trained in "Value-Based Selling" (two-day program) and "Effective Negotiation" (two-day training). As well as dealing with the same content as their teams, managers and team leaders received additional coaching tools and specially designed reinforcement tools to enable them to provide their staff with effective support after the training.

The training strategy was to always train the leaders first and then—about four weeks later—the sales professionals to allow the leaders to

FIGURE 2.1   Value-Based Selling and Pricing

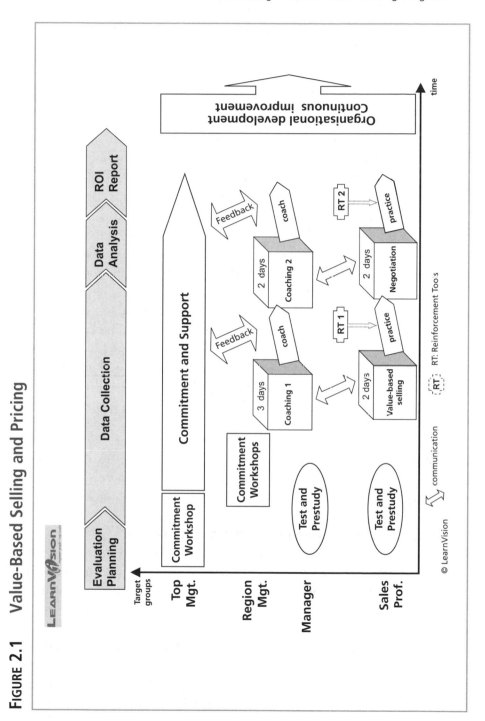

position the seminar in advance of the training and use their newly learnt coaching tools to improve the commitment and application of their staff. The time gap between the two different modules was planned as eight to 10 weeks. Figure 2.1 provides an overview of the concept "value-based selling and pricing," a combination of attitude, communication, tools, and strategic pricing.

Prior to the training, all participants filled out a skill gap test (online questionnaire) to ascertain individual skill gaps concerning Value-Based Selling and Negotiation. All managers gave additional information on their coaching skills. The summary of the analyzed skill gaps for each group, country, and region provided good hints for the regional and country-specific implementation. Furthermore, those gaps were included in the global commitment workshop (with the CEO and all business leaders) and in each regional commitment workshop to enhance support at all management levels—globally and locally.

After a pilot training four months prior to the global rollout and necessary adjustments, the global rollout started in Europe at the end of January 2007 and continued until the end of 2008 in five regions (Europe, North America, Latin America, Asia, and Special Markets) in more than 28 countries and seven languages (German, English, French, Spanish, Italian, Chinese, and Japanese). One success factor was the design of special tools for the technically minded sales professionals, which are useable in the work field right after the seminar. Figure 2.2 provides an overview of the global rollout timeline. Parallel to this initiative, the company began using pricing software to provide consolidated margin data to each sales professional and changed the incentive system from revenue to margin improvements.

Project Team and Steering Committee

One key success factor was the creation of a project team. The project team members came from each division, from HR, and from LearnVision. The objective was to plan and implement the global program effectively to support the marketing and sales strategy. The following phases helped the project team to keep track of developments: Evaluation Planning, Data Collection, Data Analysis, and ROI Reporting. Monthly meetings with direct communication from and to the business line as well as to the management and the steering committee (CEO and major leaders) were set up. The steering committee received a monthly report from the project team to be

FIGURE 2.2   Global Rollout Timeline

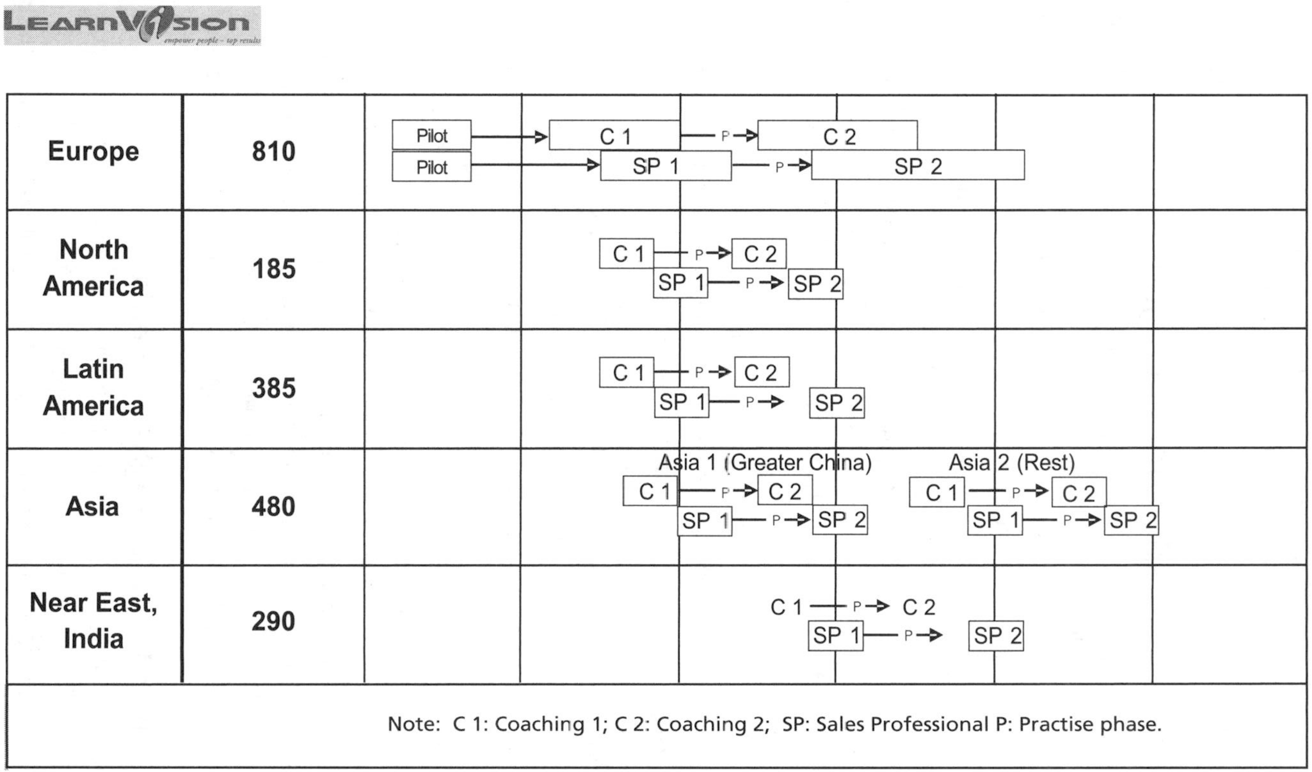

		Pilot	C 1	SP 1	P→	C 2	SP 2			

Europe 810
North America 185
Latin America 385
Asia 480
Near East, India 290

Note: C 1: Coaching 1; C 2: Coaching 2; SP: Sales Professional P: Practise phase.

© LearnVision

27

able to monitor progress, to see the barriers and enablers, and to make decisions for continuous improvement. To be able to support successful implementation, the CEO and his team decided to participate in all seminars too.

Content and Design of the Program

To save costs in the global rollout and to be able to focus the seminar on key content and methodology, an extended pilot program with a practise phase was set up in advance. A global team comprised of participants from multiple businesses went through the pilot session. The outcome was the development of specific tools for the workplace in order to be able to implement training as a global "living" system. The "Bridgetool" from the ROI Process helped to define the exact result-based content and design of the program. The result was that content for usually seven days could be focused and specialized to five days for the manager and four days for the sales professionals.

In accordance with the cost-saving approach, a comprehensive prestudy with self-tests and checklists was designed to save seminar time. A cost analysis showed that web-based training sessions were too expensive and provided no extra benefit.

Table 2.1 describes the key content areas, which were established in up to seven languages. The key tools were developed in 12 languages. After the second module, a similar practise phase with a measurement system was established.

One success factor was that all managers received the same key content and tools as the sales professionals and specialized reinforcement tools, as well as the situational coaching skills to use them in the work field. The tools were placed on the intranet for professional use. Another success factor was the concentration on the development of the necessary skills for the highest business impact and the understanding of the whole learning process (before, during, and after) on a global and individual basis.

Business Tools for Highest Impact

Tools were designed to support the implementation of the acquired knowledge in the work field. At first the key situation was identified and special tools for managers, the organization, and sales professionals were designed. The project team set objectives indicating which tool would help in which situation and integrated them on the intranet. The following tools were

TABLE 2.1   Key Content

Target Group	Module 1	Practise	Module 2
Manager, Coach	**Coaching 1, 3 days** • Prestudy up front as learning tool • Business positioning with commitment tools and test results • Value-Based Selling (VBS) content with "Profiles" to become a "solution provider" • Coaching content related to VBS with reinforcement tools to be able to develop and challenge the implementation by the sales professionals for the new "coaching culture" • Individual action plan	Learning transfer, situational coaching, tools, reinforcement, PAS, DIGL	**Coaching 2, 2 days** • Prestudy up front as learning tool • Business positioning • Identify the individual and organizational barriers and enablers in the work field and find solutions to overcome the barriers and strengthen the enablers. • Negotiation content with 16 negotiation tactics from purchasers and specially designed methodology • Coaching content related to negotiation with reinforcement tools to be able to develop and challenge the implementation by the sales professionals • Individual action plan
Sales Professionals, Marketing	**Value Based Selling, 2 days** • Prestudy up front as learning tool • Business positioning with commitment tools and test results • Value-Based Selling (VBS) content with "profiles" to become a "solution provider"—extended version • Awareness of coaching to understand the managers' perspective and develop an effective "coaching culture" • Individual action plan in conjunction with managers	Learning transfer, receiving situational coaching	**Negotiation, 2 days** • Prestudy up front as learning tool • Business positioning • Identify the individual and organizational barriers and enablers in the work field and find solutions to overcome the barriers and strengthen the enablers in conjunction with their managers • Negotiation content with 16 negotiation tactics from purchasers and specially designed methodology—extended version • Individual action plan in conjunction with managers

designed, positioned, and learned in the seminar, and then applied in the work field:

1. Tools for managers:
   - reinforcement: using short exercises based on the seminar content for the actual work environment of the employees for better impact in the workplace
   - coaching to support the situational applications
   - observer sheets for the skills to be able to change behavior.
2. Tools for the organization, participants, and managers:
   - PAS (Planning-Analysis-Strategy) to be used for the preparation of individual or sales calls/negotiation dialogues
   - DIGL (Dialogue Guidelines) to be used in front of customers to guide an effective and professional sales call or negotiation dialogue
   - "product profiles" (sales and marketing tool) to be used for quick wins in sales
   - action plan with preset objectives related to the key challenges to build the bridge between the training and higher margins (business measures).

EVALUATION METHODOLOGY

Building a comprehensive measurement and evaluation process is like a puzzle in which the pieces are developed and put in place over time. The ROI model is a step-by-step approach to develop the ROI calculation and the other measures important to stakeholders. The ROI Methodology is a trademarked process of the ROI Institute, based in Birmingham, Alabama, USA. LearnVision is the only consulting company in Germany, Austria, and Switzerland with rights to apply this evaluation process.

Evaluation Levels, Data Types

A variety of measures report elements of success of a program. The measures are categorized as levels and serve as the framework for evaluation. Measures taken for this evaluation project are categorized as follows:

- **Level 0: Preprogram Test Data**
  To involve all participants and to focus on each individual seminar, a needs analysis tool was provided. The answers from the online questionnaires were sent to the trainers in advance in order to help them focus on each individual seminar.

- **Level 1: Reaction, Satisfaction, and Planned Action**

  Measures the satisfaction of program participants, along with their intention to apply what they have learned. Almost all organizations evaluate at Level 1, usually with a generic, end-of-program questionnaire. While this level of evaluation is important as a participant satisfaction measure, a favourable reaction does not ensure that participants have learned new skills or knowledge.

- **Level 2: Learning, Knowledge**

  Focuses on what participants learned (competencies) during the program. A learning test is helpful to ensure that participants have absorbed the content and know how to use it properly. However, a positive result at this level is no guarantee that what has been learned will be applied on the job.

- **Level 3: Application and Implementation**

  A variety of follow-up methods are used to determine whether participants apply what they have learned on the job. The frequency and use of skills are important measures at Level 3. While Level 3 evaluation is important to gauge the success of the application of a program, it still does not guarantee that there will be a positive business impact in the organization.

- **Level 4: Business Impact**

  Focuses on the actual results achieved by program participants as they successfully apply what they have learned. Typical Level 4 measures include output, quality, costs, time, and customer satisfaction. Although the program may produce a measurable business impact, there is still a concern that the program may cost too much.

- **Level 5: Return on Investment**

  The ultimate level of evaluation compares the monetary benefits of the program in relation to the program costs. Although the ROI can be expressed in several ways, it is usually presented as a percentage or benefit-cost ratio. The evaluation chain of impact is not complete until Level 5, ROI evaluation, is developed.

- **Intangible Measures**

  While not a different level, intangible measures are the benefits (business impact) directly linked to the training program, which cannot or should not be converted to monetary values. These measures are still very important in the evaluation process.

Table 2.2 shows the evaluation methods for the program.

TABLE 2.2   Evaluation Methods at Each Level

Level of effectiveness	Aspects to be evaluated/controlled	How to evaluate/control
LEVEL 5	ROI—return on investment	Monetary training value to full loaded costs, intangibles
LEVEL 4	Business impact	Isolate the training effects, convert data to monetary value
LEVEL 3	Skill development in the work field, learning transfer	Performance observation from the leaders/trainers, follow-up questionnaire (esp. usage of business tools)
LEVEL 2	Skill development in the seminar	Competence test: pre and post test
LEVEL 1	Seminar and trainer acceptance, supposed barriers/enablers	Questionnaires, planned action from the participants
LEVEL 0	Involvement and learning gaps	Questionnaire online

PERFORMANCE

QUALITY

ROI Process for Quality Implementation and CIP

To be able to monitor implementation and react in time, the company has chosen the ROI Process as a quality and continuous improvement process (CIP). The ROI Process helps to strengthen the result-based approach in the Human Resource Development (HRD) program—from the planning stage to the ROI report. It involves all important target groups and gives the necessary information to monitor and steer the implementation for success. Figure 2.3 shows the key steps within the ROI Process.

Before the actual content was established, the objectives were defined on all five levels to effectively build the bridge between learning content and business impact. A Data Collection Plan and an ROI Analysis Plan were determined by the project team and the chief controller and agreed on with the steering committee. These planning documents are show in Tables 2.3 and 2.4. They detail the approach to evaluating the program.

FIGURE 2.3   ROI Methodology

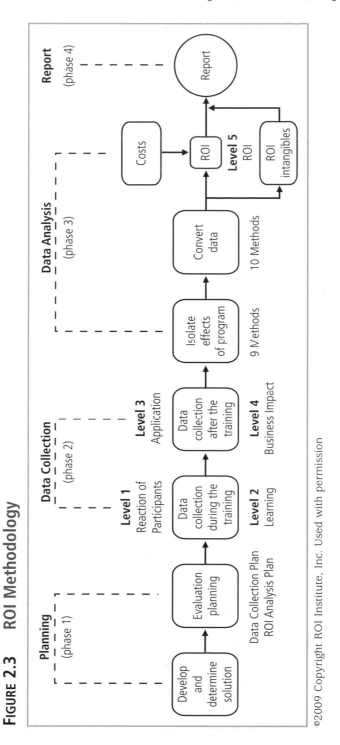

TABLE 2.3 Data Collection Plan

Program: Sales Academy: VBS —————— Responsibility: Mr. X, from company —————— Date: ——————

Level	Broad Program Objective(s)	Measures	Data Collection Method/ Instruments	Data Sources	Timing	Responsibilities
1	**REACTION/ SATISFACTION** • Positive reaction • Action items	**Manager/Sales:** • On a scale from 1 to 6 the avg. should be greater than 4.6. • 90% of all salespeople will fill out the action plans	Online questionnaire	Participants	End of each seminar (time slot 1–7 days)	Trainer → LearnVision
2	**LEARNING** • Acquisition of skills • Selection of skills	**Manager/Sales:** • 90% of the participants have an average of 4.6 (post, scale 1 to 6)	Pre/post-competence test	Participants	End of each seminar	Trainer → LearnVision
3	**APPLICATION/ IMPLEMENTATION** • Use of skills • Frequency of skill use • Identify barriers	**Manager:** • 80% of the managers are using the reinforcement tool • All have to identify possible barriers for the salespeople **Sales:** • 80% of the salespeople use the skills at an average of 4 (scale 1 to 6) • 80% of the salespeople use the PAS and DIGL tools	**Manager:** • Review **Sales:** • Observer sheet • Action plan review • Online questionnaire	**Manager:** • Manager **Sales:** • Participants • Participants • Participants	**Manager:** • Next seminar **Sales:** • 2 months after seminar during the practise phase 1 and 2 • Next seminar • 10 weeks after seminar 2	**Manager:** • Trainer → LearnVision • Top management **Sales:** • Manager → LearnVision • Trainer → LearnVision • LearnVision
4	**BUSINESS IMPACT** • Margin increase	Delta gross margin per quarter	CPI data from controlling	Business warehouse, SAP	Monthly	Controlling
5	**ROI** • Gross margin and fully loaded cost	**Baseline Data:** • Controlling will deliver the baseline data for 2006 (monthly) by end of 2006 and the margin per quarter from Q2/2006 till Q2/2008				

TABLE 2.4   ROI Analysis Plan

Program: Sales Academy: VBS

Responsibility: Mr. X, from company

Date:

Data Items (Usually Level 4)	Method for Isolating the Effects of the Program/ Process	Method of Converting Data to Monetary Values	Cost Categories
Gross margin	Control groups and estimates from experts (benchmark other ROI studies)	H storical data	Fully loaded costs, see separate cost table, e.g.: • Cost of project team and training costs (external) • Costs of time from participants • Evaluation costs

Intangible Benefits	Communication Targets for Final Report	Other Influences and Issues During Application	Comments
Will be clarified: job satisfaction, networking, one culture	Communication plan will be set up for continuous communication during the whole process, see separate plan	Organizational effectiveness (new processes) Downsizing STF (Strategic Task Force), incl. Asia Strategy	Check for baseline data (controlling)

To capture all the data from the evaluation levels during implementation, the specially designed evaluation tools were monitored (mostly online) by the project team and businesses so that they could react accordingly in time—on a local and global basis.

RESULTS

The evaluation showed results on the different levels and in different regions and countries. The evaluation tools, their implementation (time and form), and the respective data collection were designed to provide early indications to enable instant decisions on improvements. The communication of intermediate results to the responsible target group was reflected by a communication plan for general information and alarm messages. The key information derived from the evaluation and a key driver for initiating the evaluation is the impact of the program on margin.

Reaction and Planned Actions (Level 1)

After each training module, the participants completed a seminar feedback questionnaire either online or on paper. The results were presented by country (for the sales coaches, per region) and level. The scale went from 1 (minimum) to 6 (maximum).

An "after seminar alert system" was established to be able to react in a short time and to implement improvements for the next scheduled seminars or other regions. All seminars under 4,5 were under observation for a continuous improvement process. Based on this analysis, decisions were made and improvements were established for the next seminars.

Two objectives were established at Level 1:

1. The first objective related to the data collection plan was 4,6 as overall satisfaction. Benchmark data showed results for Level 1 usually being more than 4,8.

2. The second objective was that 90 percent of all salespeople would fill out the action plans, which was fulfilled (information from trainer).

Table 2.5 presents the results for the sales coaches regarding the first objective. As shown, the first objective of 4,6 was reached, and even the overall high benchmark target of 4,8 was reached globally. The best results came from Latin America, where the whole process was strongly supported by management and the training performance was perfect.

TABLE 2.5   Sales Coaches, First Objective

Region	Module 1 Average Result	Module 2 Average Result	All Modules Average Result
Europe	4,8	4,7	4,75
Latin America	5,3	5,3	5,3
North America	4,5	4,8	4,65
Asia	4,7	4,5	4,6
Special Markets	5,3	5,0	5,15
Total	**9,6**	**9,0**	**4,89**

The lowest training performance was in North America, especially in module 1. After the first module, the trainer had meetings with the local manager, which had positive effects on the training results of module 2.

Table 2.6 presents the Level 1 results on the first objectives for sales professionals. The objective of 4,6 was reached, and even the overall high benchmark target of 4,8 was reached globally. The best results came from Peru and Colombia, with an average of 5,7.

The first trainer in the UK was replaced due to bad personal performance after he had delivered one seminar. The first trainer in Germany did only two groups instead of four planned groups, and a different trainer trained the third and fourth groups.

The lowest training performance was in Japan. Meetings with management and local HR, as well as support from the master trainer during the training, were established. The main reason was the habit of the participants in Japan to rate lower than those in other countries. Management in Japan strongly supported the whole process.

Some of the comments made by participants include the following:

"I will have a customer meeting (one day after training) that I know is going to be 'price' driven. With my new learned techniques, I'm definitely better prepared to face their objections!"

"This training was a worthwhile investment for the company!!!!!!!! No doubt!!!"

"The value-based training was and is proving to be very effective when working with old and new customers."

TABLE 2.6   Sales Professionals, First Objective

Region	Module 1 Average Result	Module 2 Average Result	Region	Module 1 Average Result	Module 2 Average Result
Switzerland	4,6	4,6	China	4,3	4,3
Germany	4,3	4,4	Malaysia	5,0	4,9
France	4,8	4,2	Singapore	4,9	4,8
Italy	4,5	4,1	Indonesia	5,0	4,9
Spain	4,7	4,9	Japan	3,9	3,8
UK	4,3	4,0	South Korea	4,5	4,4
Eastern Europe	5,0	5,0	Thailand	4,7	4,8
Brazil	5,1	5,2	Australia	3,7	4,1
Mexico	5,4	5,3	Turkey	4,3	4,8
Colombia	5,7	5,6	India	5,2	5,0
Peru	5,7	5,7	Pakistan	5,3	5,3
Chile	5,4	5,3	South Africa	5,4	5,3
Argentina	5,1	4,9			
North America	5,1	4,8	**Total**	**8,62**	**9,08**

"Excellent training for salespeople."

"I have acquired new techniques that I can utilise in my day-to-day interaction with customers."

Both overall objectives were reached. Only a few difficulties occurred during the global implementation. The alert system for Level 1 gave transparency to the training implementation and showed the necessary improvements in time.

More than 85 percent of the seminars ran smoothly, and more than 90 percent of the participants planned actions for their personal work application between module 1 and 2. The objective "positive reaction" of 4,6 was overshot by 4,8 on average.

Learning, Knowledge (Level 2)

To establish data at Level 2, the participants completed a self-assessment handout before and immediately after the training to provide feedback on how they judged their skills concerning VBS, Negotiation, and Coaching. These results (mean after) were summarised per region (sales coaches) and country (sales professionals). The scale went from 1 (minimum) to 6 (maximum).

As with the Level 1 evaluation, the "after seminar alert system" allowed for quick reaction so improvements could be made for the next scheduled seminars or other regions.

One primary objective was established at Level 2: 90 percent of the participants should have reached an average competence level of 4,6. Benchmarks shows results for Level 2 being between 4,2 and 4,6.

Table 2.7 shows the results for the sales coaches. As shown, the competencies were strongly developed globally. Even if the participants were not as satisfied in some cases (see Level 1), all participants learnt the necessary competencies to be able to apply the skills to their jobs and to coach their sales professionals effectively.

As shown in Table 2.8, the competencies for sales professionals were strongly developed globally. Even if the participants were not as satisfied (see Level 1), all participants learnt the necessary competencies to be able to apply the skills to their jobs and sell and negotiate effectively.

The objective of 4,6 for the competence level was overshot by reaching almost 5,0. The alert system for Level 2 gave transparency to the training implementation and showed the necessary improvements in time.

TABLE 2.7   Sales Coaches

Region	Module 1 Mean After	Module 2 Mean After
Europe	4,9	4,9
Latin America	5,3	5,2
North America	5,0	4,9
Asia	5,0	5,1
Special Markets	5,3	5,1
Total	**5,1**	**5,04**

TABLE 2.8   Sales Professional

Country	Module 1 Mean After	Module 2 Mean After
Switzerland	4,6	4,5
Germany	4,7	4,6
France	4,8	4,7
Italy	5,0	4,6
Spain	5,2	4,9
UK	4,9	4,7
Eastern Europe	4,9	4,7
Brazil	5,0	4,9
Mexico	5,3	5,1
Colombia	5,3	5,1
Peru	5,7	5,4
Chile	5,6	5,1
Argentina	5,6	4,8
North America	5,0	5,0
China	4,9	4,7
Malaysia	4,9	4,5
Singapore	5,1	4,9
Indonesia	4,9	4,8
Japan	4,8	4,4
South Korea	4,8	4,5
Thailand	4,8	4,6
Australia	5,0	4,7
Turkey	5,3	5,1
India	5,0	4,7
Pakistan	5,2	5,0
South Africa	5,3	4,9
Total	**9,42**	**9,62**

Application (Level 3)

Two different approaches (data methods) were set up to monitor the learning transfer:

1. Quality and quantity data during the seminar: After the first module, each participant wrote down his or her personal actions for the learning transfer. That information was gathered at the beginning of module 2. Furthermore, participants were asked how their coaches implemented the coaching (Top Management → Middle Managers, Middle Managers → Sales Professionals).

2. Questionnaire for learning transfer: A learning transfer questionnaire was developed and sent to the participants about 10 weeks after their second module to collect data for Level 3.

The objectives for Level 3 were as follows:

For the managers:

- 80 percent of the managers are using the reinforcement tool ("Learning-Transfer-Tool")
- All have to identify possible barriers for the salespeople

For the sales professionals:

- 80 percent of the salespeople use the skills at an average of 4,0 on a scale between 1 and 6
- 80 percent of the salespeople use the Planning Guide (PAS) and Dialogue Guide (DIGL) tools
- Identify barriers during the on-the-job application

The results of the different approaches are as follows:

1. Quality and quantity data developed after module 1 and gathered at the beginning of module 2:

Results for the managers and coaches showed that usage of the reinforcement tool was weak. Only approximately 30 percent of the managers were using the reinforcement tool to coach the sales professionals effectively. All managers had identified possible barriers and found solutions for how to overcome them for themselves and for the sales professionals during the seminars. Especially the reinforcement tools were not used as expected.

With regard to the sales professionals, the coaches had to observe the usage of the skills by the sales professionals in their work field. Therefore, the coaches had learnt how to observe the VBS skills in the work field by using observer sheets. The usage of the Planning Guide and Dialogue Guide was voluntarily. The barriers and solutions to overcome those barriers were identified in the seminars.

2. Questionnaire for learning transfer:

The data from the questionnaire were collected in a database. This database was transferred to global HR for internal communication to show transparency in the learning process and to find improvements for skill application. The scale went from 1 (min.) to 6 (max.).

Benchmarks show results for Level 3 usually being more than 4,5. Table 2.9 shows the results for the sales coaches.

The return rate in Special Markets was lower than 60 percent. The data were not usable, and the results were not satisfying. In certain regions, the learning transfer was quite OK, but especially in Europe, the learning transfer needed more support from top management and coaches. Table 2.10 shows some reasons (barriers) for poor learning transfer by each region.

The objective "80 percent of the managers are using the reinforcement tool" was not achieved. The usage was rated with 58 percent (trainer feedback only 30 percent). The objective "all have to identify possible barriers for the salespeople" was surpassed by finding solutions to overcome existing barriers.

In addition to identifying barriers, sales managers also identified enablers. Table 2.11 presents the top three enablers for each region as identified by sales managers.

TABLE 2.9   Sales Coaches

Region	Average Learning Transfer
Europe	3,9
Latin America	4,4
North America	4,4
Asia	4,1
Special Markets	return rate too low
Total	**4,1**

TABLE 2.10   List of Top Three Barriers (Sales Managers)

Region	Top Three Reasons (Sales Managers) for Poor Learning Transfer	In Percent
Europe	Time	66
	Other priorities	48
	Organizational issues	24
Latin America	Time	71
	Other priorities	44
	Business environment	27
North America	Time	66
	Other priorities	48
	Business environment	45
Asia	Time	52
	Other priorities	39
	Business environment	27
Special Markets	No useful data available	

TABLE 2.11   List of Top Three Enablers (Sales Managers)

Region	Top Three Enablers	In Percent
Europe	Business environment	29
	My empowerment/accountability	29
	Support from my managers	24
Latin America	My empowerment/accountability	44
	Business environment	32
	Support from my managers	27
North America	My empowerment/accountability	66
	Support from my managers	34
	Business environment	34
Asia	My empowerment/accountability	46
	Support from my managers	30
	Work environment	20
Special Markets	No useful data available	

Sales Professionals:

For the sales professionals, the learning transfer data were clustered by country. The return rate in some countries was less than 60 percent. The HR in these countries was involved to increase the return rate.

The results for learning transfer were lower than the benchmark (4,5). The reasons varied and were documented in the database, which had been sent to global HR.

The objective "80 percent of the salespeople use the skills at an average of 4 (scale 1 to 6)" was almost reached. The result for the usage of Value-Based Selling skills was 4,4 (learning transfer questionnaire questions 5 to 8; result 73 percent) and for the usage of Negotiation skills was 4,4 (learning transfer questionnaire questions 9 to 11; result 73 percent). The results are show in Table 2.12.

The objective "80 percent of the salespeople use the Planning Guide for Value-Based Selling (PAS), the Planning Guide for Negotiation, and the Dialogue Guide (DIGL) tools" was not reached. The usage was rated as shown in Table 2.13.

The results were almost satisfying. In certain regions, the learning transfer was adequate, but especially in Europe (3,7), the learning transfer needed more support from the coaches. Table 2.14 shows some reasons (barriers) for poor learning transfer by region. In addition to enablers, sales professionals also identified enabling factors. The enablers are shown in Table 2.15. Table 2.16 shows the different Level 3 objectives, their data methods, and their results in general.

Business Impact (Level 4)

The business measures were defined and had to be controlled to reflect the ROI analysis plan: average gross margin per month/quarter. The development of the average gross margin was measured 12 months before the training (module 1) and then 6 months after the training to have comparable data. Figure 2.4 shows the trend line analysis.

Due to this kind of business, the margin was calculated on a quarterly basis, meaning that business development is reflected more precisely. To compare the data, the quarterly gross margin was set in relation to the quarter one year earlier. The delta margin was thus given per quarter.

The bold line indicates the trend up until Q2/2007. The turnaround happened in Q3/2007. The gray line indicates the new trend line up until

TABLE 2.12 Sales Professionals' Learning Transfer

Country	Average Learning Transfer	Country	Average Learning Transfer
Switzerland	3,6	China	4,1
Germany	3,5	Malaysia	4,1
France	3,5	Singapore	4,2
Italy	3,9	Indonesia	4,3
Spain	3,7	Japan	3,6
UK	3,3	South Korea	4,0
Eastern Europe	4,0	Thailand	4,4
Brazil	4,2	Australia	return rate too low
Mexico	4,5	Turkey	4,8
Colombia	4,6	India	return rate too low
Peru	4,7	Pakistan	4,3
Chile	4,3	South Africa	return rate too low
Argentina	4,3		
North America	4,5	**Total**	**4,1**

TABLE 2.13 Usage of Tools

Tools (Objective: 80% of Usage)	Results
Planning Guide for Value-Based Selling (Question 12)	4,1 (68%)
Planning Guide for Negotiation (Question 13)	4,1 (68%)
Dialogue Guide for Negotiation (Question 14)	3,9 (65%)

TABLE 2.14   List of Top Three Barriers (Sales Professionals)

Region	Top Three Reasons (Sales Professionals) for Poor Learning Transfer	In Percent
Europe	Time	44
	Organizational issues	30
	Business environment	30
Latin America	Time	45
	Organizational issues	31
	Other priorities	22
North America	Time	38
	Other priorities	33
	Business environment	28
Asia	Business environment	47
	Time	29
	Organizational issues	22
Special Markets	Business environment	64
	Work environment	18
	Time	13

TABLE 2.15   List of Top Three Enablers (Sales Professionals)

Region	Top Three Enablers	In Percent
Europe	My empowerment/accountability	32
	Support from my managers	26
	Business environment	19
Latin America	My empowerment/accountability	51
	Support from my managers	44
	Business environment	34
North America	Support from my managers	52
	My empowerment/accountability	43
	Business environment	30
Asia	Support from my managers	43
	Business environment	32
	Work environment	28
Special Markets	Support from my managers	80
	My empowerment/accountability	53
	Work environment	53

TABLE 2.16   Summary of Level 3 Results

Data Methods Objectives	Quality and Quantity Data During the Seminar	Questionnaire for Learning Transfer After Module 2
Manager/coaches		
80% of the managers are using the reinforcement tool	Approximately 30%	58%
All have to identify possible barriers for the salespeople	Yes	• Time • Other priorities • Business environment
Sales professionals		
80% of the salespeople use the skills at an average of 3 (scale 1 to 5)	Trainers' observations were quite positive, but the sales professionals need more coaching support in the work field	• VBS: 73% • NEG: 73%
80% of the salespeople use the Planning Guide (PAS) and Dialogue Guide (DIGL) tools	Trainers' observations were quite positive, but need more coaching support in the work field	• PAS VBS: 68% • PAS NEG: 68% • DIGL NEG: 65%
Identify barriers during the on-the-job application	Yes	• Time • Business environment • Organizational issues

FIGURE 2.4   Change in Quarterly Gross Margin

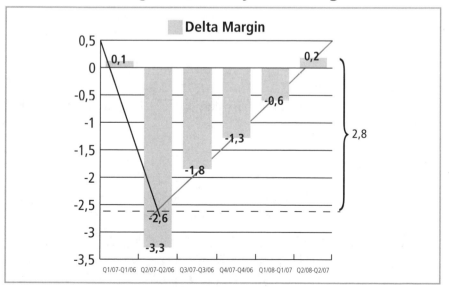

47

Q2/2008. The dotted line indicates the turnaround factor and is set at a conservative level. The delta improvement reflecting the period of the program is 2,8 percent (−2,6 to +0,2).

The original plan to use a country as a control group could not be realized due to the lack [of data per participant for a reliable comparison. Although the data from the control group signalled a good training impact (more than 30 percent), it was decided to use another method to isolate the effect for even more conservative data.

Another usually reliable source is to isolate the effect of the program with estimates from experts. The isolation effect was estimated at 35 percent. Sixty-five percent of the impact was estimated to come from other factors (top three other factors: new incentive system, better processes, and increased management attention). The confidence level of 78 percent and the isolation of 35 percent results in a total isolation training effect of 27 percent. In addition, other ROI studies used as a benchmark showed around 30 percent, which confirms the estimates from the experts.

Return on Investment (Level 5)

The purpose of the VBS initiative was to increase margin. To calculate the ROI, this increase in margin was compared with the fully loaded cost of the project.

Convert Data to Monetary Value

The data used to convert the isolated program benefit into a monetary value came from the controlling department: a 1 percent margin improvement equals a benefit of 23 million euros.

Fully Loaded Costs

The fully loaded total costs for the Value-Based Selling project were calculated as 6.672.928 euros.

ROI Calculation

The total training benefits can be calculated as follows:

Total training benefit = 2,8 percent Delta Margin × 0,27 (isolation effect) × 23 million euros (per Delta %, converting data) = 17.388 million euros

ROI calculation (%): [(Total benefits − Fully loaded costs)/Fully loaded costs] × 100

ROI (VBS) = [(17.388 million euros − 6.673 million euros)/6.673 million euros] × 100

ROI (VBS) = 160,6 = 161 percent

Training Scorecard

The Training Scorecard shown in Table 2.17 provides an overview of the methods used, the defined objectives, and the results. This scorecard was presented to the management board.

The specially designed content was accepted, and the tools were used in all countries. The Level 1 and 2 implementations went relatively smoothly. Some small disturbances were monitored in time and could be solved effectively.

The application of the VBS and Negotiation tools for Level 3 were accepted by the organization. This was critical in creating a system based on a results-based approach versus being only a training program. The coaching tools for the managers were not well implemented. The sales professionals stated that their managers only gave situational coaching in 30 percent of the cases. The managers said they had given situational coaching but did not get any coaching themselves from their managers (midlevel managers). The coaching aspect is a critical success factor in every case.

CONCLUSIONS AND RECOMMENDATIONS

Although the performance of coaching is too low on all levels and in most of the regions, the ROI of 161 percent is still impressive. Looking back from the end of 2008, we see these as the major potential tasks for the company:

- An improved use of coaching during the program (from lip service to unintentional coaching) amongst all managers as an organization development initiative would have increased the effectiveness of the program.

- Enhancing the usage of the product profiles and linking them with the marketing strategy would have made the selling solutions more effective.

It was a pleasure to see how the organization went through this learning process. It was excellent to see how the managers used the comprehensive data resulting from the training to steer the business more effectively. The first major step to develop a "global sales behavior system" has been taken successfully. The proven connection between training and business impact will help to support similar HR initiatives in the future.

TABLE 2.17   Training Scorecard

Program:	Value-Based Selling (2 days) and Negotiation Skills (2 days) and Coaching (3 + 2 days), globally (organizational development)
Target group:	1.700 sales professionals (4 days) and 450 coaches (5 days), global and regional approach
Duration:	Between January 2007 and end of 2008
Methods to isolate the training effects:	Control group; estimates from experts and benchmark from other ROI studies
Methods to convert the data to monetary value:	Historical data from controlling, direct link to delta margin
Program costs (fully loaded):	6.672.928,00 euros

Results:

Level 1: Reaction	Level 2: Learning	Level 3: Application	Level 4: Impact	Level 5: ROI	Intangible Benefits
90% of participants planned actions for application in their personal work. The objective "positive reaction" of 4,6 was exceeded by an average of 4,8.	The objective of 4,6 for the competence level was exceeded by reaching almost 5,0.	**Coaches:** • Use of the Reinforcement Tool: objective 80%, result only 30% • All have identified barriers **Sales Professionals:** • Use of the VBS and Negotiation skills: objective 80%, result 68%	Margin improvement through training: 17.388 million euros	161%	**Significant impact (%):** • Coaching practise: 73% • Sales efficiency: 70% • Employee satisfaction: 70%

DISCUSSION QUESTIONS

1. Overall, do you think the Value-Based Selling project was successful?
2. How would you have approached the evaluation of the Value-Based Selling project differently?
3. What improvements in the implementation process could have helped the team reach the Level 3 objectives? Would that improvement have had a significant impact on the Level 4 outcome, improved margin?
4. How useful is a training scorecard in presenting evaluation data?

ABOUT THE AUTHOR

Frank C. Schirmer, Dipl. Ing., holds a civil engineering degree and is a certified coach and consultant for leadership, team development, sales, service, and quality. For more than 17 years, he has supported companies as an expert to implement training solutions including evaluation and ROI, resulting in the application of ROI evaluation to a variety of projects.

Frank is managing director of LearnVision and the ROI Institute, and he is the exclusive implementer of the ROI Methodology in Germany, Austria, and Switzerland. He has published several articles on the subject of ROI in major magazines and, together with Jack J. Phillips, PhD, he has authored the first German ROI book. You can reach him at **F.Schirmer@ LearnVision.de**.

A Learning Intervention
for Work Engagement

PolyWrighton
USA

*John Kmiec, Sandra Dugas, Cyndi Gaudet, Heather Annulis,
Mary Nell McNeese, and Susan Bush*

This case was prepared to serve as a basis for discussion rather than
an illustration of either effective or ineffective administrative and
management practices. All names, dates, places, and data may have been
disguised at the request of the author or organization.

Abstract

This case study describes the evaluation of a learning intervention designed
to enhance the capabilities of immediate managers to positively influence
line employee work engagement. The study used a quasi-experimental
research design to analyze changes in work engagement for line employees
assigned to 2 of 14 business units at PolyWrighton, a manufacturer of high
quality, lightweight plastics. The test group immediate managers in the Production business unit received the learning intervention. The Maintenance
business unit managers received no intervention. Also evaluated were the
Production unit's participant reaction, learning, application, and business
impact data. Production's return on investment estimate was 399 percent,
based on a cost avoidance of $1,011,804, after adjusting for impact esti-
mates and confidence error and subtracting fully loaded program costs.

PROGRAM BACKGROUND
The Company
PolyWrighton is a manufacturer of high quality, lightweight plastics used to
package a wide variety of food, beverage, and personal care products.

Meeting rigorous hygienic, chemical, and environmental safety standards and specifications for these products requires constant monitoring and testing, state-of-the-art technology, and an extensively trained, highly skilled workforce. The chemicals used in the manufacturing process are both toxic and flammable. The plant machinery is very complex, massive in size, and hazardous in its own right. The product itself is processed under high heat and pressure. These conditions combine to demand heightened operational and safety awareness by all employees.

Adding to the complexity of the operation are the costs associated with product waste and rework. In a highly competitive market in which raw materials are expensive and frequently in short supply, it is imperative that PolyWrighton generate as little waste and rework as possible. Rework is defined as product that fails to meet customer expectations for quality and, therefore, must be reprocessed. Product waste is unusable, because it cannot be reprocessed and must be discarded. The costs associated with rework and waste result in an additional $35,000 for every 1 percent of product rework and $245,000 for every 1 percent of waste per total product produced. The larger of the two expenses, product waste, costs PolyWrighton about $600 per minute for every minute waste is generated.

As with many manufacturing processes, most waste and rework can be prevented, although a smaller amount cannot be prevented and may be considered normal. *Controllable* waste and rework, for instance, are the result of assignable causes. That is, their causes are identifiable, and they can be eliminated and prevented from reoccurring. For example, some controllable waste in the Production business unit may represent the cost of a single human error in judgment or decision making that occurred during the manufacturing process. The waste in this example can be traced to the specific cause, and the cause can be diagnosed and eliminated by appropriate intervention. The same holds true for an unexpected equipment failure that must be diagnosed and repaired by the Maintenance unit. If the breakdown is preventable, it is controllable. Depending on the nature of the problem, the cause of the mechanical breakdown may be assignable to the Maintenance unit (i.e., improperly performed or neglected servicing procedure), the Production unit (i.e., operating the equipment improperly), or both. On the other hand, *common* waste and rework are random, and their causes are unknown. Common waste and rework are considered normal by-products of production as long as they remain within normal limits of the manufacturing process.

Program Purpose

The learning program was designed to prepare the Production business unit immediate managers to more effectively create and sustain a motivational work environment in order to increase the level of work engagement in their direct reports. The program was based on the assumption that by providing a more motivational work environment, the Production business unit managers would have a positive impact on the work engagement of their 32 line employees. The program would evaluate the extent to which any improvements in work engagement led Production to higher performance, productivity, business results, or profitability.

Work engagement is a positive psychological state of mind that researchers have linked to employee satisfaction and superior job performance. Research suggests that higher levels of work engagement are associated with positive feelings of individual well-being, or *vigor*; a strong sense of commitment to the organization and its mission, goals, and objectives, or *dedication*; and the employees' full concentration and involvement with the work itself, a state in which time passes quickly, or *absorption*. Work engagement is measured by the frequency an employee experiences the three psychological substates of *vigor*, *dedication,* and *absorption* at work. The *self-coaching* skills taught during the learning program were intended to help the participating managers create and sustain a more favorable environment for work engagement in order to positively impact employee motivation and performance.

Program Objectives

Five self-coaching skills were taught to the Production business unit managers during a rigorous 90-day learning program, combining classroom and online instruction, on-the-job skills practice, journaling, and peer interaction. The objectives of the learning program were for each participant to (1) describe, relate, and apply the concepts of motivational work environments, work engagement, and organizational performance; (2) effectively employ the five skills to create and sustain a motivational environment that positively impacts work engagement and organizational performance; and

(3) develop a habit of continuous self-coaching for the personal development in, and the practice of, the five skills.

A Summary of the Five Skills

Rooted in self-coaching, or the personal practice of monitoring and assessing one's own job performance, the five skills include self-managing, reflecting, acting consciously, collaborating, and evolving. Self-managing refers to clearly knowing one's self and practicing self-discipline and control in one's actions, communications, and interpersonal relations. Self-managing requires managers to understand how they are perceived by others and how these perceptions can impact the business unit's overall performance. Reflecting is the practice of silent observation, or detaching one's self from emotionally charged situations in order to view these situations with much greater clarity. Helping the manager avoid ineffective or harmful courses of action, reflecting suspends judgment to consider the environment, the situation, and possible decision outcomes. When acting consciously, managers are more deliberate in their decision making. Because they take the time to understand the facts and nuances of a situation, these managers have a heightened awareness of the consequences and desired outcomes of alternative courses of action. By engaging in informed, conscious decision making, these managers deliberately and decisively act to achieve optimal performance and results. Collaborating managers invite team contributions, not just the opinions of a chosen few. Promoting a spirit of inclusion and abundance, these managers fully utilize the talents of their employees so they can more effectively achieve organizational goals and objectives. Evolving managers continue to purposefully grow and develop themselves, both personally and professionally. These managers are open and eager to learn, and they are quick to see work challenges as opportunities for improving their own capabilities and performance.

Basis for Linking Skills to Performance

Research suggests that immediate managers who consistently and effectively practice the self-coaching skills of self-managing, reflecting, acting consciously, collaborating, and evolving play a significant role in shaping motivational work environments that positively impact individual and group performance. Motivational work environments more effectively engage the talents and abilities of employees in ways that positively influence their behavior on the job. Specifically, because motivational work environments lead to greater levels of employee satisfaction, work engagement, and productivity, the more highly engaged employees outperform their lesser engaged peers. Effective managers afford their people the opportunity to perform well by providing them with critical resources and the information needed to do an excellent job. These managers also provide meaningful professional development and growth opportunities, recognition and rewards, and other support valued by their employees. Superior managers build trust, treat people fairly, genuinely appreciate the contributions of employees, and respect each person as a highly valued member of the team. By clearly communicating organizational plans, goals, and objectives, and by setting and enforcing high standards of performance, these managers successfully align the personal aspirations and efforts of their people with the mission, goals, and objectives of the organization.

Purpose of Evaluation

This study focused primarily on the Production business unit's performance, as measured by the four participating immediate managers' reaction, learning, and application of the five skills taught during the intervention. Also evaluated were the work engagement levels of the Production managers' 32 line employees compared with the control groups' 31 line employees assigned to the Maintenance business unit. Moreover, the study evaluated the impact and return on investment (ROI) of the intervention in terms of the Production unit's output of controllable waste and rework. The decision to evaluate the intervention to ROI was to provide information for PolyWrighton decision makers to extend the learning to the remaining 13 business units, to make improvements to the learning program, or to abandon the program altogether.

EVALUATION METHODOLOGY
General Description of Approach

The Phillips ROI Methodology was used to determine five levels of value, including participant reaction, learning, and on-the-job skills application. Also measured were business impact, intangible benefits, and return on investment in the Production unit. That is, the evaluation focused primarily on the Production unit's performance, as measured by the four immediate managers' reaction, learning, and application of the five skills taught during the intervention. Using the extensively studied and highly validated Utrecht Work Engagement Scale (UWES), the evaluation also measured the work engagement levels of the Production managers' 32 direct reports compared with the 31 direct reports assigned to the Maintenance unit. The impact and ROI of the intervention were evaluated in terms of the Production unit's controllable waste and rework.

Model or Approach

The Phillips ROI Methodology is a systematic approach for planning evaluation, collecting and analyzing data, determining intangible benefits, calculating return on investment, and reporting results to stakeholders for decision making and continuous improvement. In this context, the decision to evaluate the learning intervention to the fifth level, ROI, was to provide information for PolyWrighton decision makers to extend the learning to the 13 remaining business units, to make improvements to the learning program, or to simply abandon the learning program entirely.

Planning the intervention and its evaluation required a thorough needs assessment to ensure the intervention aligned with organizational priorities. The result of the needs assessment was the Business Alignment and Forecasting shown in Figure 3.1.

For the Production unit, aligning the intervention with organizational needs meant increasing employee work engagement and reducing controllable product waste and rework. The Production unit's work engagement was compared with the Maintenance unit's work engagement using the highly validated UWES. In a quasi-experimental research design format, work engagement comparisons were generated by taking repeated UWES measurements of both Production and Maintenance. Product quality was measured in terms of costs associated with the Production unit's monthly percentages of controllable product waste and rework. Trend analysis and participant and management estimates were the methods used to isolate the effects of the intervention. The fully loaded costs of the program were included in the ROI calculation to ensure the monetary benefits were not overstated. PolyWrighton provided standard values for converting controllable waste and rework data into monetary values. At PolyWrighton, rework

FIGURE 3.1 Business Alignment and Forecasting

Level	Needs Assessment	Program Objective	Measurement and Evaluation
5	**Payoff Needs →** Avoid costs associated with controllable waste and rework	**ROI Objectives →** Target return on investment of 15%	**ROI** Calculate ROI
4	**Business Needs →** Reduce controllable waste and rework Increase work engagement	**Impact Objectives →** Monthly percentages of controllable product waste and rework decline Increase work engagement	**Impact** Percentages of controllable product waste and rework at 8 months after completion of the program compared to the same measurements taken before the program Utrecht Work Engagement Scale (UWES) of direct reports at 6 months
3	**Job Performance Needs →** Immediate manager effectiveness in the areas of leadership, setting and maintaining standards, and developing and motivating employees	**Application Objectives →** Effectively and continuously apply the five self-coaching skills at work Effectively create and sustain motivational work environments that increase engagement	**Application** Participant self-assessment at 3 months after completion of the program Utrecht Work Engagement Scale (UWES) direct reports at 3 months
2	**Learning Needs →** Increase success skills of immediate managers in the areas of leadership, setting and maintaining standards, and developing and motivating employees	**Learning Objectives →** Immediate managers learn to effectively apply the five self-coaching skills of self-managing, reflecting, acting consciously, collaborating, and evolving Learn how to foster motivational work environments that increase engagement	**Learning** Session content summaries, participant assignments, and skill development journal entries during the program Pre/post self-assessment profile Utrecht Work Engagement Scale (UWES) of direct reports during the program
1	**Preference Needs →** Learning that is relevant and important to successful job performance	**Reaction Objectives →** Program content receives favorable rating of 4 out of 5 in relevance and importance 80% of participants identify planned actions	**Reaction** Reaction and planned action questionnaires at the end of each session of the program

Note: Adapted from *The Value of Learning: How Organizations Capture Value and ROI and Translate Them Into Support, Improvement, and Funds* by Patricia Pulliam Phillips and Jack J. Phillips, 2007. Copyright 2007 by John Wiley & Sons, Inc., San Francisco: Pfeiffer.

and waste result in an additional $35,000 for every 1 percent of product rework and $245,000 for every 1 percent of waste per total product produced. Data not converted to monetary values, including work engagement, were listed as intangible benefits.

The participating managers' on-the-job application, learning, and reaction data were also collected. The on-the-job application of participant skills was measured using immediate manager self-assessment surveys and UWES data collected from their direct reports after the intervention. During six of the seven sessions, learning was measured by the participants summarizing how they practiced the previous session's content on the job and by their completed assignments and skill development journal entries. Learning was also measured using a pre- and post-program skill assessment inventory and by UWES data collected from the direct reports during the course of the intervention. Participant reaction data pertaining to program content relevance and importance, as well as the participants' planned implementation actions, were collected at the end of each of the seven learning sessions.

Categories or Levels of Data

Corresponding to the Phillips ROI Methodology, the categories, or levels, of data included those listed in Table 3.1. Level 1 Reaction data measured participant satisfaction and planned actions for implementing the learning. The organizational need was for the participants to perceive the learning as relevant and important to successful job performance and for the participants to plan to use the learning on the job. The program objectives, in this case, included a favorable mean rating of 4 out of 5 points for content relevance and importance on participant reaction surveys, and that 80 percent of the participants would identify planned actions. Level 2 Learning measures participant acquisition of knowledge and skills, as well as changes in attitude. The need was for the immediate managers to learn how to effectively apply the five skills on the job. Program objectives were determined by facilitator assessments of participant discussions, responses to questions, and completed assignments. Also, the facilitator administered pre- and post-intervention self-assessment profiles to gauge the participants' perceptions of changes in key behaviors related to the five skills. UWES surveys of the Production unit direct reports were taken at Days 0, 45, and 90 of the intervention and compared with those of Maintenance. Level 3 Application measured the on-the-job utilization of the learning. The organizational need was for the immediate managers to consistently and effectively apply the five skills on the job. Participant self-assessments were taken at three months after completion of the learning to assess the on-the-job application of the five skills in Production. UWES data of Production and

TABLE 3.1   Categories or Levels of Data

Level	Measurement Focus	Organizational Needs	Program Objectives
1. Reaction	Measures participant satisfaction and planned actions for implementing the learning.	Participants perceive the learning as relevant and important to successful job performance. Participants plan to use the learning on the job.	Program receives a favorable mean rating of 4 out of 5 points for content relevance and importance. At least 80% of participants identify planned actions.
2. Learning	Measures acquisition of knowledge and skills, as well as changes in attitude.	Immediate managers learn to effectively apply the five skills on the job.	Facilitator assessment of participant discussions, responses to questions, and completed assignments. Pre- and post-intervention self-assessment profiles. UWES surveys of direct reports taken during the intervention.
3. Application	Measures on-the-job utilization of learning.	Immediate managers consistently and effectively apply the five skills on the job.	Participant self-assessments at 3 months after completion of the program. UWES of direct reports 3 months after completion of the intervention.
4. Impact	Measures changes in business impact.	On-the-job application of the five skills has a positive impact on reducing controllable waste and rework.	Percentage of controllable rework and waste product generated by Production. UWES of direct reports at 6 months.
5. Return on Investment	Compares the benefits of the program with its costs.	Target 15% ROI from controllable rework and waste production.	Calculate ROI.

Source: Adapted from *The Value of Learning: How Organizations Capture Value and ROI and Translate Them Into Support, Improvement, and Funds* by Patricia Pulliam Phillips and Jack J. Phillips, 2007. Copyright 2007 by John Wiley & Sons, Inc., San Francisco: Pfeiffer.

Note: UWES = Utrecht Work Engagement Scale.

Maintenance direct reports were also taken at three months after completion of the intervention to assess changes in work engagement. Level 4 Impact measures changes in business impact. The organizational need was to reduce the percentage of controllable waste and rework generated by Production, the participants' business unit. That is, the monthly percentages of controllable rework and waste product generated by Production were used to determine if program objectives were met. Also, one last UWES comparison of direct reports was taken at six months. The Level 5 Return on Investment (ROI) calculation would compare the program benefits with its costs. In this case, a conservative 15 percent target ROI for the reduction of the Production unit's controllable rework and waste was established.

Standards or Guiding Principles

The standards of evaluation were the 12 Guiding Principles of Phillips ROI Methodology depicted in Table 3.2.

TABLE 3.2   Phillips Methodology 12 Guiding Principles

1. When a higher level evaluation is conducted, data must be collected at lower levels.
2. When an evaluation is planned for a higher level, the previous level of evaluation does not have to be comprehensive.
3. When collecting and analyzing data, use only the most credible sources.
4. When analyzing data, select the most conservative alternative for calculations.
5. At least one method must be used to isolate the effects of the solution/program.
6. If no improvement data are available for a population or from a specific source, the assumption is that little or no improvement has occurred.
7. Estimates of improvements should be adjusted for the potential error of the estimate.
8. Extreme data items and unsupported claims should not be used in ROI calculations.
9. Only the first year of benefits (annual) should be used in the ROI analysis of short-term solutions.
10. Costs of a solution, project, or program should be fully loaded for ROI analysis.
11. Intangible measures are defined as measures that are purposely not converted to monetary values.
12. The results from the ROI Methodology must be communicated to all key stakeholders.

Note: Adapted from *The Value of Learning: How Organizations Capture Value and ROI and Translate Them Into Support, Improvement, and Funds* by Patricia Pulliam Phillips and Jack J. Phillips, 2007. Copyright 2007 by John Wiley & Sons, Inc., San Francisco: Pfeiffer.

Data Collection Strategy

The data collection strategy included acquiring five levels of credible, relevant evaluation data capable of showing the satisfaction of assessed organizational needs and the accomplishment of the learning program objectives previously shown in Figure 3.1. Data for Levels 1 through 3 were collected to evaluate the participants' reactions, learning, and on-the-job application of newly acquired knowledge and skills. Level 4 data evaluated the impact of the application of those skills on business outcomes and performance, while the Level 5 ROI calculation would estimate the monetary value of the learning intervention over costs.

Data Collection Plan

The data collection plan in Figure 3.2 shows the level of evaluation, broad program objectives, measures and data collected, collection methods, data sources, timing, and responsibility. Level 1 Reaction data collected at the end of each session gauged the participants' perceptions of the program and their intent to apply what they learned. In addition to Level 2 participant pre- and post-self-assessment profiles and facilitator appraisals of learning, the evaluation used work engagement data collected from the Production business unit during the intervention and compared it with the work engagement of the Maintenance unit. Participant self-assessment profiles and work engagement data taken three months after the intervention gauged the Level 3 on-the-job application of participant skills. Level 4 Impact data included work engagement measurements taken at six months after the intervention and the percentage of controllable waste and rework generated by Production at eight months. Level 5 ROI was a calculation of net program benefits over costs, expressed as follows:

$$ROI = \frac{\text{Program Benefits} - \text{Program Costs}}{\text{Program Costs}} \times 100$$

Example Data Collection Instruments

Data were collected with a variety of instruments. Figure 3.3 shows the reaction questionnaire administered to the participants at the end of each of the seven learning program sessions. Figure 3.4 includes the instrument used by the participants to self-assess their learning at the beginning and

FIGURE 3.2   Data Collection Plan

Level	Broad Program Objectives	Measures/Data	Data Collection Methods	Data Sources	Timing	Responsibility
1 Reaction	Program content receives favorable ratings from participants Participants plan to apply the learning on the job	Program content receives average favorable rating of 4 out of 5 for relevance and importance 80% of participants identify planned actions	Questionnaires	Participants	End of each session during the program	Facilitator
2 Learning	Learn to effectively apply the five self-coaching skills of self-managing, reflecting, acting consciously, collaborating, and evolving Learn to foster motivational work environments that increase engagement	Participants demonstrate successful completion of program learning objectives outlined in the facilitator and participant guides Self-assessment Work engagement	Observations of performance, guided discussions, questioning, and assignments Skill development journals Pre/post self-assessment profile Utrecht Work Engagement Scale (UWES)	Facilitator Participants Participants Direct reports	Throughout the 90-day learning program Day 0, Day 90 Day 0, Day 45, Day 90	Facilitator
3 Application	Apply the five self-coaching skills at work Foster motivational work environments that increase engagement	Self-assessment Work engagement	Questionnaires UWES	Participants Direct reports	3 months after program completion	Program manager
4 Impact	Reduce product waste and rework Increase work engagement	Percentage of controllable waste and rework generated by the Production business unit Work engagement	Organizational records/databases UWES	Business unit manager Direct reports	8 months after program compared with pre-program 6 months	Program manager
5 ROI	Target ROI 15%	*Comments:* ROI = (Net Program Benefits ÷ Program Costs) X 100				

Source: Adapted from *The Value of Learning: How Organizations Capture Value and ROI and Translate Them Into Support, Improvement, and Funds* by Patricia Pulliam Phillips and Jack J. Phillips, 2007. Copyright 2007 by John Wiley & Sons, Inc., San Francisco: Pfeiffer.

FIGURE 3.3   Session Reaction Questionnaire

Session (Circle One): I II III IV V VI VII

Name (Only if you want us to contact you):_____

Instructions: Circle the appropriate response to each statement and add any comments you have about the program below.

	Strongly Disagree				Strongly Agree
1. The content was relevant to my job.	1	2	3	4	5
2. The content was important to my job success.	1	2	3	4	5
3. I intend to use the material.	1	2	3	4	5
4. The facilitator was effective.	1	2	3	4	5
5. The materials were effective.	1	2	3	4	5
6. This was a good investment of my time.	1	2	3	4	5
7. I would recommend this to others.	1	2	3	4	5
8. Overall, I was satisfied with the program.	1	2	3	4	5

Comments:

Source: Adapted from *The Value of Learning: How Organizations Capture Value and ROI and Translate Them Into Support, Improvement, and Funds* by Patricia Pulliam Phillips and Jack J. Phillips, 2007. Copyright 2007 by John Wiley & Sons, Inc., San Francisco: Pfeiffer.

end of the 90-day intervention. The same instrument was used to self-assess participant application of the learning on the job at three months after the intervention. Figure 3.5 includes the UWES used to measure the work engagement levels of the Production and Maintenance unit direct reports three times during the intervention, three months after the

Figure 3.4 Participant Skill Self-Assessment

Savvy Self-Assessment Profile: What's Your Savvy I.Q.?					
Think you might already be a savvy manager; sharp and perceptive, someone with "know how"? Let's find out! For each statement, choose the number that best describes how consistently you practice each of these behaviors on the job. Write your score in the box provided.					
Self-Managing Behaviors	**Never (1)**	**Rarely (2)**	**Sometimes (3)**	**Usually (4)**	**Always (5)**
1. I control my emotions during the day regardless of any particular event or situation.					
2. I enjoy my job and easily maintain a positive attitude about my work.					
3. I step back from a situation and separate my personal feelings and perceptions from the facts of the issue.					
4. I speak the truth as I know it to be.					
5. My words match my actions; I walk my talk.					
Reflecting Behaviors	**Never (1)**	**Rarely (2)**	**Sometimes (3)**	**Usually (4)**	**Always (5)**
6. I think through events, appropriately identifying and filtering assumptions I am making.					
7. I play back events in order to identify learning to improve my performance the next time.					
8. I set specific goals that guide my managerial actions.					
9. I consider the best time and place for holding an important conversation or discussion.					
10. I use my experiences to guide my actions.					
Acting Consciously Behaviors	**Never (1)**	**Rarely (2)**	**Sometimes (3)**	**Usually (4)**	**Always (5)**
11. I do what is right, even when it is the harder choice.					
12. I provide specific expectations about desired outcomes and ask for questions when delegating tasks.					
13. I know when to lead and when to step back.					
14. I pay full attention to people when they are talking to me; I don't multitask.					
15. I give employees the tools they need to do their jobs well.					

FIGURE 3.4 Participant Skill Self-Assessment (Cont.)

Collaborating Behaviors	Never (1)	Rarely (2)	Sometimes (3)	Usually (4)	Always (5)
16. I give appropriate feedback to employees to drive optimal performance.					
17. I actively look for opportunities to praise others.					
18. I effectively engage the talents and skills of employees on projects.					
19. I include team members in decisions that impact their performance.					
20. I accept "no" as a starting point for uncovering barriers to success.					
Evolving Behaviors	Never (1)	Rarely (2)	Sometimes (3)	Usually (4)	Always (5)
21. I continuously seek opportunities to learn and grow.					
22. I know the difference between motivation and manipulation.					
23. I view mistakes as learning opportunities for myself and my staff.					
24. I work well with others even when I don't get my way.					
25. I use wisdom from my experiences and hindsight to make better decisions going forward.					
Calculate Your Score					
Subtotals					
Total Score					
Your Rating					
115–125	You are evolved and seamlessly integrating your savvy skills.				
100–114	You are on your way! Keep practicing your savvy skills.				
88–99	You frequently hit the mark. Assess and grow your specific savvy skills.				
87 and below	You have work to do! Let's get going on your development!				

Source: Adapted from *The Savvy Manager: 5 Skills That Drive Optimal Performance* by Jane R. Flagello and Sandra Bernard Dugas, 2009. Copyright 2009 by the American Society for Training & Development, Alexandria, VA: ASTD Press.

FIGURE 3.5   Utrecht Work Engagement Scale (UWES)

Please check the appropriate response(s):

Role: ❑ Team Member   ❑ Manager/Supervisor   ❑ Other (Specify):

Unit: ❑ Polymer   ❑ Maintenance   ❑ Other (Specify):

Instructions: The following 17 statements are about how you feel at work. Please read each statement carefully and decide if you ever feel this way about your job. If you have never had this feeling, cross the "0" (zero) in the space after the statement. If you have had this feeling, indicate how often you felt it by crossing the number (from 1 to 6) that best describes how frequently you feel that way.

	Never	Almost Never	Rarely	Sometimes	Often	Very Often	Always
	0	1	2	3	4	5	6
Note: Infrequently used words, and words needing further clarification, are described below as footnotes.	Never	A few times a year or less	Once a month or less	A few times a month	Once a week	A few times a week	Every day
1. At my work, I feel bursting with energy.	0	1	2	3	4	5	6
2. I find the work that I do full of meaning and purpose.	0	1	2	3	4	5	6
3. Time flies when I am working.	0	1	2	3	4	5	6
4. At my job, I feel strong and vigorous.[1]	0	1	2	3	4	5	6
5. I am enthusiastic[2] about my job.	0	1	2	3	4	5	6
6. When I am working, I forget everything else around me.	0	1	2	3	4	5	6
7. My job inspires[3] me.	0	1	2	3	4	5	6
8. When I get up in the morning, I feel like going to work.	0	1	2	3	4	5	6
9. I feel happy when I am working intensely.[4]	0	1	2	3	4	5	6
10. I am proud of the work that I do.	0	1	2	3	4	5	6
11. I am immersed[5] in my work.	0	1	2	3	4	5	6
12. I can continue working for very long periods at a time.	0	1	2	3	4	5	6
13. To me, my job is challenging.[6]	0	1	2	3	4	5	6
14. I get carried away when I am working.	0	1	2	3	4	5	6
15. At my job, I am very resilient[7] mentally.	0	1	2	3	4	5	6
16. It is difficult to detach myself from my job.	0	1	2	3	4	5	6
17. At my work, I always persevere,[8] even when things do not go well.	0	1	2	3	4	5	6

[1] vigorous (energetic, enthusiastic)
[2] enthusiastic (excited, passionate)
[3] inspires (motivates, encourages)
[4] intensely (passionately, with focus, with concentration)
[5] immersed (wrapped up, engrossed, absorbed)
[6] challenging (stimulating, exciting, thought-provoking)
[7] resilient (flexible, elastic, recover easily from setbacks)
[8] persevere (keep trying, persist, stick with)

Source: Adapted from *Utrecht Work Engagement Scale: Preliminary Manual*, by W. Schaufeli and A. Bakker, p. 48. Copyright 2003 by Schaufeli & Bakker.

intervention, and six months after the intervention. The UWES was used as a measure of participant learning, application, and business results; each measure depended on the timing of administration.

ROI Analysis Strategy

The ROI analysis strategy shown in Figure 3.6 is based on the Phillips Methodology. The ROI analysis for this project depended on tracking the percentage of controllable waste and rework for the Production business unit before, during, and after the learning intervention. Monetary values were calculated directly, based on the percentage of total product waste and

FIGURE 3.6   ROI Analysis Strategy

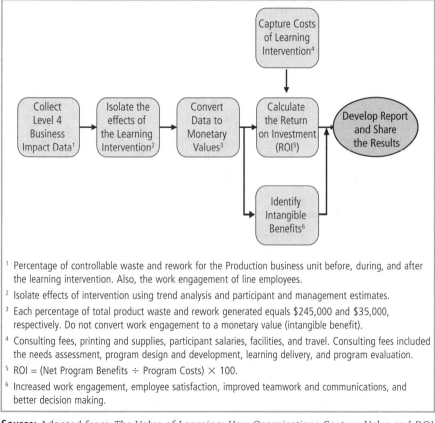

[1] Percentage of controllable waste and rework for the Production business unit before, during, and after the learning intervention. Also, the work engagement of line employees.

[2] Isolate effects of intervention using trend analysis and participant and management estimates.

[3] Each percentage of total product waste and rework generated equals $245,000 and $35,000, respectively. Do not convert work engagement to a monetary value (intangible benefit).

[4] Consulting fees, printing and supplies, participant salaries, facilities, and travel. Consulting fees included the needs assessment, program design and development, learning delivery, and program evaluation.

[5] ROI = (Net Program Benefits ÷ Program Costs) × 100.

[6] Increased work engagement, employee satisfaction, improved teamwork and communications, and better decision making.

Source: Adapted from *The Value of Learning: How Organizations Capture Value and ROI and Translate Them Into Support, Improvement, and Funds* by Patricia Pulliam Phillips and Jack J. Phillips, 2007. Copyright 2007 by John Wiley & Sons, Inc., San Francisco: Pfeiffer.

rework generated each month. The researcher used two methods to isolate the effects of the intervention on controllable waste and rework. The strategy called for trend analysis of the monthly percentage of controllable waste and rework per total product, less those outliers identified by Poly-Wrighton management as nonattributable to the Production business unit. Management and participant estimates of the impact of the intervention and the level of confidence in those estimates were also taken and adjusted. Work engagement was not converted to a monetary value but was instead listed as an intangible benefit. Fully loaded costs were calculated and verified by management to ensure the most conservative ROI possible.

ROI Analysis Plan

The data analysis and ROI plan are shown in Figure 3.7. The data items analyzed included percentage of controllable waste, percentage of controllable rework, and work engagement. All of these were Level 4 Impact data for the Production business unit.

Isolation Techniques

Participant and management estimates of the impact of the intervention on business results, corrected for estimate error, were used in conjunction with trend analyses of controllable waste and rework. Outliers identified by PolyWrighton management as nonattributable to the Production business unit were removed from the trend analyses.

Data Conversion Techniques

The conversion from percentage of controllable waste and rework to monetary values was direct. As previously noted, it costs PolyWrighton $35,000 for 1 percent of product rework and $245,000 for 1 percent of product waste. Data not converted to monetary values, including work engagement, were listed as intangible benefits.

Cost Summary

The program cost categories shown in Figure 3.7 included the consulting fees for the learning needs assessment, program design and development, learning delivery, and program evaluation. Printing and supplies, participant salaries, facilities, and travel were also planned costs of the program. In actuality, all fees and expenses were waived, leaving only the cost of participant salaries for PolyWrighton to bear. However, in order to provide

FIGURE 3.7   Data Analysis and ROI Plan

Data Items	Methods for Isolating the Effects of the Program or Process	Method for Converting Data to Monetary Values	Cost Categories	Intangible Benefits	Communication Targets for Final Report
Percentage of controllable waste Percentage of controllable rework Work engagement	Participant and management estimates Trend analysis	Percentage of controllable waste × $245,000 Percentage of controllable rework × $35,000 Work engagement not converted to a monetary value	Consulting fees (needs assessment, program design and development, learning delivery, and program evaluation) Printing and supplies Participant salaries Facilities Facilitator travel	Increased work engagement Employee satisfaction Improved teamwork and communications Better decision making	Management Participants Training Human Resources

Source: Adapted from *The Value of Learning: How Organizations Capture Value and ROI and Translate Them Into Support, Improvement, and Funds* by Patricia Pulliam Phillips and Jack J. Phillips, 2007. Copyright 2007 by John Wiley & Sons, Inc., San Francisco: Pfeiffer.

the most conservative ROI figure for decision makers, all costs were included in the calculation, even those fees and expenses that were never actually charged.

EVALUATION RESULTS

Level 1 Reaction

The four participating immediate managers from the Production unit completed reaction questionnaires (Figure 3.3) at the end of each of the seven learning sessions. The areas surveyed included content relevance to the job, content importance to job success, intent to use the material on the job, facilitator effectiveness, material effectiveness, whether the participant would recommend the program to others, and overall satisfaction. At the end of each session, the participants rated these items on a scale of 1 ("strongly disagree") to 5 ("strongly agree"). The participants also indicated planned actions for each session. Evaluation targets were set for a favorable mean rating of 4 out of 5 points for content relevance and importance, and at least 80 percent of the participants would identify planned actions (Table 3.1, Figure 3.2). The targets set for content relevance and importance, and for planned actions, were met. In this case, content relevance and importance scored mean ratings of 4.16 and 4.07, respectively. Also, all participants developed plans to apply, on the job, what they learned during the program. The reaction data are summarized in Table 3.3.

Level 2 Learning

Rooted in self-coaching, or the personal practice of monitoring and assessing one's own job performance, the five skills included self-managing, reflecting, acting consciously, collaborating, and evolving. These five self-coaching skills were taught to the Production managers during seven separate learning sessions facilitated over the course of the 90-day learning program. The seven sessions combined classroom and online instruction, on-the-job skills practice, journaling, and peer interaction, offering a variety of methods to evaluate learning. This design enabled the participants to apply newly acquired skills at work, to share their experiences and lessons learned from each outing, and to become more self-directed and confident with each new skill. Facilitator observations of participant performance through guided discussion, Socratic questioning, and completed assignments (Table 3.1); participant pre- and post-program self-assessment profiles (Figure 3.4); and UWES measurements (Figure 3.5) of the participant's direct reports were used to evaluate learning (Table 3.1, Figure 3.2).

The pre- and post-program self-assessment profile asked participants to rate how consistently they practice 25 specific work behaviors. These behaviors, shown in Figure 3.4, are anchored to the five skills covered during the 90-day learning intervention, with each behavior being rated on a scale of 1 ("never") to 5 ("always"). Scores were totaled and compared with a rating scale (Figure 3.4) for individual feedback. Administered at Day 0 of the learning intervention, the pre-program self-assessment mean score was 105.0 points (Table 3.4). The Day 90 post-program self-assessment mean score was 107.6 points (Table 3.4). An increase of 2.6 points for the mean, while statistically inconclusive, suggests the possibility that at least a modest amount of learning may have occurred during the program. The project team deemed this acceptable, as the learning was designed to become

TABLE 3.3   Participant Reactions

Reaction Questionnaire[1] Item	Mean Rating[2,3]	Target[4]
1. The content was relevant to my job.	4.16	4.00
2. The content was important to my job success.	4.07	4.00
3. I intend to use the material.[5]	4.23	
4. The facilitator was effective.	4.05	
5. The materials were effective.	4.00	
6. This was a good investment of my time.	3.98	
7. I would recommend this to others.	4.07	
8. Overall, I was satisfied with the program.	4.23	

[1] The four participating immediate managers from the Production business unit completed a reaction questionnaire at the end of each of the seven learning sessions.

[2] The participants rated each item on a scale of 1 ("strongly disagree") to 5 ("strongly agree").

[3] The mean rating is the average of participant responses collected at the end of each of the seven learning sessions.

[4] Evaluation targets were set for a favorable mean rating of 4 out of 5 points for content relevance and importance.

[5] At the end of each learning session, all participants identified planned actions to implement what they learned on the job. Follow-up sessions allowed time for each participant to discuss the implementation experience with the rest of the group.

participant self-directed and to continue to increase after the formal 90-day program ended. In essence, the plan was for the participants to become *self-coaching*. This evolution from facilitated instruction to self-coaching and self-directed learning required that learning be evaluated as it was practiced on the job. With this in mind, work engagement levels would help evaluate participant skill acquisition during the intervention.

Taken in the context of the organizational setting, work engagement readings of the Production test group and Maintenance control group line employees provided additional insight into the participants' on-the-job skill development. A highly disruptive plant fire that occurred toward the end of the learning program produced a significant gap between these two groups; a slight drop in Production work engagement compared with a much steeper decline in Maintenance (Figure 3.8). A thorough assessment of the situation found that the fire should have had no more of an adverse impact on Maintenance (control group) than it did on Production (test group). According to the senior human resource manager, the lead training manager, and the business unit and line managers at PolyWrighton, both groups experienced the same extended period of excessive overtime and intense physical labor. While work engagement was more negatively impacted in Maintenance compared with Production, no apparent reason could be identified. This may suggest that the with-intervention Production immediate managers might have been better equipped to deal with the plant fire and its negative consequences than their Maintenance business unit counterparts. In other words, it is possible that the five skills learned and practiced during the program helped keep the Production unit from being as negatively impacted.

TABLE 3.4   Pre- and Post-program Self-Assessment Profile Results

Timing[1]	Level[2]	Mean Score	Change[3]
Pre-program (Day 0)	2	105.0	0.0
Post-program (Day 90)	2	107.6	2.6

[1] The four participating immediate managers from the Production business unit completed a self-assessment profile at the beginning and end of the 90-day learning program as a measure of learning.

[2] Level of evaluation: 1 = Reaction; 2 = Learning; 3 = Application; 4 = Impact; 5 = ROI.

[3] Change is the difference between the previous and current reading.

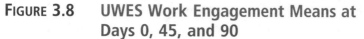

FIGURE 3.8   UWES Work Engagement Means at
Days 0, 45, and 90

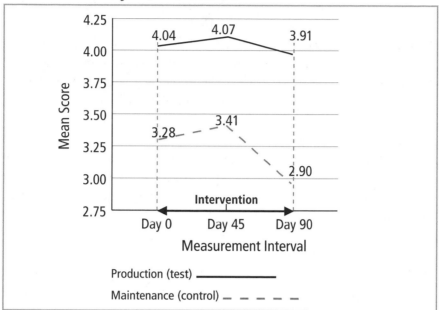

Note: An independent samples *t* test for differences between the Production (test) and Maintenance (control) means was not statistically significant at Day 0. That is, the difference between the two groups' work engagement was too small to matter at Day 0. However, the gap between these groups had widened considerably by the end of the intervention. Given the organizational context, including a disruptive plant fire during the final 30 days of the study, the intervention can perhaps be seen as being more preventive in nature. It may be that the Production managers had learned to handle the high-stress situation more effectively than their Maintenance counterparts.

Level 3 Application

Participant self-assessment profiles taken at three months after completion of the learning program (Table 3.5), as well as the UWES readings of direct report work engagement taken at three months after completion of the learning program (Figure 3.9), provided some insights into the on-the-job application of participant learning.

Application Data

As the self-assessment profile data in Table 3.5 suggest, the self-coaching participant managers from Production appeared to be applying their newly acquired knowledge and skills more frequently at Day 180, with a mean score of 112.6, than they were at Day 90, with a mean score of 107.6. This new level of application was 5.0 points higher at three months after the completion of the intervention. Shown in Figure 3.9, while work engagement in both business units was on the increase three months after the intervention, Production maintained a higher response from its direct reports than did Maintenance. Managers at PolyWrighton have suggested that the gain in the nonintervention Maintenance group was probably the result of key supervisory changes made during that period.

Barriers to Application

Engaged leadership by the lead manager in Production, also a recipient of the intervention, and closer coordination and communication among all managers in that business unit prevented any notable barriers to application.

Enablers to Application

Production unit leadership was a driving force in enabling the transfer of learning by the participating managers to the job. The lead manager participated in the learning intervention and practiced the five skills alongside her direct reports, the four line managers. Also, regular meetings between these managers to discuss the application of the five skills, and an improved

TABLE 3.5   Self-Assessment Profile Results at Three Months

Timing[1,2]	Level[3]	Mean Score	Change[4]
Pre-program (Day 0)	2	105.0	0.0
Post-program (Day 90)	2	107.6	2.6
3 months after (Day 180)	3	112.6	5.0

[1] The four participating immediate managers from the Production business unit completed a self-assessment profile at the beginning and end of the 90-day learning program as a measure of learning.

[2] The participating immediate managers completed another self-assessment profile at three months after the completion of the learning intervention as a measure of their on-the-job application of their newly acquired knowledge and skills.

[3] Level of evaluation: 1 = Reaction; 2 = Learning; 3 = Application; 4 = Impact; 5 = ROI.

[4] Change is the difference between the previous and current reading.

FIGURE 3.9   UWES Work Engagement Means at
Days 0, 45, 90, and 180

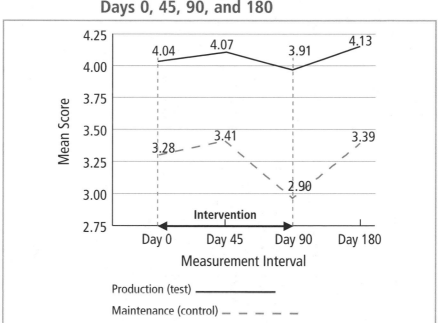

Note: An independent samples *t* test for differences between the Production (test) and Maintenance (control) means was not statistically significant at Day 0. Further, the gap between these groups had widened considerably by the end of the intervention. By Day 180, or 3 months after the intervention, work engagement in both business units was on the rise. Managers at PolyWrighton indicated the gain in the nonintervention Maintenance group was probably the result of key supervisory changes made after the plant fire.

system of tracking unit performance initiated by these managers, supported the continued use and development of the learning.

Level 4 Business Impact

The business impact measures included Production's controllable rework and waste summarized in Table 3.6. Also measured were Production's work engagement levels compared with those of the Maintenance unit (Figure 3.10). Work engagement data were not converted to monetary values and, therefore, were treated as intangible benefits. The following discussion will focus on Production controllable waste and rework.

TABLE 3.6   Production Controllable Rework and Waste

	Pre-intervention 8-Month Average[3,6]		Projected Trend[4]		Post-intervention 8-Month Average[5,6]		Percent Change[7]	Average Monthly Cost[8,10]	12-Month Cost Projection[9,10]
	Percentage	Value	Percentage	Value	Percentage	Value			
Controllable Rework[1]	2.69	$94,000	0.0	$0	1.87	$65,450	+1.87	+$65,450	+$785,400
Controllable Waste[2]	0.73	$178,850	1.5	$367,500	0.22	$53,900	-1.28	-$313,600	-$3,763,200
								-$248,150	-$2,977,800
					Total Program Benefits (Controllable Waste and Rework Combined)[11]				

Isolation of Impact on Total Program Benefits	Impact Estimate[12]	Confidence[13]	Adjusted Estimate[14]	Total Benefit Adjusted for Impact[15]
	50%	85%	42.5%	$1,265,565

[1] $35,000 is the monetary value of 1 percent of controllable rework per total product produced. Monetary values provided by PolyWrighton.

[2] $245,000 is the monetary value of 1 percent of controllable waste per total product produced. Monetary values provided by PolyWrighton.

[3] Pre-intervention monthly percentage and cost averages are based on the data collected during the 8-month period preceding the intervention.

[4] The projected trends are based on the pre-intervention percentage waste and rework data collected during the 8-month period preceding the intervention. A linear trend line, generated in Microsoft Excel and extended through the end of the post-intervention period, returned the projected percentages shown. The dollar values referenced in notes 1 and 2 were then multiplied by the trend percentages to return the projected values.

[5] Post-intervention monthly percentage and cost averages are based on the data collected during the 8-month period following the intervention.

[6] Data points, whose causes were not assignable to the Production business unit, were treated as outliers and removed from the calculation of the pre- and post-intervention 8-month averages. PolyWrighton management made the final determination of which data points would be treated as outliers. Examples of causes not assignable to Production included new product specifications, ongoing technical issues stemming from the plant fire recovery, an unexpected line freeze attributable to severe weather, and worse than usual supplier material shortages.

[7] Percent change is the post-intervention percentage minus the projected trend percentage for both controllable rework and waste.

[8] Average monthly cost is the post-intervention value minus the projected trend value for both controllable rework and waste.

[9] Average monthly cost multiplied by 12 months for both controllable rework and waste.

[10] Negative values represent PolyWrighton cost avoidances.

[11] Total benefit before factoring in participant and management impact estimates corrected for confidence error.

[12] Combined manager and participant estimate of the intervention's impact on improvement.

[13] Combined manager and participant confidence of their estimate of the intervention's impact on improvement.

[14] Combined adjusted impact estimate based on combined manager and participant estimate and confidence.

[15] (12-Month Total Program Benefit expressed as a positive value) × (Adjusted Estimate expressed as a decimal value) = (Total Benefit Adjusted for Impact): $2,977,800 × 0.425 = $1,265,565

**FIGURE 3.10   UWES Work Engagement Means at
Days 0, 45, 90, 180, and 270**

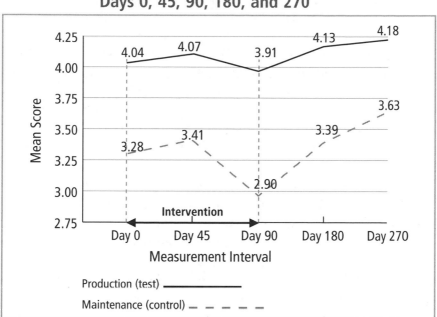

Note: An independent samples t test for differences between the Production (test)
and Maintenance (control) means was not statistically significant at Day 0. Further,
the gap between these groups had widened considerably by the end of the
intervention. At Day 270, or 6 months after the intervention, work engagement in
both business units was still on the rise. Managers at PolyWrighton indicated the
gain in the nonintervention Maintenance group was probably the result of key
supervisory changes made after the plant fire that occurred in the last 30 days of
the intervention. While the post-intervention gap continued to narrow, Production
maintained higher levels of work engagement compared with Maintenance.

Impact Data

Pre-intervention monthly percentage and cost averages, based on data collected during the eight-month period preceding the intervention, projected
trends for controllable waste and rework through the end of the eight-
month period following the intervention. A linear trend line, generated in
Microsoft Excel and extended through the end of the post-intervention
period, returned the projected percentages shown in Table 3.6. The projected trend values through the end of the post-intervention period were
0.0 percent for rework and 1.5 percent for waste.

All rework and waste data whose causes were not assignable to the
Production business unit were treated as outliers and removed from the

calculation of the pre and post-intervention eight-month averages. Poly-Wrighton management made the final determination of which data points would be treated as outliers. Examples of causes not assignable to Production included new product specifications, ongoing technical issues stemming from the plant fire recovery, an unexpected line freeze attributable to severe weather, and worse than usual supplier material shortages. All the data that follows have had the outliers removed and are deemed by Poly-Wrighton management as Production controllable waste and rework.

Referring to Table 3.6, controllable rework during the pre-intervention period averaged 2.69 percent. At a cost of $35,000 for every 1 percent, pre-intervention rework averaged $94,000 per month. The projected trend value through the end of the post-intervention period was 0.0 percent for rework, or $0.00. The post-intervention monthly average for rework, however, was $65,450, based on 1.87 percent. The difference between the post-intervention average (1.87%) and the projected trend (0.0%) represented an average monthly cost increase of $65,450 for rework.

Shown in Table 3.6, controllable waste during the pre-intervention period averaged 0.73 percent. At a cost of $245,000 for every 1 percent, pre-intervention waste averaged $178,850 per month. The projected trend value through the end of the post-intervention period was 1.5 percent for waste, or $367,500. The post-intervention monthly average for waste was $53,900, based on 0.22 percent. The difference between the post-intervention average (0.22%) and the projected trend (1.5%) represented an average monthly cost decrease of $313,600 for product waste.

The difference between rework ($65,450/month) and waste (–$313,600/month) yielded a total average monthly benefit of –$248,150/month. The negative value (–$248,150) represents the average monthly cost avoidance for rework and waste combined, before factoring in participant and management impact estimates and correcting for confidence error. The total projected annual cost avoidance, before factoring in participant and management impact estimates and correcting for confidence error, was –$2,977,800 (–$248,150/month × 12 months).

How Results Were Isolated to the Program

The combined participant and management estimates of the impact of the intervention on business results, corrected for estimate error, which are also shown in Table 3.6, were used in conjunction with the trend analyses of controllable waste and rework. In this case, the 12-month total program benefit, expressed as a positive value of $2,977,800, multiplied by the adjusted estimate of the intervention's impact on program benefits, expressed as a decimal value of 0.425, returned an annual cost avoidance of $1,265,565 before expenses. This is the total benefit, adjusted for impact, before subtracting total program costs.

How Data Were Converted to Money

PolyWrighton provided standard monetary values for each 1 percent of waste and rework. $35,000 is the monetary value of 1 percent of rework, and $245,000 is the monetary value of 1 percent of controllable waste. The average monthly percentages were multiplied by these values to determine monetary value.

Program Costs

Program costs, including the bases for these costs, are summarized in Table 3.7. It should be noted here that the learning intervention was provided pro bono, free of charge, to the participating firm. The total estimated cost for the learning intervention, however, was calculated at $253,761. While the firm's actual cost for the intervention was $3,360, this study provided the more conservative return on investment calculation, the one using the estimated cost of $253,761. The basis for this decision was to allow PolyWrighton managers to make a better informed decision when considering whether to extend the intervention to the other 13 business units.

Level 5 ROI

The total projected annual benefit adjusted for impact, before subtracting total program costs, was $1,265,565. The $1,265,565 benefit less the program cost of $253,761 was $1,011,804. The net benefit of $1,011,804 divided by the total program cost of $253,761 was 3.99. Multiplied by 100, the Level 5 ROI calculation of net program benefits over costs was 399 percent, as expressed in Figure 3.11.

Intangible Benefits

Shown in Figure 3.10, work engagement was studied throughout the intervention plus six months afterward. With no monetary value calculated, work engagement would become an intangible benefit. Work engagement is a positive psychological state of mind that researchers have linked to employee satisfaction and superior job performance. Higher levels of work

TABLE 3.7   Program Costs

Consulting fees[1]		
$249,375.00	$10,000.00	needs assessment[2]
	$218,750.00	program design/development[3]
	$8,750.00	learning delivery[4]
	$11,875.00	program evaluation[5]
	$249,375.00	total consulting fees[6]
Printing and supplies		
$606.00	$126.00	printing
	$136.00	books
	$344.00	supplies
	$606.00	total printing and supplies
Participant salaries[7]		
$3,360.00	6	participants
	$32.00	average hourly salary[8]
	17.50	hours in training
	$3,360.00	total participant salaries
Facilities[9]		
$0.00	$0.00	Leo Seal Community Center
	$0.00	total facility cost
Facilitator travel		
$420.00	140	miles round trip
	6	number of trips
	$0.50	rate per mile[10]
	$420.00	total travel
Total	**$253,761.00**	

[1] $500/hour based on $4,000 per day market average for a senior consultant with more than 5 years experience.

[2] Based on the total number of hours spent assessing client needs.

[3] Based on the market ratio of 25 hours of design/development for each hour of classroom instruction (25:1).

[4] Based on the number of hours of instruction delivered by the program facilitator.

[5] Based on the market average of 5 percent of total program budget.

[6] Cost estimates were conservative for design/development, evaluation, and needs assessment.

[7] This figure represents the actual cost incurred by the participating firm, as the learning intervention was provided without charge.

[8] Provided by participating organization's Human Resources function.

[9] The Leo Seal Community Center does not charge a fee for the use of its facilities.

[10] Based on the travel rate approved by the University of Southern Mississippi: http://usm.edu/

FIGURE 3.11   ROI Calculation

$$\text{ROI} = \frac{\text{Program Benefits} - \text{Program Costs}}{\text{Program Costs}} \times 100$$

$$\frac{\$1,265,565 - \$253,761}{\$253,761} \times 100$$

$$\frac{\$1,011,804}{\$253,761} \times 100$$

$$3.99 \times 100 = 399\%$$

engagement are associated with positive feelings of individual well-being (vigor); a strong sense of commitment to the organization, its mission, goals, and objectives (dedication); and the employees' full concentration and involvement with the work itself, where time passes quickly (absorption). Work engagement is measured by the frequency an employee experiences the three psychological substates of vigor, dedication, and absorption at work. The self-coaching skills taught during the learning program were intended to help the participating Production managers create and sustain a more favorable environment for work engagement in order to positively impact employee motivation and performance. A series of statistical tests examined work engagement in Production and Maintenance using the UWES in a quasi-experimental research design.

An independent samples *t* test for differences between the Production (test group) and Maintenance (control group) means was not statistically significant at Day 0 of the intervention. That is, the difference between the two groups' work engagement was too small to matter at Day 0. However, the gap between these two business units had widened considerably by the end of the intervention. By Day 90, mixed-design analysis of variance statistical testing indicated that the difference between Production and Maintenance work engagement was statistically significant and powerful. Further, Cronbach's alpha testing showed the statistical reliability of the UWES was high. Given the organizational context, including a disruptive plant fire during the final 30 days of the study, the intervention can perhaps be seen as more preventive in nature. That is, it may be that the Production managers learned to handle the high-stress situation more effectively than their Maintenance counterparts.

By Day 270, or six months after the intervention, work engagement in both business units was on the rise. Managers at PolyWrighton indicated the gain in the nonintervention Maintenance group was probably the result of key supervisory changes made after the plant fire that occurred in the last 30 days of the intervention. While the post-intervention gap continued to narrow, Production maintained high enough levels of work engagement to remain statistically significant at Day 180 and Day 270, when testing for differences between the two business units. In essence, Production managers held that increased work engagement led to greater employee satisfaction, improved teamwork and communications, and better decision making.

COMMUNICATION STRATEGY
Results Reporting
Face-to-face meetings with members of the PolyWrighton management team, the participants, the training function, and the director of Human Resources ensured the results were fully understood and reconciled prior to issuing the final written report.

Stakeholder Response
PolyWrighton had a positive reaction to the results and requested the intervention extend to the 13 remaining business units.

Program Improvement
Stakeholders remained engaged throughout the entire data collection, analysis, and reporting process and offered suggestions to improve future iterations of the learning intervention used to teach the five self-coaching skills. PolyWrighton agreed to collaborate with the design team to reduce the 90-day learning period without sacrificing quality and transfer of skills to the job.

LESSONS LEARNED
Process Learning
Researchers should conduct additional research into interventions, particularly in the context of organizational settings and individual business units. For instance, exploring a wider variety of applications for the highly reliable UWES, including longitudinal studies that link work engagement to tangible business results indicators, may prove useful in assigning monetary values

to calculate return on investment. Also, using intervention research to move toward a more common and practical engagement construct that links the preconditions, psychological factors, behavioral outcomes, and business results may enhance the evaluation of such interventions in an organizational setting.

The study confirmed that practitioners should first take the time and effort to assess relevant business and learner needs in the context of organizational objectives and environmental conditions before selecting an intervention. In this case, the self-coaching learning intervention was designed to meet the needs of PolyWrighton and to link program objectives and measures to meaningful business outcomes. The integration of measurement and evaluation into the intervention from the start proved invaluable, because it helped shape a more successful implementation. Finally, interventions firmly grounded in research are more likely to succeed.

Approach Modifications

No modifications to the evaluation approach were noted or recommended.

Organizational Response

Organizational response was favorable and positive. The key element in the overall success of the project was the highly engaged leadership by Poly-Wrighton managers to ensure the intervention was implemented on the job, as intended. Regular team meetings in Production, enhanced communications among participating managers, and an element of accountability for implementing the self-coaching skills on the job were leadership-driven enablers of success.

RESOURCES

Flagello, J.R., and S.B. Dugas. (2009). *The Savvy Manager: 5 Skills That Drive Optimal Performance*. Alexandria, VA: ASTD Press.

Kmiec, J. (2010). *A Study of the Effectiveness of a Pilot Training Program in an Organizational Setting: An Intervention for Work Engagement* [Ph.D. dissertation]. Hattiesburg, MS: The University of Southern Mississippi. In: Dissertations & Theses @ The University of Southern Mississippi [database on the Internet] [cited 2010 Nov 18]. Available from: http://www.proquest.com/; Publication Number: AAT 3416289.

Phillips, J.J., and P.P. Phillips. (2005). *ROI at Work: Best Practice Case Studies From the Real World.* Alexandria, VA: ASTD Press.

Phillips, J.J., and P.P. Phillips. (2007). *Show Me the Money: How to Determine ROI in People, Projects, and Programs.* San Francisco, CA: Berrett-Koehler.

Phillips, P.P., and J.J. Phillips. (2007). *The Value of Learning: How Organizations Capture Value and ROI and Translate Them Into Support, Improvement, and Funds.* San Francisco, CA: Pfeiffer.

Phillips, P.P., and J.J. Phillips. (2008). *ROI in Action Casebook.* San Francisco, CA: Pfeiffer.

Phillips, P.P., J.J. Phillips, R.D. Stone, and H. Burkett. (2007). *The ROI Field Book: Strategies for Implementing ROI in HR and Training.* Burlington, MA: Butterworth-Heinemann.

Schaufeli, W.B., and M. Salanova. (2008). Enhancing Work Engagement Through the Management of Human Resources. In K. Näswall, M. Sverke, and J. Hellgren (Eds.), *The Individual in the Changing Working Life* (pp. 380–404). New York: Cambridge University Press.

QUESTIONS FOR DISCUSSION

1. How critical do you think the business alignment and forecasting plan in Figure 3.1 was to the success of the program? Explain.

2. Given the time invested in the program, would it be practical to try it in your organization? Why was it successful at PolyWrighton?

3. How might the close coordination with the PolyWrighton stakeholders serve as a model for implementing similar interventions in other organizations?

4. Besides the UWES and self-assessment profiles taken at three months after the termination of the program, how would you have measured on-the-job implementation of the five skills? Explain.

5. Guiding Principle #8 states that "Extreme data items and unsupported claims should not be used in ROI calculations." How would you relate that principle to the elimination of nonassignable outliers from Production's waste and rework calculations? What about the use of the estimated total cost instead of the actual amount paid for the intervention? Explain.

6. The authors state that a key element in the overall success of the project was the highly engaged leadership by PolyWrighton managers to ensure that the intervention was implemented on the job, as intended. In what ways do you believe that level of involvement impacted the outcome, and how can it be nurtured in other organizations in which the environment isn't as user friendly?

ABOUT THE AUTHORS

John Kmiec, PhD, serves as research associate at the Jack and Patti Phillips Workplace Learning and Performance Institute, The University of Southern Mississippi, where he recently graduated from the Human Capital Development program. A 27-year veteran of the United States Air Force, John has broad experience training, educating, evaluating, and developing human capital resources in order to improve work processes, products, services, productivity, and performance. His recognitions include the United States Air Force Chief of Staff Team Quality Award and Rochester Institute of Technology/USA Today Quality Cup. He was in Who's Who in American Colleges and Universities in 2010. You can reach him at **john.kmiec@usm. edu**.

Sandra Dugas, PhD, is a highly respected, nationally recognized executive coach, speaker, and author with extensive professional experience maximizing workplace learning and performance in many diverse industrial settings. She is coauthor of *The Savvy Manager: 5 Skills That Drive Optimal Performance* (ASTD Press, 2009). Sandra contributed immeasurably to the seminal research of a learning intervention for work engagement and to the success of The University of Southern Mississippi's first Human Capital Development doctoral program graduate. You can reach her at **sandra@ dugas.biz**.

Cyndi Gaudet, PhD, is professor and director of the Human Capital Development doctoral program and director of the Jack and Patti Phillips Workplace Learning and Performance Institute at the University of Southern Mississippi. She was Principal Investigator for the U.S. Department of Labor's Geospatial Technology Apprenticeship Program. Her workforce development research has received awards from the National Aeronautics and Space Administration and the Southern Growth Policies Board. Cyndi made presentations at more than 100 regional, national, and international conferences, and her research has been published in *Performance Improvement Quarterly*, *Performance Improvement Journal*, and *HRD Quarterly*, among several others. You can reach her at **cyndi.gaudet@usm.edu**.

Heather Annulis, PhD, is an associate professor of Workforce Development and assistant director of the Jack and Patti Phillips Workplace Learning and Performance Institute at the University of Southern Mississippi. Heather blends teaching and training management experience to coordinate the master of science program in Workforce Training and Development and the Training and Development Certificate Program for training and human resource development professionals. She was co-principal investigator for the U.S. Department of Labor's Geospatial Technology Apprenticeship Program. Her research has garnered numerous awards, including recognition as one of Mississippi's Top 40 Under 40. You can reach her at **heather.annulis@usm.edu**.

Mary Nell McNeese, PhD, serves as associate professor in the Department of Educational Studies & Research at the University of Southern Mississippi. She has taught doctoral statistics in three of the university's five colleges. Mary served as co-principal investigator (Co-PI) on the Preparing Mississippi's Teachers to Use Technology Grant and as Co-PI on the AmeriCorps Campus Link Grant to create a corps of college student volunteers at 11 campus and community sites who will help develop campus volunteer centers focused on hurricane relief, recovery, and preparedness. Her publications include articles in *International Journal of Diversity in Organizations, Communities, and Nations*; the *International Journal on E-Learning*; and *The Journal of At-Risk Issues*. You can reach her at **mary.mcneese@usm.edu**.

Susan Bush is the Student Services Coordinator at Gulfport High School's Technology Center (GHSTC). She has been with the Gulfport School District (GSD) for 17 years. Susan's current responsibilities include identifying and assisting students who may have barriers to achieving success in their Technology Center program. Susan has served in leadership positions at GHSTC; most recently as co-chair of the SACS/AdvancEd and Office of Civil Rights committees. She received both her bachelor of science in business administration and master of education degrees from the University of Southern Mississippi and is currently a student in the Human Capital Development PhD program. You can reach her at **susan.bush@gulfportschools.org**.

4

Success Through Managers Program ROI Study

Nova Scotia Public Service Commission
Canada

Patricia Charlton, Allison Chubbs, and Caroline Hubble

This case was prepared to serve as a basis for discussion rather than an illustration of either effective or ineffective administrative and management practices. Names, dates, places, and data may have been disguised at the request of the author or organization.

Abstract

As with many organizations, the Nova Scotia government faces numerous workforce challenges, including an aging workforce and a tight labor market. To address these challenges, a comprehensive needs analysis was completed and a management development program called the Success Through Managers Program was implemented. The program was designed to provide managers with the knowledge and skills they need to fulfill their legislative and policy-related responsibilities. To determine the business impact and ROI of the program, a comprehensive program evaluation was completed. This case study illustrates the process and results of the study, how a negative ROI was communicated, and lessons learned from completing the evaluation.

PROGRAM BACKGROUND

The government of Nova Scotia is currently faced with numerous workforce challenges, including an aging workforce and a tight labor market with increased competition for skilled labor. To build workforce capacity and support recruitment and retention strategies, the government implemented a number of measures to ensure that it would have a vibrant, productive, and properly trained workforce. This includes providing continuous development for employees and leaders at all levels in the organization. Building the skills, knowledge, and competencies of new managers builds capacity and enables strong succession planning and management.

A needs analysis was conducted with all management levels in the government and also with various stakeholders to determine what knowledge and skills were necessary for a manager to be successful in the government. A survey was emailed to 1,300 stakeholders across all departments, including deputy ministers, executive directors, directors, managers, and supervisors, and 31 percent responded. Based on this needs analysis, a management development program was designed.

Success Through Managers provides managers with the knowledge and skills they need to fulfill their legislative and policy-related responsibilities. It targets new managers (those with fewer than five years in that role) and employees aspiring to management positions. The program begins with a three-day conference at which senior leaders from across government provide an overview of government strategy, policy, and process. After the conference, participants take 11 required modules that cover the processes managers use throughout the employment lifecycle. Participants choose from a selection of dates available through the Corporate Training Catalogue.

After the program was developed, a pilot program was implemented. At the end of the pilot, participant satisfaction (Level 1) and learning (Level 2) data were collected. In addition, the participants' specific input regarding the pilot was captured and incorporated into the program. Since the original pilot, three additional programs have been completed with Level 1 and Level 2 evaluations occurring. Because there was a specific interest in understanding how the participants were applying the knowledge and skills to the job, how business results are affected by the program, and the return on investment to the government, a more comprehensive evaluation was planned for the fourth offering. Table 4.1 reflects the content included for program completion by the participants of this study.

EVALUATION METHODOLOGY

Success Through Managers was selected for a comprehensive evaluation to identify business impact and ROI because it aligned with the following criteria:

- The expected life cycle of the program is at least 10 years.
- The program supports organizational goals and strategic objectives.

TABLE 4.1   Group 4 Program Content

Conference Topics	Required Courses
• Public Service Values	• Recruitment and Selection
• Government Basics: How Things Work	• Labor Relations
• Legislation, Acts, and Regulations	• Performance Management
• Managing in the Nova Scotia Government	• Occupational Health and Safety for Managers
• Corporate HR Plan	• Diversity for Leaders
• Disability Management	• Leading a Respectful Workplace
• Mentoring and Coaching	• Conflict Management
• Compensation and Classification	• Financial Management
• Freedom of Information and Protection of Privacy	• Leadership Skills for Teams
• HR Planning and Succession Management	• Coaching to Develop Others
• Understanding Benefits	• Employee Assistance Program for Managers
• Procurement	
• The Budget Process	
• Ethics, Codes, and Conflicts	
• Communicating in Government Channels	
• Healthy Workplace	
• Tour of the Legislature	

▓ The target audience is extensive, as it spans all new managers across government.

▓ The program, at a cost of $2,850 per participant, is one of the most expensive offered by government.

▓ The time commitment for attending the program, at 17 training days, is extensive.

To evaluate this program, the Phillips' ROI Methodology was utilized. The evaluation framework categorizing data by levels, as described in the methodology, is shown in Table 4.2.

The data represent measures that capture program success from the participant, system, and economic perspectives. The results answer the key questions and illustrate the chain of impact the program has within the organization. Along with the evaluation framework, the ROI Methodology Process Model is used to provide a consistent approach to completing the evaluation. This model includes a step to isolate the effects of the program

TABLE 4.2   Evaluation Framework

Evaluation Level	Measures	Key Question Addressed
Level 0: Input	Program activity, inputs and costs	What resources (human and monetary) were required to implement the initiative?
Level 1: Reaction	Stakeholder reaction and level of satisfaction with the initiative	What are the stakeholders' reactions and perceived value of the initiative?
Level 2: Learning	Changes in knowledge, skill, and attitudes	What skills, knowledge, or attitudes have changed and by how much?
Level 3: Application	Changes in job performance and application of new skills	Did teams apply what they learned?
Level 4: Impact	Changes in organizational results	Did the initiative produce tangible and intangible business results?
Level 5: ROI	Program benefits compared with costs	Did the monetary benefits of the tangible results exceed the cost for the initiative?

from other influencing factors. Figure 4.1 presents the process model, which offers a step-by-step approach for planning, collecting, and analyzing the data as well as reporting the outcomes of the study. In addition to the process model, the 12 Guiding Principles ensure that the implementation of the evaluation will be systematic and credible.

Evaluation Implementation

As referenced above, the ROI Methodology process involves four phases that provide the structure for completing the evaluation studies. Each phase has a specific purpose to ensure that the evaluation will be executed effectively while maintaining study credibility.

Evaluation Planning Phase

As part of the planning phase, comprehensive plans were put in place, including specific planning tools that provided a means for validating the direction of the study and ensured that key stakeholder needs would be addressed. For this evaluation study, there were two distinct planning deliverables:

- **Data Collection Plan:** This plan outlined the primary objectives and measures for each evaluation level and ensured that the needed data would be collected by specifying the timing, responsibility, and data sources (see Figure 4.2).

FIGURE 4.1   ROI Methodology Process Model

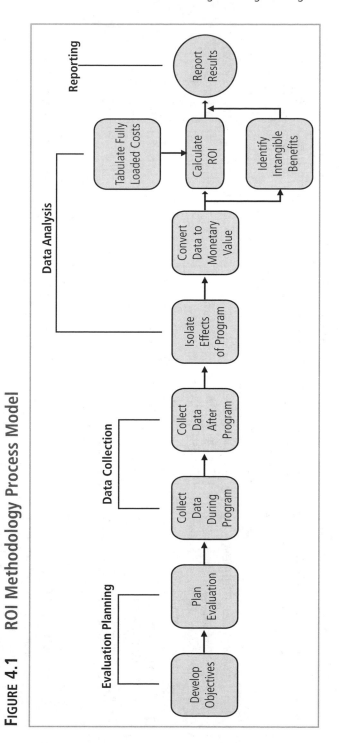

Figure 4.2   Success Through Managers Program Data Collection Plan

Level	Broad Program Objective(s)	Measures	Data Collection Method/ Instruments	Data Sources	Timing	Responsibilities
1	**REACTION AND PLANNED ACTION** Participants indicate they are satisfied with program content and facilitators.	Obtain a 4 out of 5 on a 5-point rating scale for applicable questions. Use open-ended questions.	Questionnaire	Participants	End of program	Program manager Independent consultant
2	**LEARNING AND CONFIDENCE** Participants indicate that their skills and knowledge have increased as a result of taking the program.	Increase one skill level after training on a 5-point rating scale.	Questionnaire Focus group	Participants	End of program	Program manager Independent consultant
3	**APPLICATION AND IMPLEMENTATION** Participants utilize their new or improved skills back on the job.	Use knowledge and skills on at least a monthly basis. 50% of total work time requires knowledge and skills gained from the program.	Questionnaire Focus group	Participants	3 months after program's completion	Program manager Independent consultant
4	**BUSINESS IMPACT** Participants indicate improvements in related areas of business results. Participants indicate some financial impact from these improvements.	Various business result measures are at least somewhat significantly impacted by experience in the program.	Questionnaire Focus group	Participants	3 months after program's completion	Program manager Independent consultant
5	Achieve 0% ROI (breakeven point)	Comments: A secondary purpose is to make improvements in the program as appropriate.				

■ **ROI Analysis Plan:** This plan detailed the elements needed to complete the ROI calculation, including identifying Level 4 business measures, the applicable techniques for isolating the effects of the program, converting the measures to monetary values, and the fully loaded program cost categories (see Figure 4.3).

Data Collection Phase

During the data collection phase, data were collected at two different intervals. When the program was implemented, data were collected to capture the participants' immediate reaction (Level 1) to the program as well as success with learning (Level 2). Following program implementation, data were collected to identify the success with applying the skills learned in the program (Level 3) and the resulting impact on the organization (Level 4). The following highlights the three data collection instruments used to collect the needed data:

■ **End of Program Questionnaire:** This questionnaire was designed to capture data on participant satisfaction (Level 1) and the learning that occurred (Level 2). The tool included 54 questions, mostly with answers on a Likert-type scale but some open-ended to allow comments. Thirty-four program participants completed the questionnaire.

■ **Follow-up Impact Questionnaire:** This questionnaire gathered data primarily on the application of knowledge and skills (Level 3) and the business impact of participating in the program (Level 4). Data were also collected in an attempt to determine the return on investment of the program (Level 5). The tool included 69 questions, most of which used Likert-type scales, with a few questions open-ended. Twenty-seven participants completed the questionnaire and provided data.

■ **Focus Group:** A focus group was conducted to provide an opportunity to gather qualitative data about the program. The participants were led in a guided discussion to explore the following questions:

■ How did the program *increase your knowledge and skills* related to managerial responsibilities?

■ How have you *applied* the knowledge and skills gained through Success Through Managers?

■ What has been the *impact* on your work or business unit as a result of your participation in Success Through Managers?

FIGURE 4.3   Success Through Managers Program ROI Analysis Plan

Data Items (Usually Level 4)	Methods for Isolating Effects of Program	Methods of Converting Data to Monetary Values	Cost Categories	Intangible Benefits	Communication Targets for Final Report	Other Influences/Issues During Application
Varies, depending on measures selected	Participant estimate	Participant estimate	• Program fee • Participant time • Participant travel expenses • Evaluation costs	• Increased job effectiveness • Increased ability to make decisions aligned with policies/procedures • Increased confidence in ability to fulfill job expectations • Increased capacity to coach and develop employees • Increased job satisfaction • Increased coaching capacity • Increased compliance with policies and procedures • Increased focus on a work environment that values diversity • Increased supports for employees • Increased client satisfaction	• Senior mgmt of PSC—Presentation with full report and executive summary in advance of presentation • Mgrs and supervisors—Post a copy on HR Online • Participants—Email executive summary • HR Forums—Presentation and executive summary • All PSC—Newsletter • Potential participants—Executive summary on website; incorporate results into program brochure	• Managers' support of participants • Participant selection—Proper developmental fit • Applicability of all modules (opportunity to use skill)

Unfortunately, the low participation rate (26 percent) was not conducive to drawing specific conclusions from the discussions. However, some themes emerged that were incorporated into the findings as appropriate. During the focus group, the participants were also encouraged to complete the Follow-up Impact Questionnaire and ask for clarification on the business impact questions, if needed.

Analysis Phase

Following data collection, the researchers analyzed the data. To ensure that the stakeholders' communication needs were addressed, key steps in the analysis phase were completed as outlined below.

Isolation Participants' estimates were used to isolate the effects of the program. Specifically, participants were asked to estimate the percentage of improvement related directly to the program and their level of confidence in this estimate. This isolation technique was selected due to the nature of the program being evaluated. It would not be feasible or appropriate to prevent a group of new managers from taking the program so they could serve as a control group. Trend line analysis would not be credible, as other influences besides the program have affected the improvements. Forecasting would also have been infeasible, as the other potential factors contributing to improvement were not known in advance to enable an accurate projection. Beyond the ease of use and feasibility of this method, participants' estimates were the most credible and accurate source for expert estimates as they are at the center of the change or improvement. This method had the added benefit of requiring less time and money and causing less work disruption than the previously mentioned techniques.

Converting Data to Monetary Values Participants' estimates were also used to convert the data to monetary values. This method was chosen because standard values for measures, such as output, quality, cost, or time, are not readily available within the organization. Furthermore, participants in the program ranged across many departments, regions, and types of positions—the diversity of which does not translate into the wide generalizations needed for meaningful standard values. The business impacts from participating in the program were also expected to vary widely by participant, which further complicated the application of standard values. Last, this method had the added benefit of ease of conversion.

Tabulating the Cost of the Program The next step involved determining the fully loaded cost of the program. To accomplish this step, a detailed cost summary worksheet was developed. Costs included the program fee of $2,850, participant salaries and benefits for the time away from work to attend the program, estimated travel costs for those located in regional offices, and the time associated with participating in the evaluation study.

Determining Return on Investment and Intangible Benefits Once the above steps were completed, the ROI was determined. The ROI is a comparison of benefits to cost expressed as a percentage of the original investment. During data analysis, every attempt was made to convert all data to monetary values. However, it was determined that converting some measures was either too subjective or too time-consuming, which could have impacted the credibility of the study. Therefore, some of the impacted measures were identified as intangible benefits.

Reporting Phase

The final step in the evaluation of the program was communicating the results of the study to the applicable audiences. Although communication with applicable stakeholders occurred throughout the study, it was critical to communicate the final results in a timely manner. Within the ROI Analysis Plan, key communication audiences were identified along with the applicable communication tool(s).

EVALUATION RESULTS

Reaction

At the end of the program, the reaction (Level 1) to the program was captured using the End of Program Questionnaire. The results for this level were very positive, and most of the ratings exceeded the set targets. On average, 91 percent of participants rated the program content and facilitators 4 out of 5 or higher (see Table 4.3). In addition, 100 percent of those who responded indicated they would recommend the program to others and 79 percent felt the program was the right length.

As part of the questionnaire, the respondents had the opportunity to respond to open-ended questions designed to capture more detailed reaction data. There were a few comments regarding program length (e.g.,

TABLE 4.3   Program Participants' Reaction Results

Content	Average Rating (1 = Strongly Disagree; 5 = Strongly Agree)
The program was relevant to my work.	4.3
The program was important to my success.	4.1
The program provided me with useful information.	4.5
The program was a worthwhile investment for my organization.	4.4
The program met my needs.	4.1
The program was a good use of my time.	4.2
I intend to use the information from the program modules.	4.4
	Average response = 4.3

some of the two-day modules should be shortened), and some modules were not applicable to some participants. Furthermore, there were varying requests either to increase or to decrease the time spent on various modules, which could be indicative of individual needs based on respondents' position and experience. Last, in response to the open-ended question regarding what should be added, courses regarding time management, courses covering performance management for bargaining unit employees, and expanded coverage of labor relations and financial management were recommended. Overall, the Level 1 results show that the participants were very satisfied with the content and the facilitators and planned to use what they had learned.

Learning

Learning data were also captured on the End of Program Questionnaire, and the overall results show that participants gained significant learning from the program. Participants were asked to assess their knowledge and skill levels before and after training based on the learning objectives of each program's component. Ninety-one percent of the participants' skills increased by at least 25 percent or one level (which exceeds the established target of 90 percent). When these data were broken down by program components, the three areas resulting with the largest increase in knowledge and skills level were EAP, Coaching for Generations, and the Conference. The importance of the Conference also emerged during the focus group as the group noted it was essential in helping increase knowledge about how government functions, important policies and processes, and available resources and therefore should be available to all new employees as part of their orientation to government.

The positive results in the program meeting its learning objectives were likely due to the comprehensive needs assessment that was conducted in designing the program's content, as well as the provision of a dedicated program manager to oversee the program's day-to-day operations and delivery. The use of internal subject matter experts to facilitate many of the program's components has also been key to ensuring participants receive information that is relevant to the Nova Scotia public sector.

Application

To capture application data, a Follow-up Impact Questionnaire was implemented and a focus group was conducted. The results indicate that participants are applying the knowledge and skills gained from the program back on the job, but with varying levels of frequency. The participants indicated that 69 percent of their work time requires the knowledge and skills presented in the program, which exceeded the target of 50 percent. They also reported specific actions undertaken as a result of the program. The top three were

- improved management of budgetary processes
- more effective performance management of staff
- better management of conflict in the workplace.

The results were not as strong when measuring the frequency of use for application, as only 59 percent of the participants indicated that they applied the relevant knowledge and skills on at least a monthly basis.

To further understand the application of knowledge and skills on the job, the participants were asked to indicate the barriers and enablers to application. From a list, they were asked to identify what prevented them from using the skills and knowledge gained in the program (barriers) and what supported them in doing so (enablers). The results from this question are illustrated in Table 4.4. As shown, the top three factors that prevented them from using the relevant skills were lack of time, systems and processes that do not support application, and lack of opportunity. Two of the most common barriers listed in the comments were time constraints and lack of opportunity to use because of not being in a managerial role. With regard to the enablers, the top three factors that participants reported were supportive managers, supportive work environments, and opportunity to use the skills. The most widely cited enabler in the verbatim comments was the presence of a supportive manager and a strong leadership environment. In response to a question about what additional supports could influence their ability to apply the program's skills and knowledge, respondents listed the provision of follow-up refreshers or recertification programs.

Business Impact

The results showed that the participants were able to have a positive impact on business measures due to their experience in the program. Participants

TABLE 4.4   Barriers and Enablers to Application

Factors	Barriers (Factor Is Not Present)	Enablers (Factor Is Present)
Time to apply the skills	37%	41%
Systems and processes within organization support application of knowledge/skills	22%	44%
Opportunity to use the skills	19%	70%
Content is applicable to job	15%	63%
Confidence in ability to apply the knowledge/skills	11%	63%
Work environment that supports the use of these skills/behaviors	7%	70%
Other	7%	0%
Sufficient knowledge and understanding	4%	56%
Manager supports this type of program	4%	74%

Note: Results are presented as the percentage of participants completing the survey who indicated this factor was an enabler or a barrier.

rated the level of impact regarding personal effectiveness, team effectiveness, and overall business improvements. As shown in Figure 4.4, on average, participants indicated some impact for all but two business results. The top three areas impacted were increased job effectiveness, making decisions aligned with government policies, and increased confidence. The three areas least impacted were decreased absenteeism, reduction in client complaints, and increased safety in the work environment.

Isolating the Effects of the Program

As referenced in the beginning of the study, to isolate the effects of the program, participants' estimates were used. Specifically, participants were asked to estimate the percentage of improvement directly attributable to the program and their level of confidence in the estimate. This process is in accordance with two guiding principles:

- At least one method must be used to isolate the effects of the solution.
- Estimates of improvements should be adjusted for the potential error of the estimate.

The results were then used to determine the overall business impact and monetary benefit of the program.

Participants were also asked to identify other factors that contributed to the improvements. Personal commitment and leadership support received the most responses, while other development opportunities and "other" received lower responses. Two factors, new technology and new programs/services, did not receive any responses, indicating they did not contribute to the improvement.

Converting to Monetary Value

The next step in the process is to determine the monetary value of the improvements. Again, participants' estimates were used to convert the data to a monetary value. Like the previous estimates, this information was captured via the Follow-up Impact Questionnaire.

First, to determine the specific measure, the participants were asked to identify the business result most impacted by the program and the associated value of its improvement (e.g., if absenteeism was selected, the unit of measure could be one unplanned absence). Then the value was

FIGURE 4.4 Impact of Managerial Skill

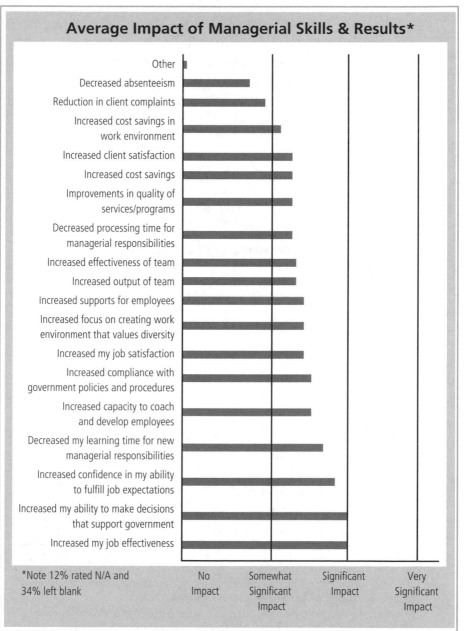

determined by asking participants to indicate the dollar value of the improvement. The yearly change in performance and its associated value was measured by next asking participants to estimate the projected annual value of improvement. The monetary results of this process, including the participants' estimates regarding the program's contribution to the improvement (isolation), are highlighted in Table 4.5.

Although 85 percent of participants (23) indicated the business results impacted and the percentage of improvement, only 37 percent (10)

TABLE 4.5　Project Benefits and Monetary Value

Calculation and Rationale			
Participant Estimated Benefits (a)	Improvement Attributed to the Program (%) (b)	Confidence in Estimates (%) Adjusted (c)	Estimates a × b × c
$7,000	20	60	$840
$5,000	100	75	$3,750
$42,120	6	70	$1,769
$1,000	100	60	$600
$16,310	25	50	$2,039
$32,620	25	70	$5,709
$3,262	100	30	$979
$23,400	20	75	$3,510
$4,800	50	70	$1,680
$1,631	100	75	$1,223
$137,143			$22,098

- Total benefits reported = $137,143 (based on 10 participants who provided estimates of annual value of improvement as a result of the program)
- The estimated values were then adjusted based on the percentage of this improvement participants attributed to the program and their level of confidence in the estimate using the following calculation: a × b × c
- Amount used for ROI calculation: $22,098

provided monetary estimates for this improvement. The reason for the lower response to this question may be because the business results that emerged as most impacted (e.g., increased confidence) were largely intangible benefits that do not translate easily to a dollar value. Other factors may be a lack of awareness or familiarity with ROI processes and placing financial measures on business results.

Determining Program Costs

The fully loaded cost of the intervention was calculated to include all expenses incurred by Success Through Managers Program participants. This included the program fee of $2,850, participant salaries and benefits for the time away from work to attend the program, estimated travel costs for those located in regional offices, and the time associated with participating in the evaluation study. Participants' salaries and benefits costs were pulled from the payroll system to calculate the average hourly and daily rate. As the evaluation was considered to be of equal value to both clients and the Public Service Commission (PSC), half of the cost of the consultants' time to conduct the ROI study was also included in the costing. As the costs included reflect the expenses or the program "fee" incurred by participants, costs pertaining to the design and administration of the program were not included. The specific calculations for all costs included are provided in Table 4.6.

Return on Investment

Utilizing the monetary value of the benefits and the fully loaded costs of the solution, the benefit-to-cost ratio (BCR) and return on investment (ROI) were determined. As shown in Figure 4.5, the ROI results were negative, and communicating these results can present challenges that must be positioned appropriately. The approach in this case focused on putting the results in context with the business need for the program. The results showed that participants found the content very relevant to their roles, they gained significant learning from the program, and they required the knowledge and skills gained to do their jobs. While they may have struggled to define the financial impact of their participation in the program, they clearly indicated many benefits that could not be measured in monetary terms. These positive outcomes support the continued provision of this program and were presented to senior management in that context.

TABLE 4.6 Fully Loaded Costs of the Program

Factors	Calculation and Rationale	Amount
Program fee	$2,850 fee charged to each participant × 43 participants	$122,550
Participant salaries and benefits (for time away from work)	This amount represents the cost of time spent in training as a proportion of the average salary and benefits cost for the 43 participants included in the study. Time spent in training = $\frac{17 \text{ training days}}{233 \text{ working days}}$ = 7.3% Average biweekly salary ($108,474/43) + Average biweekly benefits ($16,749/43) = $2,912 $2,912 × 33 pay periods = $96,096 (average salary/benefits cost) $96,096 × 7.3% × 43 participants = $301,645	$301,645
Estimated travel costs for participants	11 employees travelled from regional offices to attend the program: Average hourly wage ($72) = average biweekly salary ($2,522)/35 hrs Estimated cost of time spent travelling per participant: Average travel time per course × Average hourly wage × Training days 3.5 hrs × $72 × 17 training days = $4,284 Estimated travel expenses per participant ($1,700) = $100/day × 17 days Estimated total travel cost for 11 regional participants = ($4,824 + $1,700) × 11 = $65,824	$65,824
Evaluation costs	Participant time to complete the evaluation: 0.5 hours × 33 participants completed the End of Program Questionnaire 0.5 hours × $72 (hourly wage) × 33 participants = $1,188 0.5 hours × 27 participants completed the Follow-up Impact Questionnaire 0.5 hours × $72 (hourly wage) × 27 participants = $972 4.5 hours × 11 participants attended the focus group session 4.5 hours × $72 (hourly wage) × 11 participants = $3,564 Total participant time spent on evaluation = $5,724 Consultant time to design and conduct the evaluation: Average annual salary of 2 consultants = $73,000 Time spent on evaluation = $\frac{10 \text{ days each}}{233 \text{ working days}}$ = 4.3% Total consultant time = 4.3% × $73,000 × 2 consultants = $6,278 The value for consultants' time was seen as 50% toward participants and 50% toward program owners (PSC). Adjusted cost for consultant time = $6,278 × 50% = $3,139 Total evaluation time = $5,724 + $3,139 = $8,863	$8,863
Total costs		**$498,882**

FIGURE 4.6   BCR and ROI Results

$$BCR = \frac{\$22{,}098.00}{\$498{,}882.00} = 0.04$$

$$ROI = \frac{\$22{,}098.00 - \$498{,}882.00}{\$498{,}882.00} \times 100 = -96\%$$

Intangible Benefits

As referenced previously, the program was created to build management capacity for the future of public service, to ensure that the organization has the right people in the right place at the right time. A vibrant and productive workforce will ensure that the government is able to continue to provide efficient and effective services to enhance the quality of life for all Nova Scotians. This outcome contributes to the public good but is by nature difficult to measure in terms of a financial return. In addition, the participants identified the following other intangible benefits:

- increased confidence in their ability to fulfill job expectations
- increased capacity to coach and develop employees
- increased supports for employees
- increased their job effectiveness
- decreased learning time for new managerial responsibilities
- more able to make decisions that support government policies and procedures.

Last, as indicated in the organization's 2009 employee survey results, leadership practices were identified as the most significant driver (out of 15 drivers) of higher employee engagement. By significantly raising the skill levels for managers, they will be better prepared to lead effectively, which in turn could improve leadership practices and favorably impact employee engagement.

COMMUNICATION STRATEGY

The entire ROI study was provided to the executive management of the PSC and it was well received. The participants involved in the study have also been provided an executive summary of the report. The study and lessons learned will be shared with learning and development professionals across the government. It is the intention of the authors to share the results with managers and employees across government through use of the PSC's intranet site. The results and recommendations of the report have been used in the design and evaluation of future offerings of the program and will also be incorporated into the promotional materials for the program.

LESSONS LEARNED

The ROI Methodology was a very useful and powerful tool for both the PSC's Learning Centre and the clients it serves. The in-depth data encouraged the participants to think about and apply the knowledge and skills from the program to their jobs. This was the first time such an extensive program evaluation was undertaken, and there are some opportunities for work to be done differently next time. These include the following:

- The design of the questionnaire should be kept simple, focused, and with few open-ended questions.
- When designing a program, clear objectives and the related evaluation methodology should be completed at the same time, and the evaluation methodology should link directly to the program objectives.
- To help increase participants' response rate, the program needs an executive sponsor such as a deputy minister to engage participants in a conversation around the value of their input, including how they can contribute to making the program better for future participants and the importance of measuring the results and impact of the program to government's results.
- The completion of this study validated the importance of higher levels of evaluation for present and future programs. The government of Nova Scotia should be evaluating more of its programs beyond Level 1 (satisfaction and planned action) and Level 2 (learning) and should be incorporating a minimum of Level 3 (application) evaluation.
- Taking the ROI methodology to Levels 4 and 5 required a significant time commitment, which reinforced the importance of using the criteria outlined by the ROI Methodology for selection of programs for impact analysis.

- Sources other than participants' estimates for data collection would be a valuable addition to future ROI studies. If the government of Nova Scotia adopts the widespread use of ROI Methodology, it would be beneficial to work toward the creation of standard values.

- It was of significant value to have more than one person collaborating on this ROI study. This provided an opportunity to analyze the data and results from varying perspectives. It would beneficial to continue to work in partnership with others when undertaking future studies.

RESOURCES

Phillips, J.J., and P.P. Phillips. (2002). *Measuring ROI in the Public Sector.* Alexandria, VA: ASTD Press, Victor Graphics Inc.

Phillips, J.J., and P.P. Phillips. (2007). *Show Me the Money: How to Determine ROI in People, Projects, and Program.* San Francisco, CA: Berrett-Koehler.

Phillips, J.J., and P.P. Phillips. (2008). *Beyond Learning Objectives: Develop Measurable Objectives That Link to the Bottom Line.* Alexandria, VA: ASTD Press.

Phillips, J.J., and P.P. Phillips. (2008). *The Measurement and Evaluation Series: Volumes 1 to 6.* San Francisco, CA: Pfiffer.

Phillips, J.J., and P.P. Phillips. (2008). *ROI in Action Casebook.* San Francisco, CA: Pfiffer.

QUESTIONS FOR DISCUSSION

1. Do you think it was worthwhile to complete both the Follow-up Impact Questionnaire and the focus group to collect Level 3 application and Level 4 business impact data? If so, how would you defend the need for the resources (e.g., time, money, etc.) for these activities? If not, why not, and what would you have done differently?

2. What additional strategies could have been implemented to assist in attaining a higher number of responses regarding the business impact and monetary value information on the Follow-up Impact Questionnaire?

3. In light of the negative ROI results, what would be the best approach for sharing this information with senior management and other executives?

4. Based on the findings of the study, what additional recommendations would you make to the program designers and stakeholders?

5. If presented with a similar program and situation, which processes or steps completed in this study would you follow and what would you do differently?

ABOUT THE AUTHORS

Patricia Charlton is a learning and development consultant with the Nova Scotia Public Service Commission, where she delivers corporate programs and services designed to foster a culture of continuous learning. As an advocate of lifelong learning herself, Patty has a degree in psychology as well as postgraduate certificates in human resource management and adult education. She has also received formal accreditation from the ROI Institute as a Certified ROI Professional (CRP). In the past eight years, she has held a variety of roles within the Government of Nova Scotia in the areas of talent management, human resource planning, and strategic recruitment. She can be reached at **CHARLTPA@gov.ns.ca**.

Allison Chubbs is a manager of organizational development with the Nova Scotia Public Service Commission, where she provides consulting services to a wide range of departments across government. She has worked within the field of learning and development for the past 15 years. She has also received formal accreditation from the ROI Institute as a Certified ROI Professional (CRP). She can be reached at **CHUBBSAL@gov.ns.ca**.

Caroline Hubble is the director of consulting services with the ROI Institute. With more than 15 years of professional experience, she has focused for the last eight years on learning evaluation. At the ROI Institute, Caroline directs the implementation of complex evaluation projects, including studies on leadership development, process improvement strategies, and skills training initiatives. She holds a BA from Rollins College and is a Certified ROI Professional (CRP) and ASTD Certified Professional in Learning and Performance (CPLP). She can be reached at **caroline@roiinstitute.net**.

5

Measuring the Impact of Conflict Management Skills Training

XYZ County
USA

Patsi Maroney

This case was prepared to serve as a basis for discussion rather than an illustration of either effective or ineffective administrative and management practices. All names, dates, places, and data have been disguised at the request of the author or organization.

Abstract

In 2006, the XYZ County Human Resources (HR) Department conducted a training needs mini-assessment for supervisors. Among other items, the results of the needs assessment identified "the ability to effectively address work conflicts and hold employees more accountable" as a high priority. Therefore, the HR department decided to see whether supervisors would report a measurable difference in unresolved work conflicts if they learned and used conflict management skills. To that end, a group of 16 supervisors participated in both a Conflict Management (CM) training class and a return on investment (ROI) study designed to measure the impact of learning the CM skills.

BACKGROUND

XYZ County is located in the western United States. It employs roughly 1,500 ongoing and benefited employees in the county's 35 different departments; 275 of those employees are in supervisory positions at various levels. As a political subdivision of the state, the organizational structure of the county is set by state statutes: a three-member board of county commissioners oversees the majority of the county's departments, and seven other independently elected officials oversee their own departments. The various county departments provide a wide range of services including a landfill, a recycling center, and mountain parks, as well as more typical local government functions, such as law enforcement, social services, health and environment, road and bridge maintenance, property assessment, and tax collection.

Due to this statutorily imposed organizational structure, the county has no single "boss" or centralized management function that has authority over all county departments and employees. The only statutory authority the board of commissioners has over the county's other elected officials is budgetary; for the most part, the county's elected officials usually choose to cooperate with the board of commissioners and consistently apply various internal administrative policies and procedures to their departments.

Although the county's HR department reports to the board of commissioners, HR provides services to all county employees. These services include various staff development training classes, which cover broad themes applicable to any county function, such as leadership development, customer service, facilitation skills, improving communication skills, and enhancing supervisory effectiveness. This study is a product of the network of employee-related county services.

PROGRAM OBJECTIVES AND SPECIFICS

The focus of the program was twofold: (1) to train a group of supervisors on specific conflict management skills that could be employed in the workplace, and (2) to conduct a return on investment (ROI) study to determine if the training class could produce measurable results. The initial assumption was that the use of the conflict management (CM) skills would have a positive impact not only on the number of unresolved conflicts in the workplace, but also on the tangible and intangible costs of such conflicts.

The county's training officer selected a specific conflict management training class developed by the authors of a best-selling book. The book's authors had already certified the training officer to teach the CM class, so the county saved the cost of contracting with an outside trainer.

The training officer asked all the county's supervisors for volunteers to attend the CM class and to participate in the ROI study. A total of 16 supervisors volunteered; they were split into two different class groups.

The training officer delivered the class using a spaced-learning approach by scheduling seven sessions, each of which was 3.5 hours long (for a total of 24.5 hours) spread over an 11-week period. During the first class session, participants completed a pre-class questionnaire, shown in Figure 5.1, in which they identified the frequency as well as the tangible and intangible costs of unresolved conflicts in the workplace. Class time consisted of a combination of learning methodologies: completion of a self-assessment tool, lectures, reading, watching video segments, large group discussions, small group breakouts, individual reflection and quiet time, game activities, and role-playing exercises. In addition, each class session started with a discussion of the participants' real-life conflict situations since the last session. Between class sessions, participants were asked to review portions of the class materials and practice the CM skills in the real world. During the fifth class session, participants took a test and completed one or more action plans using the CM skills to address unresolved conflicts in the workplace. The remaining two class sessions then focused on measuring and documenting the impact of the action plans, as well as documenting participants' barriers and enablers to the use of the CM skills in a focus group format. During the last class session, participants completed a skills test, a class evaluation, and a post-class questionnaire, again identifying the frequency and tangible and intangible costs of unresolved conflicts in the workplace.

Evaluation Methodology

The training officer chose to use the ROI Methodology developed by Jack J. Phillips, PhD, to conduct the ROI study. This methodology incorporates the use of 12 Guiding Principles, as shown in Figure 5.2.

In addition, the Phillips Methodology captures the following six types of data:

- Level 1 Data: Reaction, satisfaction, and planned actions
- Level 2 Data: Acquisition of knowledge and skills, as well as changes in perceptions and attitudes
- Level 3 Data: Success with application and implementation
- Level 4 Data: Actual business impact measured in cost savings, productivity improvements, and time reductions
- Level 5 Data: The return on investment, showing the monetary benefits versus costs
- Additional Data: Intangible benefits, such as employee satisfaction and customer satisfaction

FIGURE 5.1   Pre-Class Questionnaire

"Pre-Class" CONFIDENTIAL QUESTIONNAIRE: Work Conflicts

The needs assessment done during the July 2006 Supervisory Focus Groups identified *"ability to address work conflicts and hold employees more accountable"* as a high priority. *Webster's Dictionary* defines *"conflict"* both as a noun meaning *"prolonged open warfare, a state of disharmony: clash"* and as a verb meaning *"to be opposed: differ."* We'll use the answers from this questionnaire to help quantify the business impact of unresolved work conflicts. Please be candid; note that your individual answers will be kept completely confidential! Thanks again for your help with this project!!

1. Have any of the following conflict situations occurred at work during the last 6 months involving you and/or one or more employees under your direct supervision; if yes, how often did it occur?

Conflict Situation:	How Often?	
Employee not following appropriate policies and procedures	❏ Just once ❏ 5–9 times	❏ 2–4 times ❏ 10+ times
Employee not doing his/her share of the workload	❏ Just once ❏ 5–9 times	❏ 2–4 times ❏ 10+ times
Inefficient meetings	❏ Just once ❏ 5–9 times	❏ 2–4 times ❏ 10+ times
Misunderstandings about work assignments	❏ Just once ❏ 5–9 times	❏ 2–4 times ❏ 10+ times
Employee feels micro-managed by supervisor(s)	❏ Just once ❏ 5–9 times	❏ 2–4 times ❏ 10+ times
Employee feels under-managed by supervisor(s)	❏ Just once ❏ 5–9 times	❏ 2–4 times ❏ 10+ times
Lack of honest discussion concerning problems or issues	❏ Just once ❏ 5–9 times	❏ 2–4 times ❏ 10+ times
Out-of-date polices and procedures that hinder employees	❏ Just once ❏ 5–9 times	❏ 2–4 times ❏ 10+ times
Employee engages in disrespectful behavior	❏ Just once ❏ 5–9 times	❏ 2–4 times ❏ 10+ times
Employee engages in unsafe work behavior	❏ Just once ❏ 5–9 times	❏ 2–4 times ❏ 10+ times
Employee's lack of skill in performing assigned job duties	❏ Just once ❏ 5–9 times	❏ 2–4 times ❏ 10+ times
Employee not held accountable for poor performance or problem behavior	❏ Just once ❏ 5–9 times	❏ 2–4 times ❏ 10+ times
Problematic interactions with teams or individuals outside of your direct line of supervision	❏ Just once ❏ 5–9 times	❏ 2–4 times ❏ 10+ times

Other (please describe): _____ _____ _____	❏ Just once ❏ 2–4 times ❏ 5–9 times ❏ 10+ times
Other (please describe): _____ _____ _____	❏ Just once ❏ 2–4 times ❏ 5–9 times ❏ 10+ times
Other (please describe): _____ _____ _____	❏ Just once ❏ 2–4 times ❏ 5–9 times ❏ 10+ times

2. How many employees are under your direct supervision? _____
   Do you supervise other supervisors? ❏ Yes ❏ No

3. What is the current average hourly rate of pay for your direct reports? $_____ per hour

4. What is your current hourly rate of pay? $_____ per hour

5. In the situations shown above, how many different employees under your direct supervision were involved? _____

6. Assuming the total conflicts shown above equals 100%, what percentage of those conflicts are not yet resolved? _____%

   a. On a scale of 0–10, circle the number that shows how confident you are in the percentage of unresolved conflicts that you listed for Question #6 (0 means no confidence, 10 means total certainty):

   0—1—2—3—4—5—6—7—8—9—10

7. If any, what tangible effects related to the unresolved conflicts are you and/or your direct reports currently experiencing (check as many as apply). Also, please provide actual or estimated costs for each item you check.

Tangible effects:	Costs (mark if actual or estimate):
Increased overtime payments	❏ actual ❏ estimate
Completed work needing to be redone one or more times	❏ actual ❏ estimate
Hiring facilitator(s) to help address conflict or run meetings	❏ actual ❏ estimate
Purchasing additional supplies or materials	❏ actual ❏ estimate
Increased consulting costs	❏ actual ❏ estimate
Hiring temporary employees to fill gaps	❏ actual ❏ estimate
Hiring additional regular employees to fill gaps	❏ actual ❏ estimate
Other (please describe): _____ _____ _____	❏ actual ❏ estimate (*Cont.*)

FIGURE 5.1 Continued

Other (please describe): _____	❏ actual ❏ estimate
Other (please describe): _____	❏ actual ❏ estimate

a. On a scale of 0–10, circle the number that shows how confident you are in the cost figures you gave for Question #7 (0 means no confidence, 10 means total certainty):
0—1—2—3—4—5—6—7—8—9—10

8. What, if any, intangible effects related to the unresolved conflicts are you and/or your direct reports currently experiencing (check as many as apply):

❏ Increased workload for other employees	❏ Unplanned and undesired employee turnover
❏ Low employee morale	❏ Poor teamwork
❏ Lack of innovation or new ideas	❏ Project(s) not completed in a timely manner
❏ Important information withheld from discussions	❏ Loss of productivity
Other (please describe): _____	Other (please describe): _____
Other (please describe): _____	Other (please describe): _____

9. On average, how many hours per work week do you spend addressing the unresolved conflicts and/or any related tangible or intangible effects? _____ hours

  a. On a scale of 0–10, circle the number that shows how confident you are in the number of hours you listed for Question #9 (0 means no confidence, 10 means total certainty):
0—1—2—3—4—5—6—7—8—9—10

10. On average, how many hours per work week do your direct reports spend addressing the unresolved conflicts and/or any related tangible or intangible effects? _____ hours

  a. On a scale of 0–10, circle the number that shows how confident you are in the number of hours you listed for Question #10 (0 means no confidence, 10 means total certainty):
0—1—2—3—4—5—6—7—8—9—10

11. If any, what barriers do you encounter when addressing conflicts in the workplace?

_____

_____

_____

12. If anything, what enables you to effectively address conflicts in the workplace?
_____
_____

13. What additional information or comments do you have in regard to unresolved conflicts in the workplace? Feel free to write on the back or attach additional sheets, if needed. _____
_____
_____

14. How long did it take you to complete this questionnaire in hours/minutes?_____

THANKS AGAIN FOR YOUR HELP!!!!!!!!!

The training officer employed the Phillips Methodology and the 12 Guiding Principles at every stage of the study, from initial planning to calculations to the writing of this case study.

Prior to conducting the study, the training officer developed a data collection plan (see Figure 5.3) as well as an ROI Analysis Plan (see Figure 5.4). Level 1 and Level 2 data included class evaluation scores and end-of-class test scores. (See Figure 5.5 for a blank copy of the class evaluation form.) The selected Level 1 objective was that 80 percent of class participants would give positive feedback about the class.

FIGURE 5.2   Phillips ROI Methodology 12 Guiding Principles

1. When a higher-level evaluation is conducted, data must be collected at lower levels.
2. When an evaluation is planned for a higher level, the previous level of evaluation does not have to be comprehensive.
3. When collecting and analyzing data, use only the most credible sources.
4. When analyzing data, select the most conservative alternative for calculations.
5. At least one method must be used to isolate the effects of the solution/program.
6. If no improvement data are available for a population or from a specific source, the assumption is that little or no improvement has occurred.
7. Estimates of improvements should be adjusted for the potential error of the estimate.
8. Extreme data items and unsupported claims should not be used in ROI calculations.
9. Only the first year of benefits (annual) should be used in the ROI analysis of short-term solutions.
10. Costs of a solution, project, or program should be fully loaded for ROI analysis.
11. Intangible measures are defined as measures that are purposely not converted to monetary values.
12. The results from the ROI Methodology must be communicated to all key stakeholders.

FIGURE 5.3 Data Collection Plan

Evaluation Purpose: Evaluate the effectiveness of a specific conflict management (CM) skills training class for supervisors

Level	Broad Program Objective(s)	Measures	Data Collection Method and Instruments	Data Sources	Timing	Responsibilities
1	**Reaction/Satisfaction** • 80% of participants will give positive feedback about the CM skills taught in the class.	• Average of 4.8 out of a rating scale of 6.0.	• Class evaluation form	• Participant	• 7th class session (3 weeks following 6th session)	• Instructor
2	**Learning** • 80% of participants will know the CM steps to use to successfully address unresolved work conflicts. • 80% of participants will present at least one completed CM action plan for using the CM skills in the workplace.	• Score of 80% or higher on end-of-class test. • Action plan completion.	• Test score • Action plan	• Participant • Participant	• End of 5th class session • End of 5th class session	• Instructor • Instructor
3	**Application/Implementation** • Participants will use the CM skills in work conflict situations in accordance with their CM action plans. • Participants will report the real-life barriers and enablers in regard to the use of the CM skills and will revise their CM action plan to address these items.	• 80% of participants will report that they followed their CM action plan. • 80% of participants will report these items and will revise their CM action plan accordingly.	• Follow-up session and action plan results • Follow-up session and action plan results	• Participant • Participant	• 6th class session (3 weeks following 5th session) • 6th class session (3 weeks following 5th session)	• Instructor • Instructor

#					
3	• Participants will use the CM skills in work conflict situations in accordance with their CM action plans.	• 80% of participants will report that they followed their CM action plan.	• Follow-up session, questionnaire, and action plan results	• Participant	• 7th class session (3 weeks following 6th session)	• Instructor
4	**Business Impact** • 50% reduction in the number of unresolved work conflicts identified in a pre-class questionnaire.	• Participants will report a 50% average reduction in the number of unresolved work conflicts.	• Follow-up session and questionnaire	• Participant	• 7th class session (3 weeks following 6th session)	• Instructor
	• 50% reduction in the impact of unresolved conflict(s) in the work unit identified in a pre-class questionnaire.	• Participants will report a 50% average reduction in the tangible and intangible impact(s) of the unresolved conflicts.	• Follow-up session and questionnaire	• Participant	• 7th class session (3 weeks following 6th session)	• Instructor
	• Any measurable cost savings due to use of CM skills.	• 80% of participants will report some level of cost savings in their CM action plan results.	• Action plan results	• Participant	• 7th class session (3 weeks following 6th session)	• Instructor
5	**ROI** Target => +25%	**Baseline Data:** • Will gather participant data on "current number of unresolved conflicts at work" at the beginning of class via questionnaire.				

• Participants' action plans will specifically identify one or more unresolved work conflict(s) that would have the greatest potential positive impact if they would be resolved. July 2006 supervisory focus group needs assessment identified "ability to address work conflicts and hold employees more accountable" as a high priority; addressing work conflicts effectively also ties into strategic goals as shown in vision, mission, and strategic plan language.

FIGURE 5.4   ROI Analysis Plan

Program: Conflict Management (CM) Class Study

Data Items (Usually Level 4)	Methods for Isolating the Effects of the Program or Process	Methods of Converting Data to Monetary Values	Cost Categories	Potential Intangible Benefits	Communication Targets for Final Report	Potential Other Influences and Issues During Application

• Number of unresolved work conflict(s) identified in both a pre-class and a post-class questionnaire.
• Tangible and intangible impact(s) of unresolved conflicts in the work unit identified in pre-class and post-class questionnaires.
• Action plan calculations.
	• Compare "before and after" numbers of unresolved work conflicts identified in questionnaires for two different groups:
	  – CM class participants
	  – Control group of supervisors not taking the class.
	• Ask participants for estimates of the class's impact on any reported behavior changes or cost calculations.
	• Expert or any related studies (if any)
		• Identify cost(s) of unresolved conflict in terms of time and total compensation (both salary and benefits costs)
		• Standard values from other studies (if available).
		• Participants' estimations of related costs
		• Expert input (if available).
			• Participant materials
			• Participants' salary and benefits costs
			• Cost of trainer's salary and benefits
			• Cost of food provided
			• Room costs
			• Cost of data evaluation in time spent by training officer
				• Long-run and short-run stress reduction
				• Improved communications
				• Improved teamwork
				• Increased job satisfaction
				• Carryover effect into personal life
				• Increase in successful work project completion
				• Freed-up time for other productive tasks
					• HR director
					• Assistant HR director
					• Class participants
					• Control group participants
						• Workload changes in the work unit
						• Turnover involving workplace antagonist(s)
						• New employees in the work unit
						• Funding changes for the work unit
						• Layoffs in the work unit
						• Level of management support
						• Other related training classes that may influence interactions

FIGURE 5.5   Class Evaluation Form

Conflict Management (CM) Class Evaluation Facilitator _____ Location _____ Training Date _____ **Course**	Strongly Disagree	Disagree	Slightly Disagree	Slightly Agree	Agree	Strongly Agree
This course will help me in my professional life.						
I feel prepared to use what I learned to improve some of my own conflict situations.						
The skills will help solve some of the serious problems faced every day in my organization, team, or company.						
I would recommend this course to coworkers, friends, or family members.						
Instructor						
The instructor used engaging stories to illustrate course concepts.						
I understood what to watch for in the video clips (the instructor clearly explained what to look for).						
I understood what I was supposed to do during exercises and activities.						
The instructor made clear transitions from one topic to the next, making sure that there weren't unanswered questions before moving on.						
The instructor asked open-ended questions that encouraged discussion.						
The instructor kept the course moving at an appropriate pace.						
The instructor explained concepts clearly.						
The instructor was knowledgeable about the course material.						
Facilities						
The facilities were pleasant, comfortable, and conducive to learning.						
The information I received prior to the course met my needs.						
General						
What did you like best about the training?						
What could we improve?						

Level 2 had two broad objectives. The first Level 2 objective was that 80 percent of the participants would know the steps to use the CM skills to successfully address unresolved work conflicts. To this end, the training officer designed a true-false end-of-class test to measure the participants' learning, which the officer administered at the end of the fifth session. The second Level 2 objective was for 80 percent of the class participants to show the instructor at least one completed action plan for using the CM skills in the workplace by the end of the fifth class session. (See Figure 5.6 for a blank copy of the action plan document.)

The measurement of Level 1 and Level 2 objectives was not extensive in accordance with the Phillips Guiding Principles 1 and 2. These principles state that while you do need to collect data from all five levels to calculate a program's ROI, the lower levels of evaluation do not need to be as comprehensive as the higher levels.

Level 3 had three objectives, two of which were to be measured during the sixth class session; the remaining one was to be measured in the seventh and final class session. In relation to the action plans, 80 percent of the participants were expected to report at both the sixth and seventh class sessions that they were following their action plans to use the CM skills in real-life work conflict situations. In addition, 80 percent of participants were expected to report real-life barriers and enablers to the use of the CM skills during the sixth class session and to revise their action plans accordingly, if applicable.

Level 4 also had three objectives: first, that there would be a 50 percent reduction in the average number of unresolved work conflicts from the pre-class questionnaire; second, that there would be a 50 percent reduction in the average tangible impact of the unresolved conflicts identified in the pre-class questionnaire; and third, that there would be a level of measurable cost savings due to the use of the CM skills. It was hoped that 80 percent of class participants would report measurable cost savings on their action plan results.

Finally, the Level 5 ROI target was to meet or exceed a plus 25 percent return on the investment made in providing the CM training for the class participants.

Level 3 and Level 4 data were to come from information provided on the pre-class and post-class participant questionnaires, discussion items from the sixth and seventh class sessions, and any completed action plan results. Since XYZ County had no statistical baseline data showing the cost of unresolved conflict in the workplace, class participants completed a

FIGURE 5.6   Action Plan

Action Plan

Name _____ Instructor Initials _____ Follow-Up Date _____

Objective 1: Use CM skills to _____

Evaluation Period _____ to _____

How Will I Measure Improvement _____

Current Performance _____ Target Performance _____

ACTION STEPS: I will do this ⌐→	DESIRED END RESULT: So that ⌐→
1. _____ _____	_____ _____
2. _____ _____	_____ _____
3. _____ _____	_____ _____
4. _____ _____	_____ _____

EXPECTED INTANGIBLE BENEFITS:

_____

_____

Action Plan Results

Name _____ Instructor Initials _____ Follow-Up Date _____

Objective 1: Use CM skills to _____

Evaluation Period _____ to _____

How Will I Measure Improvement _____

Current Performance _____ Target Performance _____

Action Steps Completed	Date Completed	Analysis
1. _____ _____		**A.** What is the unit of measure? _____
		B. What is the value (cost) of one unit? $ _____
2. _____ _____		How did you arrive at this value? _____
		C. How much did the measure change during the
3. _____ _____		evaluation period? (monthly value) _____
		D. What percent of this change was actually caused by
4. _____ _____		the conflict program? _____
		E. What level of confidence do you place on the "percentage change" you listed for D above? (100% = Certainty and 0% = No Confidence) _____

Intangible Benefits Realized: _____

Comments: _____

pre-class questionnaire to help create baseline data to use in the calculation of such costs. Class participants would then complete a post-class questionnaire again showing the number and cost of unresolved conflicts in the workplace. The comparison between the pre-class reported costs and post-class reported costs would show cost savings that may have occurred during the 11-week time period.

To isolate the effects of the CM class, the training officer decided to use three methods. First, a control group of 10 supervisors who did not take the CM training class were asked to complete the same pre-class and post-class questionnaires as the 16 class participants. Second, the 16 class participants themselves were asked to estimate the impact of the CM skills taught in the class on any reported behavior changes or cost calculations, as well as to state their confidence level in the numbers they would report. Last, class participants also were asked to report any other tangible or intangible influencing the results.

To facilitate the conversion of the collected data into monetary values for the Level 4 and Level 5 calculations, class participants were asked to report the tangible costs in terms of time, salary, and estimated or actual dollars spent. The training officer then planned to apply a standard value of 30 percent of salary for the cost of employer-provided benefits plans; this figure would be added to the reported salary amounts in order to identify the "total compensation" figure to use for both the program costs and program benefits sides.

EVALUATION RESULTS

Level 1 Results

The stated Level 1 objective was that 80 percent of class participants would give positive feedback about the CM skills taught in the class, and the target measure was an average of 4.8 on a 6.0 scale. The return rate for the evaluation forms was 93 percent (15 out of 16 participants completed the evaluation form). The lowest average score on any of the measurements was 5.4, so the Level 1 objective was met and exceeded. See Figure 5.7 for Level 1 evaluation results.

Level 2 Results

Both of the Level 2 objectives were also met and exceeded. The first Level 2 objective was that 80 percent of the participants would know the steps to

FIGURE 5.7   Level 1 Evaluation Results

Evaluation Items	Average Score on a 6.0 Scale
Course overall score:	**5.6**
This course will help me in my professional life.	5.8
I feel prepared to use what I learned to improve some of my own conflict situations.	5.4
The skills will help solve some of the serious problems faced every day in my organization, team, or company.	5.5
I would recommend this course to coworkers, friends, or family members.	5.8
Instructor overall score:	**5.5**
The instructor used engaging stories to illustrate course concepts.	5.6
I understood what to watch for in the video clips (the instructor clearly explained what to look for).	5.6
I understood what I was supposed to do during exercises and activities.	5.4
The instructor made clear transitions from one topic to the next, making sure that there weren't unanswered questions before moving on.	5.5
The instructor asked open-ended questions that encouraged discussion.	5.5
The instructor kept the course moving at an appropriate pace.	5.5
The instructor explained concepts clearly.	5.5
The instructor was knowledgeable about the course material.	5.8
Facilities overall score:	**5.6**
The facilities were pleasant, comfortable, and conducive to learning.	5.7
The information I received prior to the course met my needs.	5.5

use the CM skills to successfully address unresolved work conflicts, and the target measure was for 80 percent of the participants to score 80 percent or better on the end-of-class true-false quiz. This measure was met since 81 percent of the class participants (13 out of 16) scored 80 percent or higher on the quiz and the class average quiz score was 86 percent. See Figure 5.8 for class score specifics.

FIGURE 5.8   Level 2 Evaluation Results, First Objective

Quiz	Number Correct out of 24	Test Score (%)
1	20	83
2	22	92
3	19	79
4	19	79
5	21	88
6	23	96
7	21	88
8	20	83
9	21	88
10	17	71
11	23	96
12	20	83
13	20	83
14	24	100
15	20	83
16	20	83
Average number of correct answers:	**20.6**	**86**

The second Level 2 objective was for 80 percent of the class participants to show the instructor at least one correctly designed action plan for
using the CM skills in the workplace by the end of the fifth class session.
This measure was met, since 13 of the 16 class participants (or 81 percent)
correctly designed at least one action plan for using the CM skills in the
workplace by the end of the fifth class session; a few of the participants
completed more than one action plan. See Figure 5.9 for the calculation of
this measure.

FIGURE 5.9   Level 2 Evaluation Results, Second Objective

Total number of class participants:	16
Number of participants who correctly designed at least one action plan:	13
Percentage of participants who correctly designed at least one action plan:	81
Total number of action plans to be attempted by class participants:	**19**

Level 3 Results

As stated earlier, Level 3 had three objectives, two of which were to be measured following the sixth class session; the remaining one was to be measured after the seventh and final class session. For these two objectives, the measure stated that 80 percent of the participants were expected to report at both the sixth and seventh class sessions that they were following their action plans in relation to work conflict situations. The participants met the measure for these two objectives, since all 13 of the 16 class participants (or 81 percent) reported at both the sixth and seventh class sessions that they were working on the items listed in their action plans. See Figure 5.10 for this calculation.

However, the remaining objective and measure ("80 percent of participants were expected to report real-life barriers and enablers to the use of the CM skills during the sixth class session and to revise their action plans accordingly, if applicable") was only partially met. While all 16 class participants were in attendance at the sixth class session when the group discussed real-life barriers and enablers, the training officer did not count the number of participants who made any revisions or adjustments to their action plans after that discussion. Therefore, in accordance with Phillips ROI Methodology Guidelines 6 (if no data is available, assume that no

FIGURE 5.10   Level 3 Evaluation Results, First and Third Objectives

Total number of class participants:	16
Number of participants who reported working on at least one action plan:	13
Percentage of participants who reported working on at least one action plan:	**81**

improvement occurred) and 8 (unsupported claims should not be used), this study will not calculate the measure for this objective.

Level 4 Results

Level 4 also had three objectives, all to be measured after the seventh and final class session: first, an anticipated 50 percent reduction in the average number of unresolved work conflicts from the pre-class questionnaire; second, an anticipated 50 percent reduction in the average tangible impact of the unresolved conflicts identified in the pre-class questionnaire; and third, that 80 percent of class participants would report measurable cost savings due to the use of the CM skills on their action plan results.

For the first Level 4 objective, the post-class questionnaire results showed a 21 percent overall reduction in the average number of unre-solved work conflicts when compared with the pre-class questionnaire results. This result fell short of the anticipated 50 percent reduction. How-ever, the structure of the response key for this portion of the questionnaire obscured the results for this measure. The participants were asked to respond to the frequency of various potential conflict situations using the key shown in Figure 5.11.

Using this answer key, the average pre-class frequency response was 1.4, and the average post-class frequency response was 1.1, which is a 21 percent reduction. However, if a participant selected "2" as his or her response, the response did not determine whether the situation occurred two, three, or four times. Therefore, if a situation occurred four times in the pre-class questionnaire and only two times in the post-class questionnaire, the respondent would have marked "2" for both, even though there would actually have been a 50 percent reduction. The reverse would also be true;

FIGURE 5.11   Frequency Response Key

Response	Frequency
0	None
1	Just once
2	2–4 times
3	5–9 times
4	10+ times

if there were two incidents to report in the pre-class questionnaire and four to report in the post-class questionnaire, the respondent would have marked "2" for both, although there would have been a 100 percent increase. Since the question design was flawed, the training officer chose not to use this data in accordance with Phillips ROI Methodology Guideline 3 (only use the most credible data sources).

The measure for the second Level 4 objective anticipated a 50 percent reduction in the average tangible impact of the unresolved conflicts identified in the pre-class questionnaire. When calculating this measure, the training officer looked at two items: (1) tangible costs such as overtime, consultants, and additional materials, and (2) lost time for both the participants and their direct reports. In accordance with Phillips ROI Methodology Guideline 7 (estimates are adjusted for the potential error of the estimate), the training officer adjusted any reported costs by the participant's confidence rating in the estimate.

The non-time-related tangible costs showed a decrease of 81.5 percent, which well exceeded the anticipated 50 percent reduction. Figure 5.12 shows how the calculations were done for the non-time-related tangible costs.

FIGURE 5.12 Level 4 Evaluation Results, Second Objective: Non-Time-Related Tangible Costs

	Before	After
QUESTION: If any, what *tangible* effects related to the unresolved conflicts are you and/or your direct reports currently experiencing? **TOTAL** for all respondents:	$63,760.72	$9,572.50
	Average Before Response	**Average After Response**
QUESTION: On a scale of 0–10, circle the number that shows how confident you are in the tangible cost figures you listed above (0 means no confidence, 10 means total certainty):	5.1	6.3
Tangible Cost-Adjusted Comparison		
Tangible cost total adjusted by average confidence factor:	$32,517.97	$6,030.68
Total adjusted tangible cost savings:		**$26,487.29**
Percent change between "before" and "after" adjusted tangible costs:		−81.5

The time-related cost reductions showed a 15.4 percent reduction in the cost of time spent addressing unresolved conflicts by the participants and a 50.6 percent reduction in time spent by the participants' direct reports. The costs for the direct reports met the anticipated 50 percent reduction, but the costs for the participants themselves did not meet the objective. Figure 5.13 shows these calculations.

When converting the saved hours to dollar amounts for calculation of the program's benefits, the training officer noticed that participants listed

FIGURE 5.13   Level 4 Evaluation Results, Second Objective: Time-Related Tangible Costs

	Average Before Response	Average After Response
QUESTION: On average, how many hours per work week do you spend addressing the unresolved conflicts and/or any related tangible or intangible effects?	6.5	4.8
QUESTION: On a scale of 0–10, circle the number that shows how confident you are in the number of hours you listed above (0 means no confidence, 10 means total certainty):	6.3	7.1
QUESTION: On average, how many hours per work week do your direct reports spend addressing the unresolved conflicts and/or any related tangible or intangible effects?	10.3	5.0
QUESTION: On a scale of 0–10, circle the number that shows how confident you are in the number of hours you listed [for your direct reports] above (0 means no confidence, 10 means total certainty):	5.6	6.4
	Average Before Response	**Average After Response**
What is the current average hourly rate of pay for your direct reports?	$23.25	$20.69
Benefits cost per hour for direct reports:	$6.98	$6.21
Average total compensation hourly rate for direct reports:	$30.23	$26.90
What is your current hourly rate of pay?	$31.63	$32.03
Benefits cost per hour for class participants:	$9.49	$9.61
Average total compensation hourly rate for class participants:	**$41.12**	**$41.64**

Class Participants Cost-Adjusted Comparison	Before	After
Adjusted average hours per week times average total comp hourly rate:	$267.30	$200.56
Adjusted average cost per week times confidence factor:	$168.40	$142.40
Adjusted average weekly time cost savings:		$26.00
Total adjusted time savings for participants (15):		$390.01
Percent change between "before" and "after" average cost for participants:		−15.4
Direct Reports Cost-Adjusted Comparison	Before	After
Adjusted average hours per week times average total comp hourly rate:	$309.86	$134.05
Adjusted average cost per week times confidence factor:	$173.52	$85.79
Adjusted average weekly time cost savings:		$87.73
Total adjusted time savings for direct reports (100):		$8,773.37
Percent change between "before" and "after" average wage cost for the direct reports:		−50.6

a total of 100 direct reports on 15 post-class questionnaires, as opposed to 143 direct reports shown on 16 pre-class questionnaires. She also noticed that the average hourly pay rate for the direct reports decreased while the average hourly rate for the class participants who were supervisors increased.

As the training officer was double-checking the calculations for the second Level 4 objective, she realized that a vital measure was missing. While some questions were adjusted for the participant's confidence level in the numbers he or she was reporting, two critical questions were not asked in the post-class questionnaire: "What percentage of this change was caused by the CM program?" and "How confident are you in the number you reported as the percentage of change that was caused by the CM program?" Without this information, it is not possible to credibly claim that the reductions in either the time-related or non-time-related costs are directly linked to the CM program. Therefore, in accordance with Phillips ROI Methodology Guidelines 6 (if no data is available, assume that no improvement occurred) and 8 (unsupported claims should not be used), these calculated program benefits were disregarded.

The anticipated measure for the third Level 4 objective that "80 percent of class participants will report measurable cost savings" was not met. Of the 13 class participants who correctly completed one or more action plans, only three had measurable data by the end of the seventh class session. One participant had two completed action plans, and the other two participants had one action plan each, for a total of four completed plans. The action plans for the remaining 10 participants were still in progress and were not ready to calculate. Therefore, the measure for this objective was not met, since only 18 percent of the class participants were able to report some level of cost savings in their action plan results. See Figure 5.14 for this calculation, and see Figure 5.15 for the reported cost savings from the four completed action plans. These program benefits will be included in the Level 5 calculations since the action plans did include the question "What percent of this change was actually caused by the CM program?" and the calculated benefits were adjusted appropriately based on the participants' responses.

Data Analysis

Note that all calculations were done in accordance with the Phillips ROI Methodology, specifically Guidelines 3 (use the most credible data sources), 4 (use the most conservative alternative), 7 (estimates are adjusted for the potential error of the estimate), and 10 (costs should be fully loaded).

Isolating Effects of the Program

The original plan included a comparison of the data between the class participant group and a control group. A control group of 10 supervisors completed the same pre-class questionnaire as the class participants; however,

FIGURE 5.14   Level 4 Evaluation Results, Third Objective

Total number of action plans attempted by participants:	19
Number of action plans "in progress" at end of the 7th class session:	15
Number of action plans with calculable results at end of the 7th class session:	4
Number of participants with calculable action plans:	3
Percentage of participants with calculable action plans:	18

FIGURE 5.15 Level 4 Evaluation Results, Third Objective: Reported Cost Savings From Completed Action Plans

Situation in a Nutshell	Unit of Measure	Value of Unit (Total Comp)	Monthly Value of Measure Change	Reported % of Change Caused by CM Program	Confidence Factor	Calculated Adjusted Savings	Reported Intangibles
Ongoing conflict with employee's daughter causing distraction and loss of employee's at-work productivity	1 hour per month of lost productivity at work	$32.50	2 hours of increased productivity at work	90%	100%	$58.50	Less stress on entire family, better communication
Ongoing problems with data system entry and reporting, need to request changes	1 hour per month	$32.50	Saved 2 hours per month after system changes implemented	100%	100%	$65.00	Less frustration when entering data
Employee making errors on financial reports and records, need to have employee increase her accuracy	1 hour per month	$40.30	Supervisor saved 2 hours per month in looking for employee's errors	50%	75%	$30.23	Employee more accountable for own errors, supervisor freed up to perform other tasks rather than double-checking for employee's errors
Need to improve the quality of communication between employees in order to reduce backlog of work	1 hour per month	$42.90	80 hours	77.5%	95%	$2,526.81	Employees seem happier, less tension when facing discussions about work backlog, easier to talk about important issues
				Total adjusted action plan savings:		$2,680.54	

when the 11 weeks had passed and it was time to have the control group complete the post-class questionnaire, only five of the original group did so. Although control group data are considered a highly credible source, the training officer was concerned that the loss of 50 percent of the control group would jeopardize the validity of any data gathered. Therefore, in accordance with Phillips ROI Methodology Guideline 8 (unsupported claims should not be used), the control group data were disregarded.

Again, due to the flaws in the question design, the benefit calculations for the first two Level 4 objectives cannot be included in any Level 5 benefit-cost ratio (BCR) and ROI calculations; this decision is in accordance with Phillips ROI Methodology Guideline 8 (unsupported claims should not be used).

The training officer used the "participant self-reporting" isolation method in two different ways: (1) participants' self-reported impact for the action plan results, and (2) participants' self-reported confidence level in the numbers they were providing. This method does comply with Methodology Guideline 3 (only use the most credible sources of data), since self-reported impact and confidence levels are considered highly credible data sources. In addition, the use of at least one method to isolate the effects of the program met the requirement for Methodology Guideline 5.

Level 5 Results

In order to ensure the believability of the BCR and ROI calculations for any given program, it is important to use only the most conservative calculations and the most credible data from the Level 4 analysis. The training officer originally decided not to calculate either the BCR or the ROI for this program, because she had no credible data to include for three out of the originally planned four program benefit data points. The main reasons for her hesitation were (1) a fear that county officials would not look past the negative "sound bite bottom-line" number for the program, and (2) a fear that the program's intangible benefits would be overshadowed by a negative ROI calculation.

After further consideration, the training officer decided to perform the calculations since data were available to do so. The data are what they are; the process of calculating BCR and ROI should not be determined by whether or not a program sponsor perceives that the results will be acceptable to a given audience.

As mentioned earlier, the costs of time spent by both the class participants and the training officer in the CM program were calculated in terms of "total compensation"; that is, both salary and the related employer-provided benefits costs. Figure 5.16 shows a breakdown of the total compensation cost calculations included in the fully loaded costs. Figure 5.17 shows the data for program benefits and program costs to be used in the BCR and ROI calculations.

FIGURE 5.16   Total Compensation Cost Calculations

Total minutes reported to complete pre-class questionnaire:		220
Total minutes reported to complete post-class questionnaire:		232
Total minutes reported to complete and work on action plans:		3,160
Total minutes:		3612
Converted to hours:		60.2
Average total comp "after" hourly rate for class participants:	**$41.64**	
Total comp cost for participants to complete ROI paperwork for the study:		**$2,506.72**
Total hours spent in class by each participant:		24.5
Number of participants:		16
Total number of classroom hours:		392
Total comp cost for participants to attend the classes:		**$16,322.88**
Hourly wage for training officer:	$29.42	
Benefit cost per hour for training officer:	$8.83	
Total comp hourly rate for training officer:	**$38.25**	
Hours spent in class preparation and delivery:	64	
Class preparation and delivery total comp cost:	$2,448.00	
Hours spent doing ROI calculations and write-up:	94.75	
ROI calculations and write-up total comp cost:	$3,624.19	

FIGURE 5.17   Program Benefits and Costs

Conservatively Identified Program Benefits	
Total adjusted non-time-related tangible cost savings:	cannot be included
Total adjusted time savings for 15 participants:	cannot be included
Total adjusted time savings for 100 direct reports:	cannot be included
Total adjusted action plan savings:	$2,680.54
	$2,680.54
Fully Loaded Program Costs	
Total compensation costs for time spent by all participants completing the questionnaires and the action plans:	$2,506.72
Total compensation costs for classroom time spent by all participants:	$16,322.88
Total compensation costs for class preparation and delivery by the training officer:	$2,448.00
Total compensation costs for ROI calculations and report write-up done by the training officer:	$3,624.19
Class participant books and materials:	$3,360.00
Class refreshments and supplies:	$495.00
Facilities costs for the use of the training room:	$2,240.00
Total	**$30,996.79**

The BCR was calculated by dividing the program benefits by the program costs, as follows:

$$\text{BCR} = \frac{\$2,680.54}{\$30,996.79} = 0.086 \text{ or } .086{:}1$$

Then the ROI was calculated by taking the net program benefits (program benefits minus program costs) divided by the program costs times 100, as follows:

$$\text{ROI} = \frac{\$2,680.54 - \$30,996.79}{\$30,996.79} \times 100 = -91.35\%$$

Identifying Intangible Benefits

Intangible measures are results that are purposely not converted to monetary values but are nonetheless considered to be part of the benefit derived from the program. In the post-class questionnaire, participants reported that learning the CM skills had increased their confidence in their abilities to address conflict appropriately. They also reported that using the CM skills had resulted in better employee morale, increased accountability for some direct reports, improved work-group culture, better understanding and communication between co-workers, and decreased frustration in the work unit for both the participants and their direct reports. As shown in Figure 5.18, the post-class questionnaire also demonstrated a 35 percent decrease in the number of reported negative intangible effects of unresolved conflicts in the workplace. Figure 5.19 shows the full list of intangible benefits reported by participants on the post-class questionnaire.

Participants also identified various external factors in the post-class questionnaire that had an impact on the unresolved conflicts in the workplace. Examples include some staff turnover during the 11 weeks between completion of the pre- and post-class questionnaires, other staff members taking conflict management classes, and workload slowdowns. Figure 5.20 shows a full list of these reported factors.

Identifying Barriers and Enablers

CM class participants provided information on various barriers and enablers to addressing conflicts in the workplace via group discussion during the seventh class session as well as in written answers on both the pre- and post-class questionnaires. By and large, participants mentioned similar barriers in both the pre- and post-class questionnaires and in the seventh class session discussion. Reported post-class barriers included time constraints, fear, lack of trust (leading to lack of honesty in discussions), personal issues, agency culture and history, team dynamics, high levels of defensiveness, and responses such as "It's not fun." The only barrier listed in the pre-class responses that did not appear in the post-class responses was a lack of knowledge or confidence in the participant's own ability to address conflict effectively. Figure 5.21 shows barriers reported on the questionnaires.

Likewise, CM class participants reported similar enablers both pre- and post-class. Reported enablers included honest communications, regularly

FIGURE 5.18 Details of Intangible Effects Reported in Pre- and Post-Class Questionnaires

What, if any, intangible effects related to the unresolved conflicts are you and/or your direct reports currently experiencing?				
	Number of Yeses From Before	Number of Yeses From After	Change From Before to After	Change From Before to After (%)
Increased workload for other employees	11	8	−3	−27
Low employee morale	11	7	−4	−36
Lack of innovation or new ideas	4	4	−0	0
Important information withheld from discussions	5	6	1	+20
Unplanned and undesired employee turnover	1	0	−1	−100
Poor teamwork	11	6	−5	−45
Project(s) not completed in a timely manner	5	4	−1	−20
Loss of productivity	9	4	−5	−56
Other (see below for descriptions)	5	1	−4	−80
Totals:	62	40	−22	−35

Other: *From Before Questionnaires:* "being unable to delegate work because of skills that are lacking," "staff not dealing with each other directly—being passive aggressive with each other," "not low morale but uncertainty from so many new employees," "employees pitting against each other," "low motivation"

Other: *From After Questionnaires:* "not viewed as 'professional' by other department staff"

FIGURE 5.19 Intangible Benefits Reported in Post-Class Questionnaires

As a direct result of taking the CM class, what tangible or intangible benefits (if any) do you feel you've experienced? Please be specific:
Specific personnel issues finally addressed specifically and directly with appropriate documentation.
As noted above, confidence and a greatly increased skill level when deciding when and if I am likely to address the issue in almost all instances. Better at creating safety for the person. Better at identifying what issues are barriers such as ability, motivation, or structural issues. Productivity and ability of team to be inclusive and share ideas has greatly increased.
To look at overall job duties and maybe do some re-assigning.
Being able to sort out the issues and deal with the problem directly.
The ability to identify problems and the tools to more effectively resolve them.
Less time dealing with unhappy co-workers.
Less time being spent re-addressing issues with same employee because now I have the skills to resolve those issues effectively.
Knowledge of a new tool to use in a conflict situation. Specific conflicts on a path of resolution (apparently so, too early to tell yet).
Very helpful in confronting the supervisor I am having difficulty with appropriately so I don't think he is as resentful of me and has improved in some accountability areas. Has helped me give tips to other supervisors whom I supervise (especially the new one) of how to approach their staff.
I had a situation arise across sections in which one supervisor started out pointing fingers at a particular staff member whom I supervise. I requested that we step back, ask the two direct staff members that were involved to meet with us and identify the real issue. When I approached it this way, the supervisor backed off and let the two staff members communicate. The real issue was not involving them at all but altogether different staff members getting paperwork in error and staff members not talking to each other, using email rather than direct communication. I received a thank you card from staff for my participation in the situation.
Modification of direct report's attitude about "gruff" behavior and "sink or swim" approaches to their reports. Changing to a better, more responsive attitude regarding coaching and showing respect for his employees by eliminating "gruff" behavior.
The tangible benefits I experienced are related to my not jumping in to resolve all issues. The result is staff show greater confidence dealing with customers.
Common language to strategize how and if to address concerns.
Some issues are in process of being addressed, but teamwork is improving. Improved relationships.

(Cont.)

FIGURE 5.19 Continued

Knowledge, confidence, and a better understanding of dealing with conflicts. It has also helped me deal with my children and family at home.
Look at myself and how I deal with conflict.
More confidence in my abilities due to having additional tools that are concise.
Morale. The tools and abilities to finally resolve some long-standing disappointments have improved my morale in the workplace.
More comfortable and confident in addressing conflict, less stress, more job satisfaction.
More confidence to handle conflicts. Improved skills to deal with different situations. Less stress in regards to "personnel issues" as now I can deal with them confidently.
Increased confidence in how to deal with conflict.
Personally, made my conflicts much more successful. As those have kind of "roped in" one supervisor in particular, I have seen increased morale in his staff.
Skills I can use throughout all aspects of my life even when I don't see them directly influencing my life at the present time.
1. Better accountability from direct report. 2. Increased teamwork and agreement on mutual purpose. 3. Step-by-step understanding of approaching complex problems and life's difficulties.
Change of culture; mutual respect of team members; better clarity of observing and resolving conflicts within team.
Less anger and frustration regarding interpersonal relationships and better understanding of co-workers; less fear of conflict.

scheduled meetings, good listening skills, and supportive management. Post-class questionnaire responses also listed the CM class as having given participants both additional tools to address conflict effectively and a boost in their confidence in their conflict management skills. See Figure 5.22 for the enablers reported in the pre- and post-class questionnaires.

COMMUNICATION STRATEGY

In accordance with Phillips ROI Methodology Guideline 12, which requires all key stakeholders to receive the results of an ROI study, the training officer emailed copies of both an ROI Report Summary and a detailed write-up to the stakeholders in the CM program. The detailed write-up consisted of

FIGURE 5.20   Other Influencing Factors Reported in Post-Class Questionnaires

Not including the CM class, has anything occurred for you or your direct reports since the last time you completed the questionnaire that has had an impact (either positive or negative) on the number of unresolved conflicts in the workplace? Please be specific:
New staff, different dynamics, people building relationships and reframing past history.
People have health issues that have started to cause a real breakdown of the team. Some feel like they are pulling the weight of others. It seems as though everyone is becoming their own little island.
Return of an old employee that has caused lack of trust with the line staff due to incorrect assumptions.
Meetings have taken place to address the conflicts and there has been positive resolution to them. In one case, staff was allowed to actively participate in the selection of a new supervisor.
Many employees taking this class and other conflict management class. Internal staff work as a team in developing "how we work together" document. Greater emphasis being placed on relationships with both internal and external customers.
Positive: new staff since last report are more seasoned and confident in their jobs. Negative: sort of, keep adding new programs so being in a constant state of change causes conflicts because line staff feel stressed.
Half of my reports are taking another conflict management class and they are anxious to have their peers take it so that all have a mutual purpose for reaching agreement.
My lead worker assigned to another team.
Not as busy as before.

a copy of this case study report minus the "Communication Strategy" section. The training officer asked the stakeholders to read the information and reply with thoughts, comments, or concerns.

The stakeholder group consisted of 27 people: the 16 supervisors who completed the CM class; the nine remaining control group participants (one is no longer employed with the county); the assistant human resources director (who is also the training officer's direct supervisor); and the human resources director. After the training officer sent a second reminder email,

FIGURE 5.21 Barriers Reported in Pre- and Post-Class Questionnaires

What, if any, barriers do you encounter when addressing conflicts in the workplace?	
Pre-Class Questionnaire Responses	**Post-Class Questionnaire Responses**
Blaming others, not taking responsibilities, staff feeling unappreciated, thinking everyone carries a fair share of work responsibilities due to staff receiving same pay.	Personality differences, ability skill level, perceptions, interpretations of county rules and regulations.
Co-workers not under our department in which we have no input or control over the conflicts; politics over policies and levels of desired services.	Cultural/respect issue, high defensiveness.
Time available to discuss; lack of motivation to improve on employees' part; lack of confidence of impact on supervisors' part.	Time is a big one. Employees not feeling safe enough to share honest opinions.
Cultural issues of department, pit experiences of employees impacting current situation. Disciplinary process and timeliness of other departmental input/direction; multi-agency partnerships and competing supervision expectation—lack of control due to set up. Staff not being willing/able to problem solve—people stuck in problem and solution. Selfish selections not taking into account the whole process, staff not staying in role in process situation; having expertise without power to make decision.	Filling the gap.
The age difference between myself and my staff can present challenges and barriers. Inflexible rules/regulation can be a barrier. I worry too much about "not being liked"—try too hard to please everyone, which is not always effective.	Lack of honesty between workers and supervisors, which in turn creates a lack of trust. Just getting through that and making people understand how to tell the truth and address the issues is time consuming and wearing.
Lack of standards regarding coaching expectations and supervisory responsibility (some supervisors may say I learned it by doing and they should also).	Structure—ability to address conflicts with higher level people or people outside of current workgroup.
Statutory regulations, county policies, individuals who are concerned about change. Reluctant to realize that we have limited resources. Need to provide a different level of service. We often see individuals addressing change with passive-aggressive behavior and sabotaging the results. This is done by executive staff and peers.	Prior agency culture has created some obstacles. 3.75 of 5 supervisors I supervise are hardworking, good leaders. One supervisor is brand new and on the learning curve but doing well. One supervisor is a challenge and has a ripple effect throughout the agency. This one has difficulty with giving me the same feedback as what is presented to other staff.

Pre-Class Questionnaire Responses	Post-Class Questionnaire Responses
Political correctness	Other person's personal issues are the biggest barrier.
Work schedules make it difficult to get involved employees or supervisors together to resolve issues. Also, personal feelings tend to get rehashed for longer than necessary.	Workload of all staff—finding time to deal with those issues and keep regular work flow going.
People making assumptions about each other or situations. One person in particular with a tendency to step beyond their role and unwilling to accept input or decisions of team members. My lack of time to address all issues adequately.	Conflict avoidance behaviors—getting people to the table.
Lack of knowledge by everyone in how to effectively address conflicts. Complexity—one person's conflict is not another person's conflict. Difficulty in knowing the "truth"—who did what, why, etc. Lack of time to do so.	When issues cross sections, I see a finger pointing tactic starts to surface. It is best to have it be task based so staff are able to see how tasks affect the group as a whole.
Staff from other sections where conflicts exist are not exactly honest about situations because it takes conflict off them and directs to someone else. I believe we all (myself included) put up our defenses when our sections come under attack. I see several staff who want to avoid conflict so they will agree just to do so.	Silence or violence. Structured chain of command in some employees' minds. Reluctance to hold conflict conversations. Team skills and understanding of team dynamics.
Inconsistency; one day high, bubbly—next day low, depressed. Offered EAP for counseling but what can you do if refuse to use.	Sometimes structural, ability, social or culture.
The barriers encountered in the workplace deal with my lack of comfort/confidence in handling conflict. I would rather bury my head in the sand instead of dealing with conflict head on.	Structural barriers, emotional barriers.
Team works on the front line and must be available to assist the public at all times; therefore, it is difficult to pull them all together to discuss issues without having to bring them in early or make them stay late. Also, some team members feel confident in sharing issues with each other. Others "clam up" and do not want to interact with team members. Finally, health issues with team members are drastically affecting the unity of the team.	Time involved and lack of policy support.
Lack of honest communication about what the real issues are, so many different pieces in the agency. Communication boqs down.	

FIGURE 5.22   Enablers

If anything, what enables you to effectively address conflicts in the workplace?	
Pre-Class Questionnaire Responses	**Post-Class Questionnaire Responses**
Listening and getting to root cause; bringing staff together for discussion.	Experience, training, support from my boss.
County policies regarding discipline; department heads.	This class has been extremely helpful in boosting my confidence and skill level to address issues and not avoid them. I am better able to keep my stories in check, etc. Having others in our department trained in CM.
Documentation is the proper thing to do for liability; always discuss documentation with employee. Desire to improve team morale/productivity and creativity. Desire to be fair and just.	Being able to address them immediately is very effective. Having one-on-ones and sharing feedback also helps. Also, I have some employees that are very comfortable coming to me and sharing conflicts as they arise.
Culture of department; style differences between myself and other supervisors that report to me and new line staff.	The desire to teach to listen to "stories."
I am fair and honest when addressing conflict. I am sensitive to personal differences between staff members. I am open to constructive criticism and new ideas.	Listening to others to understand the deeper problem.
Training, teamwork, communication skills, tact, patience.	CM!!!
The employee and I regularly communicate so that we do not experience much conflict. Most of the conflict is with individuals outside my department.	I now have tools that will assist me in addressing conflict.
Trust, clearly established expectations.	Performance improvement plan to support my position. Adequate training to do so effectively and support of admin staff in my decisions.

Pre-Class Questionnaire Responses	Post-Class Questionnaire Responses
Our monthly meeting where we do get to pull together off of the front line to brainstorm ideas for procedure changes, training, etc. One-on-one with the employees to address issues also is very helpful. Coaching, mentoring, assigning tasks with deadlines, etc. helps keep the focus.	Use of proper tools, e.g. CM. Motivation that these conflicts must be addressed in order to keep staff/employees performing satisfactorily.
Communications training, SDI training that helped understand orientations and approaches of others. Supportive director and management team. Policies and procedures and HR processes that give guidelines to address issues.	Staff generally is pretty straight forwards about what they see as the issues. That is so helpful in getting things out in the open and is dedicated to the success of the agency.
Training about conflict management. Staff time to reduce conflicts.	I keep an open mind; address the situation not the person and know that staff's intentions are good/that they might need direction; clarification not criticism and negative talk. Treat others as I want them to treat me.
One-on-one conversations, listening skills.	Mostly a high level of professional responsibility and acceptance of assigned obligations. Peer and team interaction.
	Communication and meetings.
	The tools given me in the class.

a total of nine of the 27 stakeholders responded to the request for comments and feedback.

The comments were generally positive and reiterated the value of the intangible benefits that the program had provided the individual participants. The training officer sent additional information to anyone who asked specific questions and made note of suggestions to improve the class or the study structure for the next round of training.

LESSONS LEARNED

Despite the low BCR and negative ROI, the training officer considered the program to be a success on several levels. The reasons for this success include the following:

The participants' response to the CM class was very positive; several participants shared stories with the training officer about how the CM skills helped them to better address specific conflict situations, both at work and at home.

The positive intangible benefits noted by the participants also reflect the program's success. One county department in particular has chosen to adopt CM principles and has taken steps to make the CM skills part of the department culture. This change not only supports and reinforces the use of the skills but may reduce the likelihood of unresolved conflicts in the future.

Class participants have told co-workers and others about how the class has impacted them, so that increasing numbers of employees are interested in taking the class. In addition, the HR department had not previously attempted to measure the impact of any training classes beyond Level 1. The ROI study for the CM class has opened the door to higher levels of evaluation for the county's entire training and development curriculum.

Since this program represents the training officer's first attempt at an ROI study, the stakeholders learned several lessons. These lessons include the following:

Proper question design was vital to gathering usable and credible data. Inadequately worded and omitted questions led to unusable data, which undermined the goal of calculating a positive BCR and ROI for the CM training. The positive side of this new knowledge is that the training officer can easily adjust the wording of the questionnaires for future ROI analyses of the CM class.

The training officer must keep the control group engaged in the program in order to use any of the data they offer. In hindsight, the training officer should have taken more proactive steps to ensure the control group participants were willing to fully participate in the process. Also, the 11-week hiatus between the completion of the pre- and post-class questionnaires contributed to the 50 percent attrition rate of the control group participants. Future projects will not include the use of a control group without a specific engagement plan.

Few tangible action plan results were available, since most of the participants' action plans were focused on a longer time frame. In the future, the training officer will ask participants to develop action plans on either short-term or interim goals that could be easily calculated within the time frame for the study.

An ROI study takes time and resources. In this case, the training officer was unable to devote as much time and energy to the program as she had initially hoped due to competing priorities and her status as the sole operator of the project. As a result, a few specific tasks did not get completed, and the study ran several months behind the anticipated completion date. In hindsight, the use of a more specific project plan with clearly outlined tasks and expectations would have helped the training officer to focus on the program details and complete milestones within realistic time frames. Another intangible benefit is that the training officer now knows where specific adjustments need to be made in order for the next ROI project to yield more complete results.

QUESTIONS FOR DISCUSSION

1. Do you agree with the training officer's original idea not to calculate the BCR and ROI for this program? Why or why not?
2. What steps could the training officer have taken to ensure the continued engagement of the control group participants?
3. What, if any, other impact measures should have been included in the study?
4. What was the effect of the lack of baseline data on the evaluation process?
5. What processes, tools, or infrastructure might have helped the training officer in designing and completing the ROI study?
6. How would you have approached this study differently?

RESOURCES

Phillips, J.J. (2003). *Return on Investment in Training and Performance Improvement Programs.* Burlington, MA: Butterworth-Heinemann.

Phillips, P.P. (2002). *The Bottom Line on ROI: Basics, Benefits, and Barriers to Measuring Training and Performance Improvement.* Atlanta, GA: CEP Press.

Phillips, P.P., J.J. Phillips, R.D. Stone, and H. Burkett. (2007). *The ROI Fieldbook: Strategies for Implementing ROI in HR and Training.* Burlington, MA: Elsevier.

ABOUT THE AUTHOR

Patsi Maroney has worked for the Larimer County, Colorado, Human Resources Department for 25 years. She has been the County's Training and Organization Development Specialist for four years. Patsi has a bachelor's degree from Colorado State University in Technical Journalism/Public Relations. She is a member of both ASTD (American Society for Training and Development) and SHRM (Society for Human Resource Management). Patsi completed a weeklong ROI certification course offered by Jack J. Phillips, PhD, in October 2006. She also completed a yearlong Organizational Development Certificate Program through Mountain States Employers Council in December 2006. Patsi is a certified trainer for both Crucial Conversations and Crucial Confrontations through VitalSmarts in Provo, Utah; also, she is a certified consultant for the EQ In Action Profile developed by Learning In Action Technologies, Inc., in Bellevue, Washington. Patsi can be reached at (970) 498-5977 or **pmaroney@larimer.org**.

6

Technical Training Case Study

Aircraft Maintenance Company
Ireland

Gerry Doyle

This case was prepared to serve as a basis for discussion rather than an illustration of either effective or ineffective administrative and management practices. Names, dates, places, and data may have been disguised at the request of the author or organization.

Abstract

This case study presents the return on investment (ROI) analysis of a broad-based training program for a group of technicians to build their business awareness and skill level to achieve time savings and other business improvements. The company provides engine repair and maintenance services to the aviation sector. The study uses a systematic approach to choosing a program for an ROI analysis, applies a skill assessment process for measuring learning, uses management estimates for isolating the effect of the program, and results in a positive ROI.

PROGRAM BACKGROUND

Aircraft Maintenance Co (AMC) is one of the world's leading independent providers of technical services for the civil aviation sector. The group offers its customer airlines comprehensive and customised solutions for the technical support and management of their aircraft fleets, engines, and components. Based in Switzerland, AMC provides its services through an extensive network of international operations and sales offices in Europe, Asia, and the Middle East. About 500 airline customers currently entrust some 750 aircraft, 300 engines, and 78,000 components to its care. The company has a workforce of around 5,000 employees worldwide.

Program Need

Technical services for auxiliary power unit (APU) support covering Boeing and Airbus aircraft is provided at AMC's focused APU service center and test cell. An APU, generally located in the tail section of the airplane, is a turbo-shaft gas turbine, which supplies air and electricity to the airplane. Its main functions are to act as a starter for the main engines, meet all electricity needs of the airplane by means of a generator installed on the APU, run the anti-icing system, and provide air conditioning and pressurization of the cabin.

The maintenance and repair of these engines is a highly specialized activity requiring experienced and skilled technicians and engineers. Maintaining the optimum standard of quality and care is crucial to meeting the demands of customers and the audit and regulatory requirements of aviation authorities. An essential requirement of today's aviation industry is cost reduction. While striving to maintain the best services for its customers, AMC also needs to remain competitive on cost to retain its position in the marketplace. Cost, in this case, is a function of efficiency of operations while maintaining the highest quality standards and turnaround time. This factor is a crucial element in the operation of any airline, affecting everything from inventory levels to aircraft departures. The longer an APU remains in the repair shop, the less opportunity the airline has to make money. AMC has identified keeping turnaround times to an acceptable minimum as vital to retaining customers and growing its business.

The management team in charge of the APU repair facility (APURF) recognize this fact and have committed to growing the current level of business by improving process efficiency and striving for more competitive turnaround times. The APURF is a self-managed unit and profit center within the group with a well-established reputation for quality and service within the industry. It was acquired by AMC more than two years ago with the previous management staying in place and virtually no change in the existing workforce. Management has a good understanding of the needs of clients and the absolute requirement to meet turnaround times through efficient shop practices and effective material management, without cutting corners.

The management team commissioned the training coordinator to conduct a preliminary needs analysis of the efficiency of the repair shop technicians with a view to achieving an expansion of APU throughput with reduced turnaround times while maintaining quality and audit standards. This revealed that the technical skills of the staff were quite high as far as the core elements of the process were concerned. These include assembly/disassembly, cleaning, surface treatments, static and dynamic balancing, inspection, harness overhaul, and repairs. In addition, a review was undertaken of the functions of the supervisory staff, in particular relating to technical direction of the repair process, development of repair work-scope instructions, failure analysis, improved repair processing, documentation required, reliability, turnaround time and cost, and compliance to client policies, as well independently audited standards. In all of these matters, both the supervisory staff and their subordinates were found to have high levels of technical competence.

However, the needs analysis revealed gaps in the level of knowledge and understanding among the supervisors and technicians regarding the impetus for business expansion, the core elements in the overall business process (outside of their technical area), the lack of an adequate customer focus, awareness of the warranty process, and certain gaps in the interpretation of instructions and completion of documentation. To fill these gaps, the management team agreed to a proposal from the training coordinator to develop and deliver a customised two-day APU development program to be delivered to 12 trainees in the APURF in two separate groups of six to minimize disruption to operations.

Evaluation Objectives

The management team had for some time expressed a desire to assess the value, in financial terms, of the training, which is a necessary, integral, and ongoing part of the operations of the facility. In early 2006, the training coordinator attended an ROI Institute certification program in return on investment (ROI) analysis delivered in Europe by the Impact Measurement Centre.

The training coordinator considered a number of programs on which to apply the ROI Methodology. These were whittled down to three programs following discussions with the HR director. These were the APU development training program, a performance management training program, and a health and safety training program. In deciding which program to choose, a job aid of the ROI Institute was found to be most useful. This allows for an objective analysis to be undertaken between different programs under consideration. The results of the analysis for the three programs based on the ratings scale (see Table 6.1) applied by both the HR director and the training coordinator (averaged) are contained in Table 6.2.

TABLE 6.1   Rating Scale for Selecting Programs for Impact Studies

1. Life cycle	5 = Long lifecycle 1 = Very short lifecycle
2. Company objectives	5 = Closely related to company objectives 1 = Not directly related to company objectives
3. Costs	5 = Very expensive 1 = Very inexpensive
4. Audience size	5 = Very large audience 1 = Very small audience
5. Visibility	5 = High visibility 1 = Low visibility
6. Management interest	5 = High level of interest in evaluation 1 = Low level of interest in evaluation

TABLE 6.2   Selecting Programs for Impact Study

	Average Rating for Each Program		
Criterion	**APU Development Program**	**Management Training Program**	**Health and Safety Program**
1. Life cycle	3.5	3.5	4.0
2. Company objectives	4.5	4.5	4.5
3. Cost	3.0	3.5	3.0
4. Audience size	4.0	3.0	4.0
5. Visibility	4.5	4.0	3.0
6. Management interest	5.0	4.0	3.5
Overall Rating	**4.08**	**3.75**	**3.67**

EVALUATION METHODOLOGY

The Phillips ROI Methodology has five levels: (1) Reaction and Planned Action (of the participants to the training, usually measured in questionnaires distributed at the end of the training session); (2) Learning (gains in skills and knowledge achieved by the participants, usually measured by pre- and post-tests); (3) Application (focused on whether the skills and knowledge gained in training are applied and practiced; this is usually measured on the job some time after training); (4) Business Impact (or ultimate outcomes of the training in terms of company goals); and (5) ROI (Level 4 measures converted to money and compared to program costs) (Phillips 1996).

Calculating ROI is a practice of modern management used in the analysis of many business strategies and operations. Perhaps the most regular application of this tool is in the analysis of purchase decisions for investments in capital equipment or technology. ROI is simply a measure of benefit versus cost. Expressed as a percentage, ROI is determined by total net present benefits divided by total net present costs. Benefits and costs are converted into present values since they usually accrue over extended periods of time.

In the context of training, ROI is a measure of the monetary benefits obtained by an organization over a specified time period in return for a given investment in a training program. Looking at it another way, ROI is the extent to which the net benefits (outputs) of training exceed the costs (inputs). Because many training initiatives tend to be short-term, the most credible approach is to consider no more than first-year benefits for short-term programs and then compare those benefits to the program cost.

The Phillips ROI Methodology not only specifies the five levels at which evaluation should be conducted, but also goes on to provide a set of tools and techniques to facilitate the gathering of appropriate data and establishes a set of guiding principles to be used in analysing that data (see Annex 6.1).

Crucial to this broad-based approach is the chain of impact or linkage between the five levels. Phillips emphasizes the "chain of effect" implied in the five-level evaluation model described above. Initially, it is essential to derive the measurable results of training from participants' application of new skills or knowledge on the job over a specific period of time after training is completed, a Level 3 evaluation. Logically, successful on-the-job application of training content should stem from participants having learned new skills or acquired new knowledge, a Level 2 evaluation. Consequently, for a business-results improvement (a Level 4 evaluation), the chain of effect implies that measurable on-the-job applications (Level 3) and improvement in learning (Level 2) are achieved. Without this preliminary evidence, it's difficult to isolate the effect of training or to conclude that training is responsible for any performance improvements. Practically speaking, if data is collected on business results (Level 4), data should also be collected at the other three levels of evaluation. This applies equally to return on investment (Level 5 evaluation) (Phillips 1997).

The crucial elements in this model, for those who wish to go as far as calculating the ROI of a training program, commence at Level 4. Phillips specifies the steps thereafter as follows:

1. Collect Level 4 evaluation data. Ask: Did on-the-job application produce measurable results?

2. Isolate the effects of training from other factors that may have contributed to the results.

3. Convert the results to monetary benefits. Phillips recommends dividing training results into hard data and soft data. Hard data are the traditional measures of organisational performance because they're objective, easy to measure, and easy to convert to monetary values. They include output (units produced, items assembled, tasks completed); quality (scrap, waste, rework); time (equipment downtime, employee overtime, time to complete projects); and cost (overhead, accident costs, sales expenses). Conversely, soft data include such things as work habits (tardiness, absenteeism); work climate (grievances, job satisfaction); attitudes (loyalty, perceptions); and initiative (implementation of new ideas, number of employee suggestions).

4. Total the costs of training.

5. Compare the monetary benefits with the costs.

6. The nonmonetary benefits can be presented as additional—though intangible—evidence of the program's success.

ROI can be defined either as a benefit-cost ratio (BCR) or the return on investment (ROI) percentage. The equations are shown below:

$$BCR = \frac{\text{Program Benefits}}{\text{Program Costs}}$$

$$ROI = \frac{\text{Net Program Benefits}}{\text{Program Costs}} \times 100$$

The Phillips ROI Methodology applies a range of unique tools and techniques that enable the practitioner to complete difficult and challenging tasks such as identifying business results of training, and then converting them into monetary values, and identifying intangible benefits.

The crucial point comes before any final calculation, however. This is the point at which the improvement in business results must be attributed to the training, isolating its impact from other circumstances.

To support his approach, Phillips has established a set of guidelines so that the process is standardised. These include a rule that only the most conservative data can be included in the formulas. Phillips's formulas have taken root in thousands of private- and public-sector organisations in more than 50 countries.

EVALUATION PLAN

As can be seen in the Data Collection Plan (Annex 6.2), it was decided to collect the reaction of the participants to the program at the end of the training (Level 1) by means of a questionnaire specially designed for this purpose. At Level 2 (Learning), it was decided to apply a knowledge and skills self-assessment process just prior to the commencement of training and at the conclusion of training based on 11 competencies determined by reference to the specific training objectives. In terms of measuring application on the job after training (Level 3), it was decided to administer a detailed questionnaire to the participants one month after the training had been completed.

The Level 4 business objectives were discussed with the operations manager and the HR director, and it was agreed that these should focus on the following areas:

- increased throughput of APUs contributing to reduced turnaround times and further business expansion
- reduced paperwork errors and omissions
- improved quality of report writing
- improved customer satisfaction and customer retention arising from a better business understanding and focus on the part of the technicians.

The ROI Analysis Plan (Annex 6.3) sets out the steps for completing the Level 5 evaluation. In relation to techniques to be used for isolating the effects of the training from other factors, it was decided that the use of a control group was not appropriate since all of the technicians were participating in the training. The next best option for isolation as defined in the ROI Methodology is to use a trend line analysis. The main condition attaching to the use of a trend line analysis, that no other significant factor apart from the solution occurred during implementation, could not be observed since a number of other factors were found to be present. The only realistic method of isolation was, therefore, to apply estimates, and it was decided to invite the operations manager and the HR director to submit estimates in this case.

The method for converting data to monetary value was to use historical costs and standard values in the work units. In terms of calculating the cost of the program, it was noted that the company usually applies a standard value for cost per training day for internal training, but in this case it was decided to analyse all of the costs in detail and ensure that the costs were fully loaded. A range of intangible benefits arising from the training were identified initially, including customer satisfaction and customer retention. Other intangibles were discovered during the data collection process.

EVALUATION RESULTS

Level 1 Reaction

As can be seen in Table 6.3, the overall reaction of the participants to the training was satisfactory at 3.75 on a scale of 5 (maximum) to 1 (minimum). The reaction to questions A and B indicated that the preparation for the training program had been carried out satisfactorily and the participants knew what the course was about and what was expected of them in this regard. The rating for the trainer in relation to questions C, D, and E was also quite good. The overall results at Level 1 were in line with the targets set.

Level 2 Learning

The primary method for determining the level of learning on the program involved using a list of 11 competencies developed in consultation with the training facilitator and applied to the participants immediately at the commencement of training, before they had received any instruction, and then at the conclusion of the training. The results are shown in Table 6.4. It can

TABLE 6.3   Participants Reaction Survey: Average for
All 12 Participants

	Response	Average Score
A	I understood the course objectives well.	4.5
B	The objectives of the course, as I understand them, were met.	4.5
C	The information was clearly presented.	4.75
D	There was enough time for the training.	3.5
E	The trainer helped me learn.	4.75
F	I am satisfied that I can apply what I learned on the job.	3.75
G	Overall the training was beneficial to me.	3.75

be seen that in all areas, there was an improvement as assessed by the participants in their skills and knowledge. What was somewhat surprising was the generally low level of knowledge and skills in almost all of the areas prior to the commencement of the training. The overall improvement of 32 percent as a result of the learning was considered to be satisfactory since it was ahead of the 25 percent target specified in the Data Collection Plan. However, the analysis indicates that further training may be needed in respect to the competencies identified, and the company continues to keep this matter under review.

Level 3 Application

Two months after the training had been completed, a survey was administered to all of the participants and 100 percent returned the questionnaire. The results are contained in Table 6.5. It can be seen that there was a very high level of reported application of the skills and knowledge learned in the training course. All of the participants report a high level of work improvement since attending the training, as well as overall improvement in job satisfaction, which also scores very high. In addition, participants have been able to help other work colleagues to improve their knowledge and skills by using what they learned in the training course.

In the same survey, the participants were asked to identify the key barriers to the application of learning on the job after the training. A total of

TABLE 6.4 Change in Skills and Knowledge Self-Assessed by Participants Before and After Training

Item	Knowledge and Skills Area	Before Course	After Course	Change (%)
A	Knowledge of the organisation structure	2.75	3.75	36
B	Knowledge of the APU business process	3.00	4.00	33
C	Understanding of the importance of each step in the business process	2.75	3.50	27
D	Knowledge of the regulations governing APU overhaul	2.50	3.50	40
E	Ability to correctly interpret APU overhaul manual instructions	3.50	4.00	14
F	In-depth knowledge of the APU purpose	4.00	4.50	13
G	In-depth knowledge of the APU construction and systems operation	3.25	4.25	31
H	In-depth knowledge of the APU aircraft interfaces	2.75	3.75	36
I	In-depth knowledge of the APU overhaul technical processes	2.50	3.50	40
J	In-depth knowledge of APU paperwork and an understanding of its importance	2.25	3.50	56
K	Good knowledge and understanding of the APU warranty process	2.25	3.25	44
Average change from before to after course for all areas:		2.86	3.77	32

five anticipated barriers where specified, and the participants were asked to rate the relevance of each of these to application. As can be seen from the results in Table 6.6, "not enough time" was the most important barrier, while the other items identified had only a negligible effect.

The participants were also asked open-ended questions in the survey in an attempt to elicit the enablers that were present in the workplace to facilitate implementation. In general, the support of the supervisor was

TABLE **6.5**   **Average Results from the Application Survey for All Participants Two Months After Training**

Item	Response	Average Score
A	I have been willing to use most of the skills/knowledge that I learned on the course.	4.5
B	I have been able to apply what I learned on the course to my job.	4.2
C	I have been able to retain most of the skills/knowledge that I learned on the course.	4.2
D	My work has improved since I attended the course.	4.8
E	My overall satisfaction with my job has improved since I attended the course.	4.7
F	I have been able to help work colleagues to improve their skills/knowledge by what I have learned.	4.3

Note: 5 = strongly agree; 1 = strongly disagree.

identified as the key enabler. A number of participants pointed to the helpfulness of the supervisor in identifying how to use the various manuals and in coaching the participants in completing the paperwork assignments. Some participants identified an ongoing need for support in implementing paperwork and in the use of computer systems, and one participant

TABLE **6.6**   **Barriers to Application Described by Participants Two Months After Training**

Item	Difficulties Applying Learning	Average Score
A	Not enough time	2.7
B	Not enough interest from my work colleagues	1.2
C	Not enough support from my supervisor	1.3
D	No structured way to incorporate what I learned to my job	1.3
E	The course was not directly relevant to the job I do	1.5

Note: 1 = least difficulty; 5 = most difficulty.

recommended that there should be more repetition of practical work in the days immediately following the training to facilitate familiarization with the systems and techniques. A number of participants recommended further training along the lines of the course. Eighty-six percent of the participants reported that the training was a worthwhile investment in their career development, while 90 percent considered the training a worthwhile investment for the company.

Level 4 Business Impact

At the planning stage, it was anticipated that the primary business result arising from the training would be linked to the increased throughput of APUs, which would lead to shorter turnaround times and thus a larger number of units being processed over a 12-month period. Because the company keeps a careful record of the labour cost of repair and maintenance of APUs within the work units, it was possible to determine the change in labour cost over a four-month period following the training program. It was considered that it would be both time-consuming and difficult to gather data on, and convert, the other anticipated business outputs, such as improvements in paperwork errors and omissions and improved quality of report writing, to monetary values. The improvements in customer satisfaction and customer retention were also difficult to convert to monetary value and could not in any event be determined in the four-month period following the training course. In relation to all of these matters, it was decided that these should be considered intangible benefits of the program.

Table 6.7 shows the cost savings achieved by staff working on APUs (85 series) fitted to Boeing 737-300, -400, and -500 aircraft in the four-month period (June–September) following the training course. There were 25 APUs processed during this four-month period, which lead to a saving in the period of €12,000. According to the Phillips ROI Methodology, only the first year of benefits (annual) should be used in the ROI analysis of short-term solutions (ninth guiding principle). The four-month savings, therefore, must be annualized, giving a total annual saving over a full year of €36,000. There are no significant seasonal variations in the flow of APUs through the facility, so the data in the post-training period need not be adjusted to account for such variations.

For the completion of a valid ROI in accordance with the Phillips ROI Methodology, the fifth guiding principle specifies that at least one method

TABLE 6.7   Analysis of Cost Savings Arising from Training

Basic cost of labour	€32/hr
Average hours per APU prior to training	160
Average hours per APU after training	145
Improvement hours on APUs after training	15
Savings per APU	€480
Number of APUs processed in 4 months	25
Savings over 4-month period	€12,000
Savings annualized over 12 months	€36,000

should be used to isolate the effects of the training from other factors. The methodology specifies the use of control groups, and where this isn't possible, the use of trend line analysis, as the most credible methods for isolation. However, as stated earlier, neither of these methods could be used in this case. The only practical method available was to obtain estimates of isolation.

Phillips's third guiding principle emphasizes that one should use only the most credible sources when collecting and analyzing data. In this instance, those best able to identify and provide estimates of all the factors contributing to the improvement were the operations managers and the three shift supervisors. To achieve this, the training coordinator invited the ROI consultant, who had provided ongoing coaching during the completion of the ROI study, to conduct a focus group with the personnel concerned.

The ROI consultant started the focus group by explaining to four participants the purpose of the estimation exercise and the process involved. At this point, the overall improvement in savings had been calculated, and these were reported to the group as a starting point. The group was also taken through the content of the training, and since they had been involved in collecting data at Level 3, they were already aware of the main impacts in terms of behaviour change among the trainees.

Each person in turn was invited to estimate the percentage of the savings achieved that they would attribute to the training program. They were asked to write this down on a sheet of paper. Their names were not to be included on the sheets. In accordance with the seventh guiding principle, they were then invited to make their own estimate of the "error" of their own estimate. This was expressed as their "level of confidence" in their estimate, and they were also asked to list this on the same sheet of paper. The group was then invited to identify any other factors that could have contributed to the savings and to list these also. Finally, the group was asked to make an assessment of whether the time saved, an average of 15 hours on each APU (or about one and a quarter hours per technician), was time that the participants were now using productively on other areas of work. The group provided feedback and examples of what other activities the participants were now engaged in. These related mostly to greater time and care being taken on completing documentation. Based on this exercise, the adjusted amount of the improvement attributed to the training by the group (averaged) was 45 percent, which gives an annual adjusted amount of €16,200. The results are shown in Table 6.8.

The program costs are outlined in Table 6.9 and represent a comprehensive assessment of the detailed cost of the training in accordance with the tenth guiding principle. They include a cost for conducting the evaluation.

Intangible Benefits

The benefits originally determined at Level 4, which were too costly and difficult to convert to monetary value (guiding principle 11), were considered to be important intangible benefits of the program. These included improved quality of work in terms of preparation of reports, reduction in paperwork errors and omissions, and, most important, improved customer satisfaction arising from a better business understanding and focus on the part of the technicians.

TABLE 6.8   Isolation of Training from Other Factors

Percentage of savings attributed to training by operations manager and supervisors	60
Confidence level (%; error adjustment)	75
Adjusted percentage attributed to training	45

TABLE **6.9**   Costs of the Training Program

Costs			
	Days	**Rate**	**Total €**
Training Time			
Development	6	300	1,800
Preparation	3	300	900
Delivery	2	300	600
Evaluation	4	300	1,200
Trainee Time			
12 trainees	24	280	6,720
Training materials			100
Total costs			€11,320.00

Level 5: ROI

As can be seen in the calculations below, the program resulted in a benefit cost ratio of 1.4 to 1 and an ROI of 43 percent, which is ahead of the target ROI of 25 percent.

Total benefits: €16,200

Total costs: €11,320

$$BCR = \frac{\text{Program Benefits}}{\text{Program Costs}} = 1.43{:}1$$

$$ROI = \frac{\text{Net Program Benefits}}{\text{Program Costs}} \times 100 = 43\%$$

COMMUNICATION STRATEGY

The results of the ROI study were formulated into a detailed report setting out the background to the study, the details of the methodology employed, and the results achieved. The report contained a number of appendices including copies of the questionnaires distributed to the participants and details of the cost calculations.

The detailed report was presented to the management team and resulted in a review of training operations generally. The management team expressed their strong support for training, which is an integral part of the operation of the facility, and they were surprised that a relatively small investment in terms of training could net a substantial and identifiable return on investment.

In line with the twelfth guiding principle, it was also decided to present a summary of the report to selected customers and to the regulatory authorities. A verbal briefing on the outputs of the training was also given to the trainees.

CONCLUSIONS

The management team, as a result of this report, has agreed that the training coordinator will prepare an ROI study on at least one program in each year going forward. A number of improvements to the APU training program will be implemented as a consequence of this study, and the program itself will be delivered on an annual basis.

LESSONS LEARNED

In general, the training coordinator found the ROI Methodology to be both practical and workable. Despite the fact that at the beginning the process seemed to be daunting, once the job aids were implemented and the activities were broken down into the relevant subsets, the task turned out to be manageable. The coaching support provided by the ROI consultant proved invaluable, not in terms of carrying out the work but in terms of guiding the training coordinator to take the right steps and pursue the right data gathering strategies at the appropriate juncture.

Gathering data on business output variables was not as easy as first thought. Only one business area could be credibly identified, and the data for the other areas did not appear to be either present or readily accessible.

This is an area for further consideration going forward in terms of how the company gathers and processes nontechnical data.

The outcome of the study allowed the company to make an informed decision and to do so with confidence relative to the continuation of this training program in subsequent years. The fact that the program was linked to a clear change in output strengthened the position of the training coordinator and the training department generally. It also enabled the management team to base their decision on identifiable fact rather than general feedback as had been the case heretofore.

QUESTIONS FOR DISCUSSION

1. Was the data collection at Level 3 adequate? Could other means of data collection have been applied at this level?
2. Were there other methods for determining change in skill and knowledge at Level 2, and how could these have been applied?
3. Were there other sources that would be able to provide credible estimates, and if so, how would this exercise have been conducted?

RESOURCES

Phillips, J.J. (1994). *Measuring Return on Investment: Volume 1*. Alexandria, VA: American Society for Training and Development.

Phillips, J.J. (1996). ROI: The Search for Best Practices. *Training & Development* 50 (February) 2: 42–47.

Phillips, J.J. (1997a). *Handbook of Training Evaluation,* 3rd edition. Houston, TX: Gulf Publishing.

Phillips, J.J. (1997b). *Measuring Return on Investment: Volume 2*. Alexandria, VA: American Society for Training and Development.

Phillips, J.J. (1997c). *Return on Investment in Training and Performance Improvement Programs*. Houston, TX: Gulf Publishing.

Phillips, P.P. (2002). *The Bottomline on ROI*. Atlanta, GA: CEP Press.

ANNEX 6.1   12 Guiding Principles

1. When conducting a higher level evaluation, collect data at lower levels.

2. When planning a higher level evaluation, the previous level of evaluation is not required to be comprehensive.

3. When collecting and analyzing data, use only the most credible sources.

4. When analyzing data, select the most conservative alternatives for calculations.

5. Use at least one method to isolate the effects of the program or project.

6. If no improvement data are available for a population or from a specific source, assume that little or no improvement has occurred.

7. Adjust estimates of improvements for the potential error of the estimates.

8. Avoid use of extreme data items and unsupported claims when calculating ROI calculations.

9. Use only the first year of annual benefits in the ROI analysis of short-term solutions.

10. Fully load all costs of the solution, project, or program when analyzing ROI.

11. Intangible measures are defined as measures that are purposely not converted to monetary values.

12. Communicate the results of the ROI Methodology to all key stakeholders.

ANNEX 6.2   Data Collection Plan

Program: APU Development Program   **Responsibility:** Training Coordinator

Level	Objective(s)	Measures	Data Collection Method	Data Sources	Timing	Responsibilities
1	**REACTION/SATISFACTION** • Positive reaction	• Average rating of at least 4.0 on 5–1 scale on objectives, usefulness, and effectiveness of program.	• Reaction questionnaire	• Participants	• End of 2nd day	• Facilitator
2	**LEARNING** • Acquisition of skills and knowledge	• Self-assessment of 11 competencies to be trained. • Target improvement of 25%.	• Skill/knowledge assessment sheet	• Participants	• At start and end of program	• Facilitator
3	**APPLICATION/IMPLEMENTATION** • Use of skills • Identify barriers	• Self-reported use and effectiveness of skill application. • Reported barriers and enablers to implementation.	• Questionnaire	• Participants	• One month after program	• Training coordinator
4	**BUSINESS IMPACT** • Improved turnaround times • Improved quality of reports • Reduced errors and omissions in paperwork	• Labour cost savings.	• Performance monitoring	• Company records	• 4 months after program	• Training coordinator
5	ROI Target ROI → 25%					

Baseline data: Data is available from company records for labour costs prior to training.

Comments:

ANNEX 6.3   ROI Analysis Plan

Program: APU Development Program   **Responsibility:** Training Coordinator

Data Items (Usually Level 4)	Methods for Isolating the Effects of the Program or Process	Methods of Converting Data to Monetary Values	Cost Categories	Intangible Benefits	Communication Targets for Final Report	Other Influences and Issues During Application
• Labor cost savings per APU	• Management and supervisory staff estimates	• Direct conversion: labor cost per hour	• Training costs • Development costs • Delivery costs • Program materials • Participant salaries/ benefits • Cost of evaluation	• Customer satisfaction • Customer retention • Employee satisfaction	• Program participants • Management team • Supervisors • Training staff	

ABOUT THE AUTHOR

Gerard M. Doyle is the managing partner of the Center for Creative Change, a consultancy that specialises in change management, coaching, and personal and business development. He is a Fellow of the Institute of Management Consultants of Ireland. He has wide experience as a manager in the construction, security, and software sectors and as a change management consultant and trainer in the ICT and pharmaceutical sectors. He has consulted with Diageo, Novartis, Ericsson, Abbott Laboratories, Hertz, Braun-OralB, Irish Management Institute, Enterprise Ireland, Skillnets, Financial Services Ireland, ICT Ireland, and Bank of Ireland.

Mr. Doyle was founder and first director of the Impact Measurement Center, which brought the Phillips ROI Methodology to scores of companies in Ireland, from 2003–2008. He is a specialist in applying the Phillips methodology to measuring impact and return on investment in training and human resources programmes.

7

The ROI in Using Colleagues as Coaches

HortResearch
New Zealand

Cynthia Johnson, Leslie Hamilton, and Craig Jensen

This case was prepared to serve as a basis for discussion rather than an illustration of either effective or ineffective administrative and management practice. Names, dates, places, and data may have been disguised at the request of the author or organisation.

Abstract

HortResearch is a New Zealand government-owned fruit science company.[1] At the beginning of the decade, HortResearch realised the urgent need to reposition its science and take advantage of emerging opportunities in the international market. The organisation acknowledged the strategic importance of developing leadership capability in order to meet this challenge as well as address low levels of staff morale. This case describes the development and implementation of an affordable and credible leadership programme based on strengths development and a mastery approach to peer feedforward coaching. The case identifies the improvement in overall leadership effectiveness and employee morale using this approach.

PROGRAMME BACKGROUND

In 2003, HortResearch employed 550 staff. Eighty percent of the staff were directly involved in scientific research focused largely on the development of innovative fruit and fruit products and environmentally sustainable production systems. HortResearch earned revenue through commercial sources and received funding from the New Zealand government that was obtained

---

[1] In 2009, HortResearch and Crop & Food Research, another government-owned research institute, merged to form Plant & Food Research.

through a competitive investment process open to other government-owned research institutes, universities, and the private sector.

In the early part of this decade, HortResearch had experienced significant reductions in funding. Consequently, the organisation was forced to quickly reposition its science to become more responsive to emerging market opportunities, the industries it served, and its largest customer. While most of the staff were positive about the repositioning, results of an organisation-wide employee satisfaction survey provided confirmation that staff morale was at a low ebb in comparison to other New Zealand scientific research organisations.

NEED FOR THE PROGRAMME

Leadership effectiveness, as assessed through 360° survey instruments, is highly correlated with profit, customer satisfaction, staff turnover, employee intention to stay, and employee commitment (Zenger and Folkman 2002). Furthermore, those great leaders whose effectiveness is assessed by 360° surveys as being in the top 20 percent provide an extraordinary return even in comparison to those whose effectiveness is assessed as good or average.

The board of directors, newly appointed chief executive, and staff all acknowledged that in order to successfully reposition the organisation and rebuild staff confidence and morale, it would be critical to develop more great leaders. Leadership development therefore became one of four initiative streams required to support the new strategic pathway.

Programme Objectives

Drawing further on the evidence of Zenger and Folkman (2002), each leader was asked to develop three leadership strengths.[2] Furthermore, leaders were advised to build strengths by developing two competencies in which they were already seen as having at least average ability.

Two programmes were initiated: a team leader programme and a senior leader programme. The senior programme began with a full 360° survey of 22 leadership competencies and was then divided into two phases. Phase 1 focused on understanding leadership research and involved approximately eight hours of classroom activity over a two-week period. Phase 2 concentrated on developing leadership competency strengths on

---

[2] A strength is defined as a competency that is assessed via a 360° survey as being in the top 20 percent of the comparison group.

the job via a process of feedforward coaching. It is this latter aspect of the senior programme that is the focus of this chapter.

Feedforward Coaching

Feedforward coaching is a Marshall Goldsmith methodology (Goldsmith and Morgan 2005). The name "feedforward coaching" implies an emphasis on what the leader needs to do in the future to develop, as opposed to relying on feedback, which is a review of the past. It draws on the insights of people who work alongside the leader. It is argued that these people know best what is required for the leader to build leadership strengths.

Drawing on the results of the 360° surveys, each leader nominated two competencies to improve using feedforward coaching. Each leader then chose four to six managers, peers, or staff to act as feedforward coaches. Every four to six weeks, the leaders asked their feedforward coaches for two suggestions for actions they could take to improve their leadership in the competencies they chose to develop. Each feedforward conversation took no more than 10 minutes, and the maximum time a leader spent in these conversations each month was about one hour.

From the range of suggestions given by the feedforward coaches, the leader chose two or three suggestions to implement. Each leader was advised to choose suggestions that energised and made sense to them and which could be fairly easily implemented. Feedforward coaches were advised that any suggestion not immediately taken up could be offered again in future or new suggestions made.

Leaders received coaching from external coaches to support their efforts in understanding their 360° leadership feedback survey, identifying the leadership competencies that would develop into strengths, and how to manage the feedforward coaching process. This support was provided at the beginning of the process, after the leaders had completed their first cycle of feedforward coaching and at the end of the six-month coaching programme. Toward the end of the feedforward coaching programme, leaders were invited to attend a facilitated group meeting to discuss their experience with feedforward coaching and other parts of the programme. A "Heads Up" 360° review was conducted at the end of the feedforward coaching programme to give leaders feedback about their progress.

The structure of the feedforward part of the programme is shown in Figure 7.1. Feedforward coaches received training in developing and communicating their suggestions. They were taught to think of behaviours that

FIGURE 7.1   Feedforward Coaching Programme

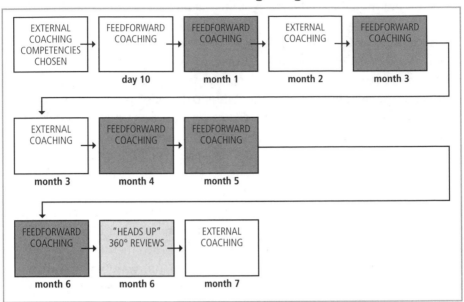

could be integrated into the leader's everyday practice and would make a significant difference to the leader's effectiveness.

The results reported here are based on the first 43 leaders who took part during the first two years of the programme.

NEED FOR EVALUATION

HortResearch was under pressure to improve its financial performance and long-term viability. Spending time, money, and effort on any initiative needed to be justified. Given that leadership development had been identified as an important strategic initiative, it was critical to demonstrate a business impact and effective results. In particular, evaluation was needed to demonstrate the following:

- Participants could successfully improve their leadership effectiveness using on-the-job learning. As Goldsmith and Morgan (2005, p. 75) note, "For most leaders, the great challenge is not understanding the practice of leadership: It is practicing their understanding."
- The leadership programme, including feedforward coaching, would create measurable results and was a sound investment of time and money.

- The programme was affordable.
- The HR department was accountable to the organisation.

EVALUATION METHODOLOGY
General Description of Approach
The evaluation focused on the leaders' effectiveness in developing two competencies in order to raise their overall leadership ability. Because leaders needed to play an important role in the repositioning of the company and the improvement in employee morale at a critical time in the development of the organisation, more focus was placed on the implementation and impact of the feedforward coaching process than on the leader's reaction to the training or the training process. Thus, the training and evaluation methods were based on a criterion-referenced, mastery framework. This focus was balanced by the fact that several senior leaders and opinion leaders in the organisation were involved in the development and, as the first cohort of the programme, had given it their enthusiastic support.

Data Collection Strategy
Leadership effectiveness was first assessed using a 360° survey. Table 7.1 displays the data collection plan for the feedforward coaching programme. The approach to the evaluation process is reported using Kirkpatrick's (1998) model of four levels of evaluation. Ongoing evaluation at Levels 1 through 4 was used to enhance the continuous development of the programme. The information was used to assist incoming cohorts in determining where to focus their efforts, to modify the programme, and to include additional support following the programme.

Measuring Level 1: Reaction and Satisfaction
To measure at Level 1 of Kirkpatrick's (1998) model of evaluation, the participant's reaction and satisfaction with the feedforward coaching process was indirectly assessed by the number of cycles of coaching the leader completed. The feedforward coaches were asked in the "Heads Up" 360° review to identify how many times their leader had engaged in the process, ranging from "not at all" to "four times."

Leaders' satisfaction with the process was also assessed by their anecdotal comments. Leaders had the option of sharing their reaction to the programme in one-on-one meetings they could initiate with the Human

TABLE 7.1   Data Collection Plan for Feedforward Coaching Programme

Level	Objectives	Measure	Data Collection	Data Source	Timing	Responsibility
1	**Response**	Number of times leader completed FF cycle (0–4)	"Heads Up" 360° review	Post-programme 360° survey raters and feedforward coaches	End of feedforward programme	HR
		Anecdotal comments	Follow-up focus group meetings with leaders	Facilitator	During and after the programme	
2	**Learning:** • Developing specific leadership competencies • Taking a strengths-based approach to leadership development • Managing the peer feedforward coaching process	Type of competencies chosen to develop against 360° survey Report to HR	Report to HR	Leaders	1 week after the programme start	HR
		Anecdotal comments	One-on-one meetings with external coaches	External coaches	End of month 1 and month 3 after the start of the FF coaching process	HR
			Follow-up focus group meeting with leaders	Facilitator	During and after the feedforward programme	

Level	Objectives	Measure	Data Collection	Data Source	Timing	Responsibility
3	**Application, implementation:** • Developing specific leadership competencies • Taking a strengths-based approach to leadership development • Managing the peer feedforward coaching process	Various questions	"Heads Up" 360° review	Feedforward coaches and "Heads Up" 360° review rates	End of feedforward programme	HR
		Anecdotal comments	Follow-up focus group meeting with FF coaches	Facilitator	2 months after the programme start	
			Follow-up focus group meetings with leaders	Facilitator	1 to 2 months after the end of the programme	
		Rating on scale (−3 to +3)	"Heads Up" 360° review	"Heads Up" 360° review rates	End of feedforward programme	
		Number of times leader completed FF cycle (0–4+)	"Heads Up" 360° review	Feedforward coaches		
4	**Business impact:** • Change in employee morale • Change in overall leadership effectiveness	Direct report survey questions Stakeholder survey question	"Heads Up" 360° review	Leader's direct reports	End of feedforward programme	HR
5	**ROI:** Cost of direct programme costs	Expenses paid out	Budget	Budget	After programme finish	HR

Resource (HR) staff any time throughout and following the programme. Approximately one-third of the leaders gave their comments as participants in post-programme follow-up focus group meetings.

Level 2: Learning

One learning objective for leaders to master in the feedforward coaching process was to understand the theory and logic of the strengths-based approach to leadership development in order to identify the competencies that would be effective and efficient for the leader to enhance in order to raise his or her capability. The second learning objective was for the leaders to understand the feedforward coaching process.

Leaders had the opportunity to clarify and verify their level of mastery of the learning objectives in the coaching sessions they had with an external coach. The purpose of the first meeting was primarily to debrief the 360° survey and to identify the two competencies for the leader to develop through the feedforward coaching process. After the debrief meeting, the leader reported to HR the two competencies he or she had chosen to develop in the feedforward coaching process.

The second coaching session was held after the first cycle of feedforward coaching and just before the leader was starting the second cycle. The third and final session, held at the completion of the programme, was to review the "Heads Up" 360° review results and plan for ongoing self-development. After these sessions, the external coach reported to HR on the leader's progress.

As with the Level 1 evaluation, Level 2, mastery learning, measurements were also gathered from anecdotal comments made in the one-on-one meetings with the HR staff throughout the programme and in follow-up focus group meetings that were held for leaders after the completion of the programme.

Level 3: Application

To evaluate the application of learning, Level 3 of the Kirkpatrick (1998) model, it was necessary to assess how well the leaders succeeded. To measure this, a "Heads Up" 360° review that focused on improvement in each leader's targeted competencies, overall changes in leadership effectiveness, and changes in the morale of the people the leader manages was used at the end of the programme. The survey assessed the level at which the leader had improved on the leadership competencies using a seven-point scale. It was completed by the people who completed the original 360° survey plus any additional people whom the leader had selected to be feedforward coaches. In the survey, the respondents were asked if they had acted as feedforward coaches for the leader and, if so, how many cycles of feedforward coaching the leader had completed. The approach and format of the survey was based on the work of Marshall Goldsmith. See Figure 7.2 for an example.

Feedforward coaches were invited to attend a focus group meeting two or three months following the start of the feedforward process. This was an opportunity to clarify their role and responsibilities and share feedback on their participation in the process, including the ability of the leader to implement the process. The meeting clarified these comments, which were then shared with the HR staff in a summary report from the facilitator and used to enhance the programme structure and materials.

Leaders had the opportunity to share their successes and issues managing their feedforward coaching process at a focus meeting taking place one to two months after the end of the feedforward coaching programme. These comments were shared with the HR staff and were used to enhance the programme and materials while reflecting back to all the leaders in the programme.

Level 4: Business Impact

Measuring Level 4, the business impact of the leader's change in performance, was done using the same "Heads Up" 360° review used to measure the Level 3 learning application. The leader's improvement in overall leadership effectiveness and relationships was rated by everyone who completed the survey. The leader's direct reports were also asked to rate their change in morale.

ROI Analysis Strategy

Because the need to raise leadership capability was recognised by Hort-Research to be a key strategic initiative, resources were budgeted to fund the programme. However, funding reductions and competing priorities meant that financial and human resources for the programme were limited. Performing a return on investment (ROI) analysis was not identified as a priority need. The focus was on building a programme that was based

FIGURE 7.2   "Heads Up" Leadership Development Review for (Leader)

1. Are you a feedforward coach for (Leader)?	❏ Yes	❏ No

2. If Yes: How often has (Leader) sought feedforward from you?

❏ He hasn't sought any feedforward from me   ❏ 3 or 4 times

❏ 1 or 2 times   ❏ more than 4 times

3. Beside each statement below, put an X in the box which best represents your answer with regard to (Leader's) development in the last 6 months. Please provide some examples where you can. Leave blank any questions that you can't answer.

	Got worse			Stayed the same			Got better
	−3	−2	−1	0	1	2	3
a. Has (Leader's) ability to build relationships							
What changes in the way in which (Leader) builds relationships are making a difference?							
b. Has (Leader's) ability to develop others							
What changes in the way in which (Leader) develops others are making a difference?							

4. Thinking more generally about (Leader's) development in the last 6 months

	Got worse			Stayed the same			Got better
	−3	−2	−1	0	1	2	3
a. Character, which includes: generosity, courage, humility, being positive, trustworthy, self-aware							
b. Personal capability, which includes: professional expertise, problem solving, innovation, business acumen, professional development							
c. Focus on results, which includes: taking responsibility, organising, setting standards							
d. Interpersonal skills, which includes: communication, collaboration, building relationships, developing others, inspiring people							
e. Lead change, which includes: having a strategic perspective, being a change champion and connecting to the outside world							

	Got worse		Stayed the same			Got better	
	−3	**−2**	**−1**	**0**	**1**	**2**	**3**
f. Has the trust between you and (Leader) . . .							
g. Has the honesty in what you talk about . . .							
h. Has the understanding between you . . .							
i. Overall their leadership ability has . . .							

5. Would you say (Leader) has:
   - **a.** made a significant and real attempt to develop and improve
   - **b.** made some attempt to develop and improve
   - **c.** made no real or significant attempt to develop and improve
6. If (Leader) is your manager, in the last 6 months has your morale:
   ❑ got worse   ❑ stayed the same   ❑ got better

on best practice and that by gaining the acceptance and support of scientists, could achieve the required business impact and deliver the anticipated performance results. The programme was also intended to be open to continuous improvement and structured in such a way that it could be readily adopted across the organisation.

The evaluation measures from the leadership programme provided strong evidence of its impact on the business and led HortResearch to continue to fund the programme. In retrospect, a more detailed ROI analysis would have provided additional data on the financial value of the programme.

EVALUATION RESULTS

The data presented in the following sections are based on feedback from the "Heads Up" 360° review completed by 34 of the 43 leaders who started the programme in the first two years.[3] Of the 232 reviews returned, 134

---

[3] Those who did not complete the mini-survey included one person who left the organisation before the six-month review period, three people who declined the invitation to take part in the survey (and who do not appear to have done any feedforward coaching), one person who dropped out of the programme for personal reasons, and four people, all from one cohort, who were unavailable for work reasons to participate.

were completed by feedforward coaches. Findings from the various focus groups are also included.

Level 1: Reaction

Based on the number of feedforward coaching cycles leaders engaged in, as reported by their feedforward coaches on the "Heads Up" 360° review, the response to the programme was mixed. Approximately half of the leaders participating in the programme engaged in three or more feedforward coaching cycles, while the remaining leaders either engaged in one or two cycles of coaching or didn't engage in feedforward coaching at all.

The anecdotal comments from leaders who attended the focus groups included comments indicating their satisfaction with the programme:

- All felt the first six months went really well; they were really enthused and found the process valuable.
- The majority of the leaders felt the external coaching was very valuable.

The areas for programme improvement included:

- making the focus of the coaching relevant to goals or work activities, not just the characteristics of a good leader
- being able to choose the external coach.

Level 2: Learning

Because the programme design was based on a mastery approach to learning, all of the leaders on the programme, through the support of the HR staff and external coaches, were able to understand the theory of strengths-based leadership development and feedforward coaching in order to engage and manage the process.

Feedback given to the HR staff from the leaders throughout the programme confirmed that the greatest learning came from understanding what behaviours the people who worked closely with the leaders needed to observe in order for them to view their leaders as having strengths in particular areas.

Level 3: Application

Two leaders did no feedforward coaching and did only one or two cycles. The remainder did three or more cycles.

Information shared by the feedforward coaches in the focus groups indicated that most leaders had understood the process themselves and had communicated the process in enough detail for feedforward coaches to understand what to do. What was not addressed well were the concerns some feedforward coaches had about being put in a position in which they had to tell their leader what to do, exactly what kind of suggestions would be appropriate, what to do if the leader didn't like or use the suggestion they made, and whether or not the feedforward coach was responsible for giving feedback to the leader.

Comments from leaders participating in the focus groups indicated that barriers to applying the feedforward coaching process focused predominantly on issues of timing and convenience.

Comments from the HR staff based on the one-on-one meetings and informal conversations indicated that barriers to using the feedforward coaching and getting the skill development results were due to

- leaders' beliefs that people who reported to them would not be able to teach them about leadership skills
- leaders being afraid of what they might hear if they asked for suggestions to improve from those around them.

The factors that enabled leaders to develop, as shared by leaders in the one-on-one informal conversations with HR staff, included the following:

- HortResearch employees' desire to learn and grow
- the enthusiasm of the CEO, who supported and modelled the programme and encouraged all of his direct reports to get involved
- the encouragement of the feedforward coaches
- the simplicity and short amount of time required for the process that enabled leaders to conveniently hold feedforward conversations in conjunction with their daily activities, such as after meetings
- the support of the external coach in helping to identify the competencies to improve and giving support through the first cycle.

To better support the feedforward process and the leadership skill development, leaders in the focus groups suggested the following additional support:

- more reminders to focus on leadership and the process, such as meetings with readings to discuss

- more external coaching
- emails to remind them it was time to engage in a new cycle
- sharing the data about the leaders' progress and the impact on the organisation and bottom line
- encouragement from the CEO about how important the programme was for achieving the organisation's vision.

Level 4: Business Impact

The anticipated business impact was to raise the leadership capability of the organisation in order to lift overall performance and to better employee morale. The results of the data, as measured in the "Heads Up" 360° review programme, indicate that both these effects occurred (Tables 7.2 and 7.3).

Further analysis isolated the effects of feedforward coaching. The more feedforward coaching leaders did, the more likely they were to change perceptions of their leadership effectiveness. Figure 7.3 shows that leaders who engaged in four or more feedforward cycles were twice as likely to shift the perception of their effectiveness positively as those who did not engage in any feedforward activities. Even completing just one or two feedforward cycles with a set of coaches resulted in a marked improvement in perceived leadership effectiveness.

A similar effect was noticed for changes in the morale of direct reports. The more feedforward coaching a leader did, the more likely it was that staff would report that their morale had improved. The most marked result seen in Figure 7.4 is that none of the staff who did not engage in feedforward coaching reported an improvement in morale.

Table 7.4 reports the differences in the assessments of those who were feedforward coaches and those who were not. For example, 77 percent of

TABLE 7.2   **Changes in Leadership Effectiveness at the End of the Feedforward Coaching Process**

Leadership Effectiveness in the Last Nine Months (*n* = 34 Leaders, 232 Surveys)		
Got Worse (%)	**Stayed the Same (%)**	**Got Better (%)**
3	20	77

TABLE 7.3   Changes in Morale Nine Months After the Start of the Leadership Programmes

Changes in the Morale of the Direct Reports of the Leader (*n* = 34 Leaders)		
Got Worse (%)	Stayed the Same (%)	Got Better (%)
11	41	48

all the "Heads Up" 360° reviews reported an improvement in overall leadership effectiveness. Eighty percent of people who were feedforward coaches reported an improvement, while 73 percent of those who were not feedforward coaches noticed an improvement. These results suggest that the

FIGURE 7.3   Amount of Feedforward Coaching and Changes in Overall Leadership

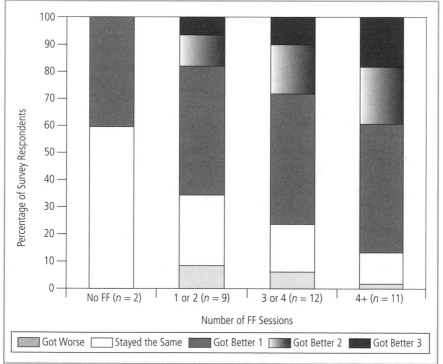

FIGURE 7.4   Amount of Feedforward Coaching and Changes in Morale of Direct Reports

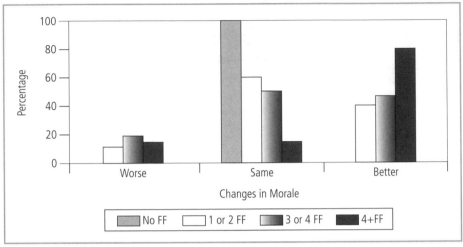

changes were real and observed by all and not just by those who were more closely involved in the leader's development.

Programme Costs

Invoices paid for Phase 1 and Phase 2 of the programme were 1800 New Zealand Dollars (NZD). This cost included the initial 360° survey, materials for Phase 1 and Phase 2, and external coaching fees. Excluded was the cost of the leader's time in Phase 1 and Phase 2, the cost of the feedforward coach's time, and that of the HR department. Assuming a senior person's charge-out rate at 150 NZD per hour, and assuming each leader involved six people and feedforward coaches, and that each leader engaged in six cycles, the cost of feedforward coaching would be 1800 NZD per leader.[4]

Level 5: ROI

A full ROI analysis was outside the scope of the mandate from the executive, which was to deliver results within budget in a timely manner. There was no authorisation to spend limited time and energy on anything that did

---

4 This is a maximum figure; for example, junior scientists and technicians who acted as feedforward coaches have charge-out rates starting at 50 NZD per hour.

TABLE 7.4   Improvement in Leadership Effectiveness and Target Competencies at the End of the Feedforward Coaching Programme: Feedforward Coaches and Others

	All Survey Respondents (%) $n = 232$	Assessment by Feedforward Coaches (%) $n = 134$	Assessment by Other People (%) $n = 98$
Improvement in overall leadership effectiveness	77	80	73
Improvement in two competencies chosen for development	70	79	60
Improvement in morale of direct reports	48	56	36
Improvement in trust, honesty, and understanding	60	65	61

not further the design, development, implementation, and evaluation of an effective programme.

Intangible Benefits

One of the most significant impacts of the programme was that, for the first time, leadership effectiveness was placed firmly on the organisation's agenda. Thirty-four leaders completed the feedforward coaching programme, and a large number of the staff had acted as feedforward coaches. This meant that every four to six weeks there were pockets of leaders engaging in conversations about their leadership effectiveness.

The research of Zenger and Folkman (2002) established that leadership effectiveness is a driver of both employee turnover and revenue. Other research cites the impact that leadership effectiveness has on employee engagement (Fleming, Coffman, and Hartner 2005; Corporate Executive Board 2004). Following the implementation of the leadership development programme, HortResearch achieved significant growth in both revenue and earnings and overall staff satisfaction levels, which, as measured in an independent benchmarked climate survey, rose from 46 percent to 57 percent in the period from 2003 to 2007. Although it is not possible to directly correlate the impact of the leadership development programme or the feedforward coaching phase with these changes in productivity and climate, it is reasonable to consider that there is a relationship between the two.

COMMUNICATION STRATEGY
Target Audience

The results of the leadership development programme were communicated to a large number of audiences and for a variety of purposes.

Internally, results were communicated to

- The HR staff:
  - Enhancements to the programme were continuously made throughout the programme based on the feedback from all levels of the evaluation feedback.
- The individual leaders who participated in the programme:
  - In one-on-one meetings, the individual results of the "Heads Up" 360° review were communicated to provide leaders with Levels 3 and 4 evaluation feedback.
- The cohort and following cohorts:
  - In the programme meetings, the collective results of the "Heads Up" 360° review were communicated to assist leaders to stay motivated to invest their time and energy into the programme and the process by illustrating the impact that feedforward coaching has on leadership effectiveness and employee morale.
- The board of directors and senior management:
  - Overall patterns were reported two or three times a year.

Externally, results were communicated to

- The New Zealand minister of science:
  - As part of an official visit to the organisation, a presentation on the programme and the results was made to the minister and officials.
- The Human Resource Institute of New Zealand:

- The Leadership Development Programme was submitted to the national professional HR society and won both the local and national award for the 2005 HR Initiative of the Year.
- More than 600 members of the coaching community internationally:
  - A poster session on the feedforward coaching process and results were presented at two international professional coaching conferences, the International Coach Federation of Europe (2006) and of Australasia (2007).
- More than 750 members of the New Zealand HR community:
  - Meeting presentations on the process and the results were given by the HR staff to members of the professional HR community and the general public.
- Visitors from local organisations:
  - Approximately six organisations visited HortResearch to meet with HR staff and discuss the process and results of the programme.

Stakeholder Feedback

The most visible response from the stakeholders was continued and increased recognition and support for the programme, despite ongoing pressure to trim costs and improve profitability. Senior management, with the endorsement of the board of directors, was willing to provide ongoing funding for the programme and the development of a companion programme at the team leader level. The chief executive continued to support and promote the programme.

Increasing interest shown by HortResearch staff to participate in the programme provided further confirmation of its impact and value. Scientists and their managers were impressed by the measurable results generated and were proud to participate in its success.

The minister of science was pleased to have a "good news" story to share about the programme and its impact in the organisation.

Data Use for Programme Improvement

Initially the programme encouraged six feedforward cycles in a six-month period. Trends from the "Heads Up" 360° review suggested that changes in the perception of leadership effectiveness could be achieved with four cycles, and hence this became the recommendation. More detailed examination of the "Heads Up" 360° review patterns showed that leaders who did not involve members of their team as feedforward coaches, or involved only one of them, were unlikely to change the morale of their team. As a result, leaders were given greater encouragement to include more of their direct reports as feedforward coaches.

Feedback from the focus groups and meetings was incorporated into briefings, support materials, and processes; for example, email reminders to leaders that it was time for another cycle, more initial support to complete the first cycle of coaching, and training sessions for feedforward coaches.

Having results that demonstrated the value of the programme enabled the HR staff to receive the support to enhance and expand the programme, which has recently been adopted as the core organisational development platform in Plant & Food Research. It has also enriched HR processes at HortResearch. Leaders now recognise that leadership is just as important a skill to look for in selection and succession planning as technical skills. In recruitment, the leadership programme also serves to distinguish the organisation from other science organisations competing for aspiring great scientists and leaders.

LESSONS LEARNED

The feedforward coaching process is a simple, cost-effective tool that works. However, it is not for everyone. When it does work, it can have powerful results. And it seems to work better when the leaders are told in advance that they will be measured, in line with the principle that what gets measured gets done.

The support and active involvement of opinion leaders among the organisation's science staff were critical to the successful introduction of the feedforward coaching process. Their initial involvement in the design of the programme and the subsequent discussion of results achieved built support for feedforward coaching as a vital and effective element in the leadership development programme. In retrospect, the involvement and support of these opinion leaders was almost as important as the involvement and support of the chief executive, who made it known that he too was receiving coaching, both from within the organisation and externally.

The most prevalent lesson learned about the evaluation process is that measuring effectiveness is not as difficult as it might seem. Mostly what is needed is the willingness to do it. Measurement doesn't have to be sophisticated to go beyond Level 1 or 2 evaluation. As a general rule, we don't do it enough.

Given the relative ease of measuring the success of the organisation, the logical next step would be to build a strong and robust ROI process to include in the programme planning. This would provide a new challenge to the HR staff, new information for the leaders to measure their success, and added understanding of how HR initiatives add value to the organisation.

Senior management and scientists responded very positively to the evaluation methodology. As scientists, they understood the issues involved and analysis methods. Many contributed their research experience to the methodology design. It helped the HR department build a different relationship with them. Having data to show the basis of the model, the process, and the results created much enthusiasm and interest. It created a very interesting story that attracted attention from many people and places.

RESOURCES

Corporate Executive Board. (2004). *Driving Performance and Retention Through Employee Engagement.* www.corporateleadershipcouncil.com

Fleming, J.H., C. Coffman, and J.K. Hartner. (2005). Managing Your Human Sigma. *Harvard Business Review* (July–August):107–114.

Goldsmith, M., and H. Morgan. (2005). Leadership Is a Contact Sport: The Follow Up Factor in Management Development. *Strategy + Business* (Fall): 71–79

Kirkpatrick, D.L. (1998). *Evaluating Training Programs* (2nd edition). San Francisco, CA: Berrett-Koehler.

Zenger, J., and J. Folkman. (2002). *The Extraordinary Leader.* New York: McGraw-Hill, pp. 29–38.

QUESTIONS FOR DISCUSSION

1. How can you identify simple measures of success, such as change in morale, that have meaning and interest to your organisation?

2. How can you simplify the scales used to measure change and impact?

3. How might the project have been scoped differently if an ROI analysis had been planned from the onset of the initiative?

4. What are the benefits of a robust ROI? What value would the ROI have added to this programme?

5. Given the interest generated by the success of the programme, what are some cost-effective ways of sharing the information without overtaxing a small HR staff?

ABOUT THE AUTHORS

Cynthia Johnson, MA, previously worked for HortResearch, where she led the leadership development programme design and evaluation programme. She is now Organisational Development Leader and is currently the Group Manager of Organisational Development and Learning Programmes for Fonterra Co-operative Group Ltd., where she continues to pursue her interests in leadership development, research, and evaluation.

Leslie Hamilton, BA, MEd, MSB, supports organisations and individuals to maximise the impact of coaching and leadership development and has been an independent international leadership coach and facilitator for 18 years. Working with the Human Resource staff, senior leaders, and feedforward coaches, Leslie assisted in the external coaching and enhancement of the leadership development programme at HortResearch.

Craig Jensen, BA, Dip. Bus., is General Manager, Human Resources at the New Zealand Institute for Plant & Food Research. With more than 900 staff, the Institute is one of New Zealand's largest research organisations. It was formed in 2008 following the merger of HortResearch with the New Zealand Institute for Crop & Food Research. Craig has a particular interest in the relationship between leadership and organisational culture and performance. He was the project sponsor for this work, securing support throughout the organisation and managing relationships at the board and executive level.

8

Lean Concepts in Healthcare: A Return on Investment Study

Home Town Care
USA

John D. Piccolo

T his case was prepared to serve as a basis for discussion rather than an illustration of either effective or ineffective administrative and management practices. Names, dates, places, and data may have been disguised at the request of the author or organization.

Abstract

Healthcare organizations are continually looking for ways to improve quality and efficiency through new and innovative initiatives. Along with the quality and efficiency movement, return on investment (ROI) also has become a topic of interest across the healthcare system. This case study examines the impact of lean manufacturing techniques in a long-term care facility. The study utilizes the Phillips ROI Methodology to evaluate three projects that were completed during a reVIEW (Realizing Exceptional Value In Everyday Work) seven-week training and implementation program. The results begin to validate what many already know through experience; that implementing lean principles in healthcare can have a positive impact.

PROGRAM BACKGROUND

Home Town Care

Home Town Care is a senior services organization in rural Pennsylvania. The long-term care facility is the skilled nursing and rehabilitative division associated with a continuum of care retirement community. The health center offers three levels of skilled nursing care: comprehensive, rehabilitative, and memory support. The facility consists of 90 beds and 168 employees.

The reVIEW Program

The reVIEW course is seven weeks in duration. Each course consists of 16 participants. The participants meet once a week for three hours of interactive classroom time, plus additional time for one-on-one coaching. Through the seven weeks of the course, participants are introduced to the following lean principles and tools:

- Toyota Production System Model and Lean Healthcare
- Power of Observation
- Value Stream Mapping (current state and future state)
- A3 Problem Solving

During the program, participants identify a specific area or problem they wish to improve. They can choose to work individually or in teams. Participants have a homework assignment each week, and each week's assignment builds on the previous week's work. Each participant is expected to complete one observation exercise, one current-state and one future-state value stream map, and one A3 Problem Solving activity.

The primary improvement tool utilized in the reVIEW program is the A3 Problem Solving form. The A3 process teaches the participants to identify problems through the observation process. After participants report their observation during week two, they are taught to draw a value stream map, which helps identify through visualization the issues or projects to work on. Once a value stream map is completed, the participants are taught to identify the root cause of a problem by using the *5 Why* process.

Need for Program

An executive overview of the reVIEW program was first offered to the senior leadership group of Home Town Care and six other healthcare organizations from the local healthcare industry partnership. Following the overview, a needs assessment was conducted to determine if a need existed for such a program within the above-mentioned healthcare organizations. The needs assessment revealed a need for and a true interest in the reVIEW process; therefore, an open enrollment program was offered to the partnership.

This case study focuses on three projects completed by eight employees of Home Town Care during their participation in the open enrollment reVIEW program. The program ran from June 2, 2009, through July 21,

2009. The final data were collected during the months of December 2009 and January 2010.

Project Description
Project 1: Dressing Change Delays
This project concerned the delays that took place when a resident required a dressing change. The residents' dressings are naturally changed in the privacy of their rooms. Typically, when a nurse would have a dressing change, delays would occur because the dressing supplies were stocked in three different locations. Inconsistency in what was stocked in each location meant that the nurses would have to travel from location to location to obtain the required supplies. Often, when needed supplies could not be located, a nurse would walk to the main stockroom in a different part of the building to acquire the needed supplies. During the observation phase of this project, the two project leaders (the nurse manager and a unit nurse) discovered that this process meant that a simple five-minute dressing change took anywhere from 10 minutes to one and one-half hours.

Problem Analysis
During the problem analysis phase, project leaders determined that a typical dressing change process should take approximately five minutes. Due to supply issues, the process was often delayed, taking time away from nurses who needed to conduct other critical and important quality-of-care activities.

During the root cause analysis, the project leaders found that the nurses were not always able to locate the needed supplies to perform a dressing change.

Why? The supplies were stocked in three different locations and not always available in any of the three locations.

Why? The nurses had their own preferences about where to keep certain supplies and would remove them unbeknownst to the supply personnel.

Why? The dressing supply process was not specified.

Target Condition, Countermeasures, and Implementation Plan
The target condition for this project was to have a process in place that allowed a nurse to perform a dressing change without supply delays. The project leaders discussed the process with the nurses on their wing. The countermeasure identified by the group was to implement a dressing

supply cart that was fully stocked with all the supplies needed to change a dressing.

The dressing supply cart was implemented. It is located in the supply room near the nurses' station. When a dressing change is needed, a nurse wheels the cart into the patient's room. When the change is completed, the cart is immediately placed back in the supply room. To ensure that supplies remain fully stocked, the cart has an inventory checklist that is maintained on a daily basis by the head nurse.

Project 2: Short-Term Rehab Discharge to Home

The second project focused on part one of a three-part project to address the delays experienced when a short-term care rehabilitation patient is discharged to home. This project leader addressed the process with three successive A3 Problem Solving forms. The project leader followed a logic model approach, in which the completion of one project triggers the beginning of the next.

The social workers always used a standardized form to collect information necessary for a short-term care discharge. The issue was that a standardized process for obtaining the information had never been created. Therefore, gathering information for a short-term rehab discharge is sometimes a lengthy process, which causes delays in the discharge process. At times, this delay forces the patient to stay longer than required, which in turn creates missed opportunities to fill that bed with another short-term rehab patient.

Problem Analysis

During the problem analysis phase, the project leader found that gathering information for a short-term rehab discharge was sometimes a lengthy process.

Why? The social services coordinator was often unable to obtain the required discharge information in a timely manner.

Why? Staff members were busy doing other tasks.

Why? A process was not specified concerning staff input needed for a short-term rehab discharge.

Target Condition, Countermeasures, and Implementation Plan

The target condition for this three-phase process was to discharge a short-term rehab patient with no rework on the part of the social workers and no delay in the discharge date.

This first phase established a process for obtaining family input prior to the weekly rehab meeting. This phase also created a process in which nursing input is provided during the weekly meeting. Both steps were coordinated with social services and the rehab nurses and implementation was completed. Phase two of this project is now under way and will be captured in a future document.

Project 3: Chart-to-Go

The third project addressed the documentation system used by the certified nurse assistants (CNAs) to capture the activities of daily living (ADL) information for each resident in the long-term care unit. The documentation system that was in place had the CNAs handwriting the ADLs for each resident in a chart at the end of the shift. The CNAs would have to remember what they did with each resident throughout the day. This process tended to create a copycat approach, in which the CNAs would look at what was written on the prior day and often rewrite very similar information. This process was not just time consuming; it also created a situation in which the ADL information might not have been accurate. Inaccurate ADL information can create reimbursement inaccuracies, since the case mix index (CMI) might not reflect the true amount of work required for each resident.

Problem Analysis

During the problem analysis phase, the project leaders found that the existing ADL documentation system was inaccurate and time consuming.

Why? The CNAs documented ADL information in a book at the end of the shift from memory.

Why? That was the only time they had to do it.

Why? No other time or process was specified for ADL documentation.

Target Condition, Countermeasures, and Implementation Plan

The target condition for this project was to have CNAs accurately document the ADL information for each resident while the activities were being conducted.

The countermeasure put in place was the purchase of a Palm Pilot for each CNA. The new system allowed the CNA to document ADL information in the resident's room while the activities were taking place.

The implementation plan included training for each CNA on the proper way to document on the Palm. Once that step was completed, the director of nursing added different components of the ADL documentation process week by week until the implementation was complete.

Need for Evaluation

In recent years, return on investment (ROI) has become a topic of interest in healthcare, with policymakers and consumers demanding greater accountability for dollars spent on healthcare. Medicaid, state officials, legislators, health plans, and other stakeholders are increasingly challenged to identify programs that both improve quality and control costs. One of the best ways to demonstrate this accountability is through evaluation.

As Home Town Care continues to invest both dollars and human resources in this new quality and efficiency program, evaluation will be paramount. Home Town Care will continue with quarterly follow-up meetings during their lean implementation, to better build a comprehensive cost-benefit analysis of a healthcare organization's lean transformation.

EVALUATION METHODOLOGY
The Phillips ROI Methodology

The use of evaluation processes and models, including the Phillips framework, continues to grow. The Phillips ROI Methodology has been replicated hundreds of times with more than 30 books published to support the methodology. The Phillips ROI process is used by more than 2,000 organizations in 44 different countries. The methodology has been the basis for many studies, providing a step-by-step guide from initial planning through data collection and evaluation (Figure 8.1). The four-phase, 10-step process generates six types of data and is the only documented ROI methodology to require a step be taken to isolate the impact of the program. The Phillips methodology is a time-tested, consistent, and credible approach for ROI studies and one with a track record of success in both for-profit and nonprofit organizations. The Phillips ROI Methodology utilizes five levels of evaluation (Table 8.1) to provide a framework to categorize the different types of data.

Any process or research study should clearly define the standards and principles by which data is collected and analyzed. Without such a protocol, one cannot ensure consistency from study to study or within the same study. The Phillips ROI Methodology provides guiding principles that form

FIGURE 8.1   ROI Process Model

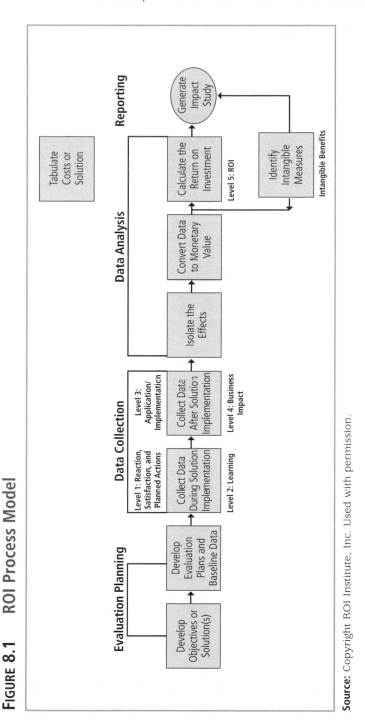

TABLE 8.1   Five Levels of Evaluation

Level	Brief Description
1—Reaction and Planned Action	Measures participants' reaction to the program and outlines specific plans for implementation. Participant reaction questionnaires are typically completed at the end of the program.
2—Learning	Measures skills, knowledge, or attitude changes. Learning is typically assessed through observations, exercises, role-plays, and subjective assessments from the program faculty and mentors.
3—Application and Implementation	Measures changes in behavior on the job and specific application and implementation. Follow-up evaluation data are usually obtained from questionnaires, observations, and focus groups.
4—Business Impact	Measures business impact of the program, linking key performance measures directly to the program. Business impact is often obtained from participants as they apply what they learn.
5—Return on Investment	Compares the monetary value of the results with the costs for the program, usually expressed as a percentage.

Source: Phillips, Phillips, Stone, and Burkett (2007).

the basis for the ROI operating standards. The 12 Guiding Principles are as follows:

1. When a high-level evaluation is conducted, data must be collected at lower levels.

2. When an evaluation is planned for a higher level, the previous level of evaluation does not have to be comprehensive.

3. When collecting and analyzing data, use only the most credible source.

4. When analyzing data, choose the most conservative among the alternatives.

5. At least one method must be used to isolate the effects of the solution.

6. If no improvement data are available for a population or from a specific source, it is assumed that little or no improvement has occurred.

7. Estimates of improvements should be adjusted (discounted) for the potential error of the estimate.

8. Extreme data items and unsupported claims should not be used in ROI calculations.

9. Only the first year of benefits (annual) should be used in the ROI analysis of short-term solutions.

10. Costs of the solution should be fully loaded for ROI analysis.

11. Intangible measures are defined as measures that are purposely not converted to monetary values.

12. The results from the ROI methodology must be communicated to all key stakeholders.

Evaluation Planning

During this stage, a detailed data collection plan and an ROI analysis plan are assembled. The data collection plan lays the initial groundwork for the ROI study. This plan answers the questions (a) what do you ask, (b) how do you ask, (c) whom do you ask, (d) when do you ask, and (e) who does the asking. The data collection plan for this study is shown in Table 8.2.

The second planning document is the ROI analysis plan, which requires the researcher to identify (a) methods for isolating the effects of the program, (b) methods for converting data to money, (c) cost categories, (d) intangible benefits, (e) communication targets for the final report, (f) other influences and issues during application, and (g) researcher comments (Phillips and Phillips 2005). The ROI analysis plan for this study is shown in Table 8.3.

Data Collection

Data collection is central to the Phillips ROI Methodology. Both *hard data* (e.g., output, quality, cost, and time) and *soft data* (e.g., job satisfaction and customer satisfaction) are collected. This study utilized a combination of action planning, assignments, questionnaires, interviews (individual coaching sessions), observation, and on-site follow-up visits to obtain relevant data. A case study database was developed by maintaining a copy of all the forms and instruments used for each project. A succession of evidence was demonstrated by collecting and maintaining chain-of-impact data at each of the five levels of the Phillips framework.

TABLE 8.2 Data Collection Plan

Purpose of this evaluation: To evaluate the impact of the reVIEW program

Program/Project: reVIEW program   Responsiblity: John Piccolo   Date: 06/29/2009

Level	Broad Program Objective(s)	Measures	Data Collection Method/ Instruments	Data Sources	Timing	Responsibilities
1	**Satisfaction/Planned Action** • Rate the facilitators as effective • Perceive the reVIEW program as relevent to the job • Recommend this program to other healthcare providers • Indicate an intent to use the reVIEW skills on the job	Average ratio of 4.0 out of 5.0 on quality, quantity, and usefulness of the reVIEW program	Standard questionnaire	Participant	End of program	Researcher
2	**Learning** • Define IDEAL, and recognize when their organization's outcome is not IDEAL • Explain the importance of studying work as it is actually done rather than work as espoused • See patient care and supporting systems as processes • Explain what "specify an activity" means, and identify when a given activity is not sufficiently specified • Explain the term "connection," and identify when a given connection is not simple or direct • Explain the term "pathway," and identify when a care pathway is complex	Ability to explain and demonstrate the learning objectives through application and articulation during the program	Skill practice Facilitator assessment Participant assessment on questionnaire Assignments Coaching sessions	Participant Facilitator	During the program	Facilitator

3	**Application/Implementation** • Observe an organization's activities and create an understandable, pictorial description of the current condition • Create a "map" of a process, collect data to quantify processing times and interval times between process steps, and use the data to determine process performance measures • Create a future state map of flow of processes that is a visualized improvement over the current state map • Diagnose a workplace "problem" by seeking out root causes in terms of activity specification, connections, and pathways • Envision a target condition that moves the organization closer to IDEAL by improving activities, connections, and/or pathways	Completion of all steps of the action plan	Standard questionnaire Action plan Assignments Observation Coaching sessions On-site meetings with researcher	Participant	During the program	Researcher
4	**Business Impact** • Redesign work activities by specifying the content, sequence, and timing of individual steps, and desired outcomes; and document the new design • Redesign workplace connections to establish simple, yes/no communications along patient care pathway • Redesign pathways such that delivery of the good or service is simple, direct, and consistent • Design improvement activities as experiments, with explicit hypotheses about expected outcomes and specific outcome measures	Each project will be different and identified on the action plan	Action plan Coaching sessions On-site meetings with researcher	Participant	During the program	Participant Researcher
5	**ROI 18%**	Comments:				

TABLE 8.3 ROI Analysis Plan

ROI Analysis Plan: reVIEW program

Program/Project: reVIEW ROI Study   Responsiblity: John Piccolo   Date: 05/29/2009

Data Items (Usually Level 4)	Methods for Isolating the Effects of the Program and Process	Methods of Converting Data to Monetary Values	Cost Categories	Intangible Benefits	Communication Targets for Final Report	Other Influences and Issues During Application	Comments
Three business impact measures identified in conjunction with management and the reVIEW facilitator	Control group Participant estimate Management estimate Customer input	Standard value Expert input Participant estimate Management estimate External studies	Program administration, implementation, facilitation, and overhead Program materials Travel and lodging Participant salaries and benefits Project team salaries and benefits Evaluation	Leadership development Standardized process improvement method Employee confidence and satisfaction	Board of directors Management team Workforce investment board PSUCE units		

Instrumentation

This study used several instruments as the basis for data collection, such as questionnaires, action plans, and observation templates. Central to the study is the action planning form depicted in Table 8.4.

The action planning process has several inherent advantages for data collection. First, "for business impact data, the action plan is more focused and credible than a questionnaire" (Phillips and Phillips 2007, p. 221). Also, since much of the data is collected by the participants, it will have the credibility needed for the analysis. And, with data collection responsibility shifted to the participants, a study such as this can be conducted with limited resources (Phillips and Phillips 2007).

TABLE 8.4   Action Plan

Name: _____ Instructor Signature: _____ Follow-Up Date: _____

Objective: _____ Evaluation Period: _____ to _____

Improvement Measure: _____ Current Performance: _____ Target Performance: _____

Action Steps		Analysis

Steps   **Date**
 1. _____ _____
    _____
    _____
 2. _____ _____
    _____
    _____
 3. _____ _____
    _____
    _____
		A. What is the unit of measure? _____
		 B. What is the value (cost) of one unit? _____
		 C. How did you arrive at this value? _____ _____
		 D. How much did the measure change during the evaluation period? (monthly value) _____
		 E. What factors influenced the change in performance? _____ _____

Intangible Benefits:		**F.** What percent of this change was actually caused by this program? _____% **G.** What level of confidence do you place on the above information? (100%=Certainty and 0%=No Confidence) _____%
Comments:		

This study followed the Phillips action planning sequence of activities:

1. Before the reVIEW program, the researcher
   - communicated the action plan requirement at the executive overview
   - discussed the importance of identifying operating measures for improvement.
2. During the reVIEW program, the researcher
   - described the action planning process at the beginning of the program
   - taught the action planning process as part of the reVIEW program
   - allowed time to develop the plan
   - had the facilitator approve the action plan
   - required participants to assign a monetary value to the plan
   - reviewed each plan during a coaching session
   - explained the follow-up mechanism.
3. After the reVIEW program, the researcher
   - required participants to provide improvement data
   - asked participants to isolate the effects of the program
   - asked participants to provide a level of confidence for estimates
   - collected action plans at the predetermined follow-up time
   - summarized the data and calculated the ROI.

Prior to the first reVIEW class, an executive overview was offered. During the overview, a brief introduction of the action planning process was delivered to senior leaders, managers, and training coordinators. Also, the importance of identifying operating measures for improvement was discussed. On the first day of the program, the action planning process was described to the participants during a 10-minute overview of the evaluation process, setting the stage for program expectations. Also, on day one, each participant received a handout on which to capture cost data throughout the program (see Figure 8.2).

The action planning process was discussed in greater detail during a one-hour session on week five of the program. This discussion included an overview of the Phillips ROI Methodology, action plan forms, guidelines for developing action plans, a worksheet to help convert data to money, and examples to illustrate what a complete action plan should look like. A complete packet of this information was provided to each participant. Each item on the action plan was discussed to ensure that the participants

Figure 8.2 Cost Sheet

Name

	Week 1		Week 2		Week 3		Week 4		Week 5		Week 6		Week 7	
	Time	Dollars	Time	Dollars	Time	Dollars	Time	Dollars	Time	Dollars	Time	Dollars	Time	Dollars
How many hours did you spend on your project?	hrs		hrs		hrs		hrs		hrs		hrs		hrs	
How many hours did others spend on your project?	hrs		hrs		hrs		hrs		hrs		hrs		hrs	
What is the average dollar amount spent in salaries (Get salary from HR)		$		$		$		$		$		$		$
Average salary and Benefits × Time														
Did you purchase or utilize company supplies for your project? Yes or No														
If yes, what are they and what did it cost?														
1)		$		$		$		$		$		$		$
2)		$		$		$		$		$		$		$
3)		$		$		$		$		$		$		$
4)		$		$		$		$		$		$		$
Are there any other costs associated with your project? Yes or No														
If yes, what are they and what did it cost?														
1)		$		$		$		$		$		$		$
2)		$		$		$		$		$		$		$
3)		$		$		$		$		$		$		$
4)		$		$		$		$		$		$		$
Total		$		$		$		$		$		$		$

understood how to answer all questions. A form that offered information on each item was also included with the handouts.

Participants were asked to complete the action plan, through item C (see Table 8.4) prior to the start of class on week six. This step allowed for meetings with participants on week six to ensure that they understood how to fill out the form.

After a predetermined amount of time (three months for this study), participants completed the remainder of the form, parts D, E, F, and G (see Table 8.4), as well as listing any intangible benefits and comments. This process was monitored through on-site follow-ups.

Reaction and Learning

Reaction data were collected using a standard questionnaire during week six of the program. The questionnaire focused on issues such as relevance of the material to participants' jobs, if the participants felt they had learned new skills, and participants' intention to use the skills in the workplace. The course content, delivery, and facilitation were also evaluated.

Learning

Learning improvement was measured throughout the program by participants conducting report-outs on the previous week's assignment. This allowed the facilitator to assess the amount of learning by each participant and document the results on the form displayed in Figure 8.3. Learning data were also captured on the end-of-course questionnaire.

Application and Implementation

The end-of-program questionnaire included application and implementation data. On-site visits by the researcher were also used to determine the extent to which the skills were being used and to check progress on the action plan. During the visits, the participants were also asked about the following topics:

- skill usage and frequencies
- additional linkage to organizational business measures
- barriers and enablers to implementation
- progress with the action plan
- additional intangible benefits.

FIGURE 8.3   Observation Template

Workshop Name: reVIEW Program
COMPETENCY: Learning
Workshop Participant's Name:_____

Skills to Be Demonstrated	Unsatisfactory	Needs Improvement	Satisfactory	Role Model
Define IDEAL and recognize when their organization's outcome is not IDEAL				
Explain the importance of studying work as it is actually done				
See patient care and supporting systems as processes				
Explain what "specify an activity" means, and identify when a given activity is not sufficiently specified				
Explain the term "connection," and identify when a given connection is not simple or direct				
Explain the term "pathway," and identify when a care pathway is complex				

EVALUATION RESULTS

Level 1

To what extent did the program participants have a favorable experience with the reVIEW program?

Reaction data was collected at the end of the reVIEW program using an end-of-course questionnaire. The overall average response for all questions was 4.5 out of 5 on a Likert-type scale, with 1 being "strongly disagree" and 5 "strongly agree." A visual summary of the Level 1 (reaction) responses from the end-of-course questionnaire can be found in Figure 8.4. The following Level 1 responses relate directly to the participants from the target organization:

- To what extent did the reVIEW program and materials meet participant expectations?
    a. (Q2) The reVIEW course met my expectations. The participants responded 4.5 out of 5 on a Likert-type scale.
    b. (Q12) The material was organized logically. The participants responded 4.4 out of 5 on a Likert-type scale.
- To what extent did the instructor meet participant expectations?
    a. (Q3) The instructor was prepared and organized for the class. The participants responded 5 out of 5 on a Likert-type scale.
    b. (Q4) Participants were encouraged to take part in class discussions. The participants responded 5 out of 5 on a Likert-type scale.
    c. (Q5) The instructor was responsive to participants' needs and questions. The participants responded 4.8 out of 5 on a Likert-type scale.
    d. (Q6) The instructor was knowledgeable about the subject. The participants responded 4.6 out of 5 on a Likert-type scale.
    e. (Q7) The instructor related the training to my work. The participants responded 4.4 out of 5 on a Likert-type scale.
- To what extent was the program relevant to participants' jobs?
    a. (Q10) The program content was relevant to my job. The participants responded 4.8 out of 5 on a Likert-type scale.
    b. (Q19) What percentage of your total work time requires the knowledge and skills presented in this program? The participants stated that, on average, 51 percent of their total workday requires the knowledge and skills taught in the review program.
- To what extent was the program important to participants' jobs?
    a. (Q11) The program content was important to my job. The participants responded 4.8 out of 5 on a Likert-type scale.
    b. (Q20) On a scale of 0 percent (not at all) to 100 percent (extremely critical), how critical is applying the content of the reVIEW program to your job success? The participants stated that, on average, 65 percent of their job success comes from applying the content taught in the reVIEW program.

- To what extent will participants recommend the reVIEW program to others?
  a. (Q8) I will recommend this program to others. The participants responded 4.8 out of 5 on a Likert-type scale.
- To what extent is there room for improvement with facilitation, materials, and the learning environment?
  a. (Q9) The learning environment was conducive to learning. The participants ranked the learning environment 4.5 out of 5 on a Likert-type scale.
  b. This was an open-ended question: Please provide us with suggestions for improving the program's facilitation, content, and utility.
     (a) Perhaps developing a way to ensure that weekly report-outs remain within the specified time frame.
     (b) Spend more time on instruction and less time on the report-outs.
     (c) Spend less time on the report-outs.

FIGURE 8.4 End-of-Course Questionnaire Responses for Level 1 (Reaction)

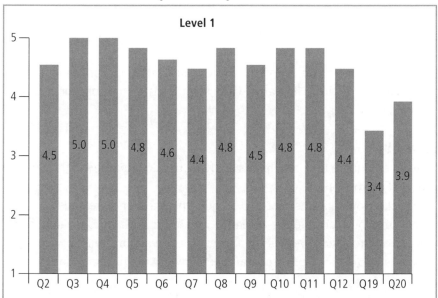

Level 2

To what extent did the participants learn the skills taught in the reVIEW program?

Learning improvement was measured several ways: (a) through the participant's demonstration of knowledge learned during weekly project report-out sessions, (b) at the end of the program using a self-assessment, and (c) through a facilitator assessment. The instructor ranked all participants with an average of 3.35 out of 4 on a Likert-type scale, with 1 being "unsatisfactory" and 4 being "a role model." A visual summary of the Level 2 (learning) responses from the end-of-course questionnaire can be found in Figure 8.5. The following Level 2 responses relate directly to the participants from the target organization:

- (Q14) To what extent did the program provide new information?
  The program content provided me new information. The participants responded 5 out of 5 on a Likert-type scale.

- (Q16) To what extent did participants gain new knowledge and skills?
  I learned new knowledge and skills from the reVIEW program. The participants responded 4.8 out of 5 on a Likert-type scale.

- (Q13) To what extent do participants know how to apply what they learned?
  The exercises and examples helped me understand the material. The participants responded 4.3 out of 5 on a Likert-type scale.

- (Q17) To what extent are participants confident to apply what they learned?
  I am confident that I can effectively apply the skills learned in the reVIEW program. The participants responded 4.5 out of 5 on a Likert-type scale.

Level 3

To what extent are the participants applying the skills learned in the reVIEW program on the job?

Application data was captured on both the questionnaire and the action plan form. To determine the extent to which the skills were actually being utilized, and to check progress of the action plan, an on-site follow-up interview was also conducted three months following the program completion.

FIGURE 8.5   End-of-Course Questionnaire Responses for Level 2 (Learning)

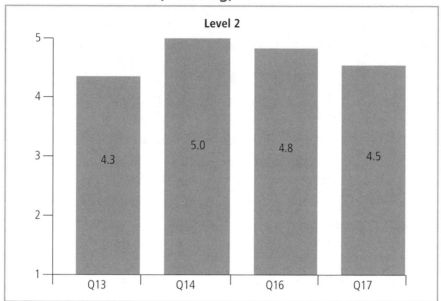

The interview included all the program participants, the HR manager, and the CEO of the organization. The follow-up questions included the following topics:

- skill usage and frequencies
- additional linkage to organizational business measures
- barriers and enablers to implementation
- progress with the action plan
- additional intangible benefits.

The projects captured on the A3s and action plans could focus on any observation, as long as they were consistent with the skills required in the program and related to the business improvement measures established between management and the instructor. The most difficult part of developing the action plan was for the participants to convert the measure to a monetary value. Several approaches were offered to the participants and a "converting data to money" handout with examples was provided. For the majority of the items converted, standard values were available and used. If a standard value was not available, the participants were encouraged to use expert input or to estimate using the conservative process defined by the Phillips ROI Methodology. It was important to require this value to be developed during the program, or at least have it developed soon after the program was completed, so that the follow-up could focus on the improvement. A visual summary of the Level 3 (application) responses from the end-of-course questionnaire can be found in Figure 8.6. The following Level 3 responses relate directly to the participants from the target organization:

- (Q18) How effectively are participants applying what they learned?

  I will effectively apply what I have learned in this program. The participants responded 4.6 out of 5 on a Likert-type scale.

- To what extent do participants intend to use what they learned?

  a. (Q15) I intend to use what I learned in this program immediately. The participants responded 4.8 out of 5 on a Likert-type scale.

  b. (Q21) The participants estimate that they will apply 75 percent of the new knowledge and skills learned from the reVIEW program on their job.

- How frequently are they applying what they learned?

  The participants are all actively working on projects using the reVIEW techniques. Three projects are completed, three are near completion, and at least five other projects have been started.

- If they are applying what they learned, what is supporting them?

  a. Senior-level management support is helping keep the program alive and working, not only at the long-term care facility, but also across the organization.

  b. The project leaders are including all employees in the projects, which in turn has created buy-in.

- If they are not applying what they learned, why not?

  The participants are applying the reVIEW tools as of the three-month follow-up.

Level 4

What is the business impact as a result of utilizing the skills learned in the reVIEW program?

FIGURE 8.6   End-of-Course Questionnaire Responses for Level 3 (Application)

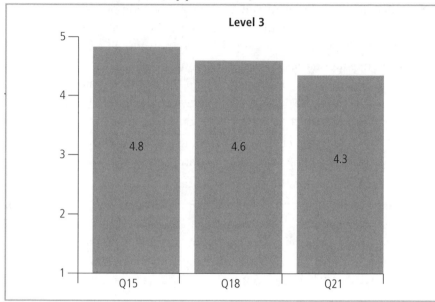

During the follow-up, the participants were asked to provide five items:

1. The actual monthly change in the measure as indicated in part D of the action plan (see Figure 8.5). This is the value used to develop an annual improvement.

2. An estimate of the percentage of improvement resulting from the application of the skills required in the reVIEW training program. An isolation technique used to determine the effects of the program included an estimate directly from the participants. As they monitor the business measures and observe their improvement, the participants likely know the actual influences driving a specific measure, or at least the percentage improvement related to their actions detailed on the action plan. Understanding that other factors could have influenced the improvement, the reVIEW participants were asked to estimate the percentage of improvement resulting from the application of the skills required in the reVIEW training program (the action steps on the action plan). Each participant was

asked to be conservative with the estimate and express it as a percentage (see parts E and F on the action plan).

3. Participants' level of confidence in their allocation of the contribution of this program. Understanding that the value in item 2 is an estimate, the participants were asked to indicate the level of confidence in their allocation of the contribution of this program. This is included in part G on the action plan (100% for certainty and 0% for no confidence). This process reflects the degree of uncertainty in the value and frames an error range for the estimate.

4. Intangible measures observed or monitored during the three months that were directly linked to this program.

5. Additional comments including explanations.

Figure 8.7 shows a sample of an action plan that was completed for this study. The example focuses on project 2, which is phase one to reduce the delays created during a short-term rehab discharge. The A3 Problem Solving form from which this example is taken is located in Appendix 8.A.

The following Level 4 responses relate directly to the three projects from the target organization:

- To what extent does participants' application of what they learned improve the measures the program was intended to improve? To date, the completed projects have done the following:

  a. **Project 1: Dressing Change Delays.** Reduced the combined nursing time spent looking for dressing supplies by 3.75 hours per day (24-hour day). This is time that is now spent providing resident care. This process has also reduced the amount of wasted medical supplies due to an inaccurate inventory.

  b. **Project 2: Short-Term Rehab Discharge to Home.** Reduced the amount of time the social services department spends coordinating short-term rehab discharges by 25 percent. Phase one has also reduced the number of missed short-term rehab patients due to a delay in another patient's discharge by approximately 20 percent. If a short-term rehab patient is turned away for admission because the facility cannot guarantee the bed of someone being discharged, that bed will become unoccupied for an average of seven days once it is available. Missed short-term rehab admittance opportunities were costing the organization more than $23,000 per year.

TABLE 8.7   Action Plan

Name: _____ Instructor Signature: _____ Follow-Up Date: _12-3-09_

Objective: **_Reduce delays in short-term discharge_**   Evaluation Period: _9-1-09_ to _12-3-09_

Improvement Measure: **_Missed short-term admissions_** Current Performance: **_Once per month_** Target Performance: **_No misses_**

Action Steps	Analysis
Steps **Date** **1.** Family input will be sought before rehab meeting. **2.** Nursing input will be provided during the rehab meeting.	**A.** What is the unit of measure? *1 missed short-term admit* **B.** What is the value (cost) of one unit? *$388.17 per day* **C.** How did you arrive at this value? *Standard Value* **D.** How much did the measure change during the evaluation period? (monthly value) *20% reduction*
Intangible Benefits: *Employee and Patient Satisfaction*	**E.** What factors influenced the change in performance? *The reVIEW Program* **F.** What percent of this change was actually caused by this program? *100%* **G.** What level of confidence do you place on the above information? (100%=Certainty and 0%=No Confidence) *75%*
Comments: 	

c. **Project 3: Chart-to-Go.** Reduced the average amount of time the CNAs were spending documenting ADLs by 45 percent. Documentation has become more accurate and the CMI has increased by 2.8 percent, thus increasing the reimbursement amount. The process is now entirely paperless and environmentally friendly.

- How do we know it was the program that improved these measures? Each of the three projects in the target organization used two isolation techniques. The following techniques were used: (a) participant estimates on all projects, (b) control group on project one, (c) expert estimates on project two, and (d) trend-line analysis on project three.

Level 5

What is the ROI associated with implementing the skills learned in the reVIEW program?

Calculating ROI requires two steps: (1) calculating monetary benefits by converting Level 4 data into a monetary value, and (2) determining the fully loaded cost of the program. When the ROI is calculated, the following standard formula should be used:

$$\text{ROI (\%)} = \frac{\text{Net Program Benefits}}{\text{Program Costs}} \times 100$$

ROI uses the net benefits divided by program costs. The net benefits are the program benefits minus the costs. This is the same basic formula used in evaluating other investments in which the ROI is traditionally reported as earnings divided by investment (Phillips, Phillips, Stone, and Burkett, 2007).

According to Phillips and Phillips (2007, p. 257), while results at the lower levels are important, converting the positive outcomes into monetary figures and weighing them against the cost of the program is more valuable from an executive viewpoint. This is the ultimate level in the five-level evaluation framework.

The following Level 5 responses relate directly to the three projects from the target organization:

- Do the monetary benefits of the improvement in business impact measures outweigh the cost of the program?

    a. **Project 1.** Yes (590%). The benefit and cost information for this project is listed in Figure 8.8. The cost information is fully loaded to include all the expenses associated with the program. The benefit information is conservative and includes confidence adjustments for any potential error.

    b. **Project 2.** Yes (154%). The benefit and cost information for this project is listed in Figure 8.9. The cost information is fully loaded to include all the expenses associated with the program. The benefit information is conservative and includes confidence adjustments for any potential error.

c. **Project 3.** Yes (31%). The benefit and cost information for this project is listed in Figure 8.10. The cost information is fully loaded to include all the expenses associated with the program. The benefit information is conservative and includes confidence adjustments for any potential error.

BALANCED DATA

The three projects also include several intangible measures (resident satisfaction, employee satisfaction, teamwork, reduced waste, and environmentally friendly processes) that were considered important and helpful to the facility. Therefore, several types of data points are generated from this project:

- reaction, satisfaction, and planned action
- learning
- application and implementation
- business impact
- ROI
- intangible benefits.

Collectively, the six types of data provide a balanced viewpoint of the success of the reVIEW program.

COMMUNICATION STRATEGY

The results of this study were communicated to a variety of stakeholders. First, the senior leadership at Home Town Care was briefed in detail on each project by the project coordinators. The leadership team was impressed to the point of making the reVIEW program the primary quality initiative in their organization. They have also assigned a senior leader the responsibility of coordinating and tracking each project so as to create a database that documents a long-term care organization's transformation to a lean enterprise.

FIGURE 8.8 Cost Benefit Worksheet (Project 1)

Project 1 Dressing Change Delays

Project 1 Cost		Actual Cost
Tuition = $2,390 per student	# of students = 2	$1,593.33
(Includes lodging, meals, instructor travel, room costs, supplies, and program admin. cost)	*Prorated over = 3	
Lost Wages (Provided by HR)		$974.60
(Includes salary and benefits while in training and while working on the project)		
Evaluation Cost		$617.18
(Includes researcher time, travel, and benefits pro-rated for all the projects in the study)		
Tuition = $2,390 per student	**Total Cost**	**$3,679.77**

Project 1 Benefit	Annual Benefit	Proj. Leader Confidence	Actual Benefit
Nursing time saved	$33,833.80	75%	$25,375.35
(adjusted for confidence by each nurse and then averaged)			
		Total Benefit	**$25,375.35**
BCR = Program Benefits / Program Cost		**BCR = 6.90**	
ROI = Net Program Benefits / Program Cost × 100		**ROI = 590%**	

Note: Numbers containing salary information are intentionally kept vague to retain anonymity and confidentiality.

* Tuition is prorated over the number of projects that each participant estimates that they will conduct in a one-year period and adjusted for the confidence in their estimate.

FIGURE 8.9   Cost Benefit Worksheet (Project 2)

Project 2 Short-Term Rehab Discharge to Home

Project 2 Costs		Actual Cost
Tuition = $2,390 per student	# of students = 1	$487.00
(Includes lodging, meals, instructor travel, room costs, supplies, and program admin. cost)	*Prorated over = 5	
Lost Wages (Provided by HR)		$590.00
(Includes salary and benefits while in training and while working on the project)		
Project Implementation Cost		$210.18
(Includes salaries and benefits of project participants and any material and equipment purchases)		
Evaluation Cost		$617.18
(Includes researcher time, travel, and benefits prorated for all the projects in the study)		
	Total Cost	$1,895.36

Project 2 Benefit	Annual Benefit	Proj. Leader Confidence	Actual Benefit
Social worker time saved (adjusted for confidence 75% by social worker)	$1,360.17	90%	$1,224.15
The annual missed opportunity due to delays **(adjusted for confidence by the admissions coordinator)	$23,476.52		
This project is preventing 20% of the missed opportunity	$3,991.01	90%	$3,591.91
(adjusted for confidence 85% by the admissions coordinator)		Total Benefit	$4,816.06

BCR = Program Benefits / Program Cost   **BCR = 2.54**

ROI = Net Program Benefits / Program Cost × 100   **ROI = 154%**

Note: Numbers containing salary information are intentionally kept vague to retain anonymity and confidentiality.

* Tuition is prorated over the number of projects that each participant estimates that they will conduct in a one-year period and adjusted for the confidence in their estimate.

** Miss on average one referral per month - 90% conf. When a referral is missed the bed will be empty on average seven days - 80% conf. Reimbursment rate per day for short-term rehab = $388.17 [(1 miss × 90% conf) × ((7 days × $388.17) × 80% conf.)] × 12 to annualize = $23,476.52 per year.

FIGURE 8.10   Cost Benefit Worksheet (Project 3)

Project 3 Chart-to-Go Program

Project 3 Cost		Actual Cost
Tuition = $2,390 per student	# of students = 2	$1,195.00
(Includes lodging, meals, instructor travel, room costs, supplies, and program admin. cost)	*Prorated over = 4	
Lost Wages (Provided by HR)		$3,961.30
(Includes salary and benefits while in training and while working on the project)		
Project Implementation Cost		$31,486.85
(Includes salaries and benefits of project participants and any material and equipment purchases)		
Evaluation Cost		$617.18
(Includes researcher time, travel, and benefits prorated for all the projects in the study)		
	Total Cost	**$37,260.33**

Project 3 Benefit	Annual Benefit	Proj. Leader Confidence	Actual Benefit
** CNA time saved (adjusted for confidence by each CNA)	$22,219.28	95%	$21,108.32
*** Change in CMI (2.8% change)	$45,990.00	60%	$27,594.00
$(((.7 \times 4) \times 365) \times 45) = \$45,990$ per year			
		Total Benefit	**$48,702.32**
BCR = Program Benefits / Program Cost		**BCR = 1.31**	
ROI = Net Program Benefits / Program Cost $\times$ 100		**ROI = 31%**	

Note: Numbers containing salary information are intentionally kept vague to retain anonymity and confidentiality.

* Tuition is prorated over the number of projects that each participant estimates that they will conduct in a one-year period and adjusted for the confidence in their estimate.

** CNAs were asked if they were spending more, less, or the same amount of time using the new Chart-to-Go system. The time was then adjusted for each CNA's confidence in the number, and then averaged.

*** CMI number is based on two months of data and will be revisited at the three-, six-, and nine-month points. (CMI = $.70 per day for each .01 change, CMI increased by .04 for the 45 residents on medical assistance).

The second communication strategy involved a presentation of this case study to the state healthcare industry partnership. The presentation was well received and has since led to other long-term care organizations investing in the reVIEW program for their organizations.

LESSONS LEARNED

It is critical to build the action planning process into the program. The process should not be seen as just a means to collect data, but rather as a mandatory part of the program to help manage project results. Providing participants with the knowledge to answer all the questions on the action plan requires a training session with specific directions on how and where to find the needed information. It is also important to appoint an internal point of contact to help answer any questions on action planning forms as they arise.

RESOURCES

Chen, A., M. Au, and A. Hamblin. (2007). *The ROI Evidence Base: Identifying Quality Improvement Strategies With Cost-Saving Potential.* Hamilton, NJ: Center for Health Care Strategies.

Phillips, J.J., and P.P. Phillips. (2003). Using Action Plans to Measure ROI: A Case Study. *Performance Improvement Journal* 43(1): 1–20.

Phillips, P.P., and J.J. Phillips. (2005). *Return on Investment (ROI) Basics.* Baltimore, MD: ASTD Press.

Phillips, P.P., and J.J. Phillips. (2007). *The Value of Learning: How Organizations Capture Value and ROI.* San Francisco, CA: Pfeiffer.

Phillips, P.P., J.J. Phillips, R.D. Stone, and H. Burkett. (2007). *The ROI Fieldbook: Strategies for Implementing ROI in HR and Training.* Burlington, MA: Butterworth-Heinemann.

QUESTIONS FOR DISCUSSION

1. Is this an appropriate program for Level 5 evaluation? If so, why? If not, why not?

2. How would you critique the evaluation design and method of data collection?

3. What other strategies could have been used to isolate the impact of the reVIEW program?
4. Discuss the use of action planning as a data collection tool. Is action planning a credible source of data collection?
5. Were the estimates used in this study conservative enough?

ABOUT THE AUTHOR

John D. Piccolo, PhD, is the director of Continuing Education at Penn State DuBois. Continuing Education (CE) is the outreach unit of the campus, with the primary mission of helping individuals, organizations, and communities obtain a competitive workforce advantage through education and training. Prior to joining the university, John was a sales engineer for GKN Sinter Metals. He also worked as a project manager for Windfall Products, Inc., and as a production manager for Metaldyne Sintered Components. John spent seven years as a pilot in the United States Army, where he reached the rank of captain. He served as Aviation Company Operations Officer in Berlin, Germany, during the unification of East and West Germany, and he flew missions in support of Operation Desert Storm. He has a PhD in workforce education and development from Penn State University, a master's in public administration from Troy State University in Alabama, and a BS in business administration from Clarion University of Pennsylvania.

9

Store Operations Development Workshop

Premier Retail
South Africa

J. H. Owens

T his case was prepared to serve as a basis for discussion rather than an illustration of either effective or ineffective administrative and management practices. All names, dates, places, and data may have been disguised at the request of the authors or organization.

Abstract

This case looks at the implementation of a skills assessment and development program designed to improve store manager capability and in-store operating efficiencies. The evaluation of the program was conducted on a _post facto_ basis and did not form part of the original design, delivery, and evaluation strategy. Data for evaluation Levels 1, 2, and 3 were collected through the use of a questionnaire. Level 4 data were collected through the use of an action plan template designed to provide impact information. Costs were compiled from company records, using standard costing where appropriate. The corporate standard or goal of 4.2 on a 5-point rating scale for all training initiatives was attained on most dimensions measured. A return on investment (ROI) of 12.54 percent was achieved for the program.

PROGRAM BACKGROUND

The retail industry in South Africa remains dominated by several large holding companies, operating in various categories ranging from grocery to clothing and footwear to furniture and furnishings. Premier Retail, a division of one of these dominant holding companies, operates primarily in the clothing, footwear, and textile sector (CFT). They operate nationally and service mainly the lower- to middle-income groups. From humble beginnings in 1965, Premier Retail has expanded to more than 220 outlets, with an expansive outlet footprint covering shopping malls, city centers, and rural main streets. Store-based retailing continues to be the preferred shopping mode for local consumers. Premier Retail boasts a 30 percent share of the CFT sector in the market in which they operate.

As part of their strategy to improve store manager capability, in-store operating efficiencies, and overall productivity, Premier Retail decided to embark on a comprehensive skills development program. This was in line with two of their corporate values, namely, *professionalism* and *performance*. To achieve this end, Premier Retail contracted with a local training supply company (Supplier) to develop a three-day skills enhancement workshop for key store operations staff. The program became known as the Store Operations Development Workshop (SODW, or the workshop). The objectives of the workshop were to improve the depth of understanding and skill level in the following areas deemed critical to the success of a retail outlet:

- increasing *sales volumes*
- understanding and managing *cost of selling*
- understanding and managing *in-store productivity*
- understanding and managing *customer satisfaction*
- understanding and managing *employee satisfaction.*

Unfortunately, a comprehensive evaluation process was not considered as part of the original training design and implementation strategy. This negated the opportunity to engage with the designers and Premier Retail management to establish meaningful evaluation criteria. It was only after the majority of staff members had gone through the workshop that the question of evaluation arose. This also occurred at a time when the performance of the group was below expectation, and numerous questions were being asked as to the value of the training and many other initiatives that were taking place at the time. It was at this stage that a request was made to provide an independent assessment of the efficacy and value of the workshops, including a benefit–cost analysis. It was suggested to the Premier Retail executive that the ROI Methodology developed by Phillips (Phillips 2003) be used for evaluation purposes, as this would provide a proven and comprehensive framework for the collection and reporting of data. The ROI Methodology was suggested as it provides a structured five-level approach as follows:

Level 1:   Delegate reaction to the workshop

Level 2:   Learning during the workshop

Level 3:   Application of knowledge/skill

Level 4:   Impact of the workshop on the business

Level 5:   Return on investment

A sixth set of data, notably other intangible data, which cannot easily be converted to a monetary value, is also collected and reported (Phillips 2003, p. 235, and Phillips, Phillips, Stone, and Burkett 2007, p. 27).

In addition to the five levels of evaluation indicated above, the ROI Methodology, selected as the evaluation process, incorporates a set of 12 Guiding Principles that guide decisions in data collection, data analysis, and reporting of data, as measurement and evaluation takes place. The Guiding Principles, as advocated by Phillips (Phillips 2003), are as follows:

1. When a higher level evaluation is conducted, data must be collected at lower levels.

2. When an evaluation is planned for a higher level, the previous level of evaluation does not have to be comprehensive.

3. When collecting and analyzing data, use only the most credible sources.

4. When analyzing data, select the most conservative alternative for calculations.

5. At least one method must be used to isolate the effects of the solution/program.

6. If no improvement data are available for a population or from a specific source, the assumption is that little or no improvement has occurred.

7. Estimates of improvements should be adjusted for the potential error of the estimate.

8. Extreme data items and unsupported claims should not be used in ROI calculations.

9. Only the first year of benefits (annual) should be used in the ROI analysis of short-term solutions.

10. Costs of a solution, project, or program should be fully loaded for ROI analysis.

11. Intangible measures are defined as measures that are purposely not converted to monetary values.

12. The results of the ROI Methodology must be communicated to all key stakeholders.

EVALUATION METHODOLOGY

It was made clear to Premier Retail that the ROI Methodology was being applied on a *post facto* basis and that this would make the data needed for evaluation at all five levels cumbersome to collect. As a consequence, it was agreed to conduct the evaluation in two phases; Levels 1, 2, and 3 initially, and then Levels 4 and 5 once the information required to do an effective evaluation at these levels was ascertained.

Questionnaires (see Appendix 9.A and Appendix 9.B) were developed and emailed to all delegates and their respective line managers, based on participant information provided by Premier Retail. Separate questionnaires were sent to delegates and line managers to ascertain any differences in opinion of the efficacy of the workshop, from a delegate versus a line manager perspective. The same questions were used, but asked from the two perspectives.

Participant questionnaires were dispatched on 18 September, requesting all participants to complete and return the questionnaire by 25 September. Line manager questionnaires were dispatched on 20 September, with a request to return by 22 September. The evaluation was conducted eight months after the first and three months after the final workshop. This time frame should have provided participants with sufficient opportunity to apply their newly acquired skills.

The Level 4 and 5 evaluations were based on assignments that were meant to be part of the original SODW process. Action plans were to be developed, but the response to the process was poor. As a consequence of this poor response and the fact that the template used did not allow for adequate collection and verification of the financial data, it was decided to reinitiate the action plan exercise. A copy of an action plan is shown in Appendix 9.C.

In consultation with the vice president of operations, special templates were developed to provide appropriate financial data to support evaluation at these levels. The vice president of operations was involved in designing the new template as well as initiating a new drive to complete and return the action plans. A requirement that each submission would be reviewed and signed off by respective line managers was instituted to ensure the reasonableness of the assignments and accuracy of the reported information. A further process of verification was conducted with the vice president of operations, whereby each submission was again evaluated to ensure that the formulae used were in line with company operating procedures and that there was verifiable evidence of improvements. In line with Guiding Principles 3 and 4, only those submissions that met these criteria were included in the final analysis. In addition, this process ensured the evaluation methodology adhered to Guiding Principle 8: "Extreme data items and unsupported claims are not included in the ROI calculation."

EVALUATION RESULTS

Questionnaire and Participant Details

Table 9.1 provides an overview of the participants (store managers) and respective line managers who were involved in the workshop. It also provides an indication of response rates and other useful summary information on the training budget, fully loaded costs for the workshops, data collection methods, and some detail about the reinitiation of the action plans that appeared to have lost some momentum.

Level 1 Evaluation: Reaction and Satisfaction

Table 9.2 provides a summary of the data relating to both participant and line manager responses to the Level 1 questions. This provides a useful comparison of how the participants versus their line managers perceived the workshop. Also included here are the aggregated responses from participants to the initial questionnaire circulated by the Supplier and Premier Retail immediately after each workshop. Because the questionnaires were different, direct comparisons are not possible. They do, however, provide a useful indication of general reaction to the workshop over different time frames.

Premier Retail has set a corporate objective of attaining a rating of 85 percent, or 4.2/5, on all training initiatives. The overall participant reaction and satisfaction rating of 4.56/5 (91.2%) is in line with this objective. This result is also aligned with the reaction and satisfaction rating (89.85%)

TABLE 9.1   Questionnaire and Participant Details

Total number of participants: Number surveyed:	93 90 used in the analysis (one subsequent resignation and two questionnaires not delivered)
Number of line managers:	24
Number of workshops run:	Eight workshops were run between January and September; only the first five are included in this evaluation
Number of respondents (participants):	31, of which 30 were useable. Not all respondents answered all the questions as required. Only information that was useable was included in the calculations.
Number of respondents (line managers):	Seven; all were used in the evaluation
Response rate: Participants: Line managers:	35% (33.3% useable) 30% (30% useable)
Workshop duration:	Three days per workshop, or 279 person days of training (five workshops)
Training budget:	R7,411,000.00
Fully loaded costs:	R2,803,594.00* *This is a "fully loaded" cost that includes development, program, participant cost to company, travel, administration and management, and assessor cost to company. Some of these costs are reflected in cost/budget centers other than the training budget. Costs have been calculated on the eight programs run between January and September.
Cost as a percentage of budget:	38%** **Bearing in mind the comment made above that some of the costs were allocated from other operating budgets and not exclusively from the training budget.
Data collection method: Timing for participant data collection: Timing for line managers data collection:	Email survey using a structured questionnaire Specifically designed template for action plans Dispatched on 18 September requesting all participants to complete and return the questionnaire by 25 September. Eight months following Workshop 1; three months following Workshop 5. Dispatched on 20 September with a request to return by 22 September; eight months following Workshop 1; three months following Workshop 5.

TABLE 9.2   Level 1: Reaction and Satisfaction

Question	Level 1: Reaction and Satisfaction	Participant Rating	Manager Rating
1	Worthwhile investment of participant's time	4.58	4.14
2	Relevance to job	4.67	4.43
3	Importance to job success	4.97	3.86
4	The workshop held interest	4.5	
4M	Speak enthusiastically about the workshop		3.86
5	Recommend to others	4.04	3.71
	Total	**4.56**	**4.0**
	Premier Retail Level 1 immediately after workshops	89.85%	N/A
	Supplier Level 1 immediately after workshops	4.5	N/A

achieved in a survey conducted by Premier Retail on conclusion of the workshops. It is also in line with the 4.5/5 reaction and satisfaction rating in the survey conducted by the Supplier. Both of these evaluations were conducted immediately after the workshops. The fact that participant ratings have been similar after a three- to eight-month time lag indicates a consistency of response to the SODW.

In the case of line managers, the overall reaction and satisfaction rating is slightly lower than the participant rating, but it still complies with the expected Premier Retail objective of 85 percent on all training interventions.

Of interest is the significant difference between the participant and line manager scores on Question 3, the importance of the workshop to job success: 4.97 versus 3.86. This indicates a need on the part of the Supplier to ensure closer line management involvement in the workshop development, objective setting, and after-course implementation and coaching process.

A line management perspective was not sought in the initial Premier Retail or Supplier surveys.

Level 2 Evaluation: Learning

Table 9.3 provides a summary of the responses to the Level 2 evaluation questions. The overall ratings for both participants and line managers are similar and compare favorably with the Premier Retail objective of 85 percent on all training initiatives.

The participant rating of 4.21/5 and line manager rating of 4.0/5 in terms of learning new knowledge and skills during the workshop is in line with the Premier Retail objective of 85 percent, or 4.2/5. The participant rating of the improvement in knowledge/skill in the ROI study is lower than that reflected in the Supplier study conducted immediately after the

TABLE 9.3   Level 2: Learning

Question	Level 2: Learning	Participant Rating	Manager Rating
6	New knowledge and skill learned from this workshop	4.04	3.71
7	Confidence in ability to apply the new knowledge/skills learned	4.42	4.14
8	Value of the feedback and input provided by the business coaches during the workshop in adding to the learning	4.17	4.14
	Total	**4.21**	**4.0**
9	Rating of improvement in knowledge/skill	75%	61%
	• Increasing "sales volumes"	60.0%	60.0%
	• Understanding and managing "cost of selling"	77.5%	65.5%
	• Understanding and managing "productivity"	75.0%	68.57%
	• Understanding and managing "customer satisfaction"	79.17%	68.57%
	• Understanding and managing "employee satisfaction"	83.33%	65.71%
	Supplier rating immediately after the workshop	4.54	N/A
	Participants' perception of change in understanding of concepts:		
	• Cost of selling	4.48	
	• Employee satisfaction	4.55	
	• Customer satisfaction	4.58	
	• Productivity	4.52	

workshops (4.21 versus 4.56). Again, one needs to bear in mind that the two questionnaires were different. The difference in ratings could also be attributed to the time delay in the ROI study.

More important, though, is the difference between the participants' ratings and the line managers' ratings (75% versus 61%) on overall improvement in knowledge/skills. Again this reflects the need to ensure that training of this nature is seen as a process and new learnings are reinforced, coached, and integrated into the job performance functions.

To facilitate learning, the workshop included participation by internal retail experts who acted as coaches and mentors during the training process. A rating of 4.17 by participants and 4.14 (see Question 8) by line managers indicates the value of this component of the workshop.

Level 3 Evaluation: Application

An evaluation of the workshop at Level 3, application, was not considered in the initial evaluation strategy. Table 9.4 summarizes the findings relating to the questions at this level. Of concern was the lack of useable data from the line managers on Question 13. This could have been due to a lack of an understanding of the concept of rank ordering.

On Question 10, To what extent have you/they applied the knowledge/ skills learned during the workshop, the line manager rating is significantly lower than the participant rating (3.13 versus 4.17), indicating a perceived lack of application of the learnings in the workplace. Again, this reflects a concern that the SODW was not developed as a fully integrated and managed training/learning/application/evaluation and coaching intervention.

The purpose of Questions 11 and 12 was to get an understanding of the criticality of the key components of the workshop and compare this to the perceived level of effectiveness. Both rate the application of the content as critical to the success of the business. Both rate application effectiveness as lower (indicating a potential performance gap), with the manager rating being significantly lower than the participant rating.

The relevance of Question 13 was to assess the relative use of the predetermined key critical components as strategies in the success of their businesses. Managing the impact of customer satisfaction was considered by the participants as a major focus in the success of their businesses. Unfortunately, the data provided by the line managers were not useable.

TABLE 9.4   Level 3: Application

Question	Level 3: Application	Participant Rating	Manager Rating
10	To what extent have you/they applied the knowledge/skills learned during the workshop?	4.17	3.13
11	How critical is applying the content of the workshop to your/their job success in terms of		
	• Increasing "sales volumes"	4.67	4.29
	• Managing the critical components of "cost of selling"	4.5	4.14
	• Managing the elements affecting "productivity"	4.67	4.29
	• Managing the impact of "customer satisfaction"	4.54	4.43
	• Managing the factors influencing "employee satisfaction"	4.54	4.29
12	How would you rate your/their level of effectiveness in applying the knowledge/skill learned during the workshop in terms of		
	• Increasing "sales volumes"	3.67	3.71
	• Managing the critical components of "cost of selling"	4.17	3.71
	• Managing the elements affecting "productivity"	4.07	4.0
	• Managing the impact of "customer satisfaction"	4.54	3.68
	• Managing the factors influencing "employee satisfaction"	4.0	3.43
13	Rank order the five critical components listed in terms of their use as a strategy in managing your/their business:		
	• Increasing "sales volumes"	3	Data not useable
	• Managing the critical components of "cost of selling"	4	
	• Managing the elements affecting "productivity"	2	
	• Managing the impact of "customer satisfaction"	1	
	• Managing the factors influencing "employee satisfaction"	5	

Action Plans

Questions 14 to 17 dealt with the action plans and learner diaries that were meant to be part of the SODW to apply and enhance learning. Table 9.5 provides the detail pertaining to the completion and submission of the action plans.

TABLE 9.5   Action Plan Details

Question	Level 3: Application—Action Plans	Participant	Line Manager
14	**Submission of action plans:** Immediately following the ODC Action plans complying with requirements	22, or 24% 7, or 8%	Data not useable
15	Reasons why learner diary and Action Plan were not submitted/signed off	Time pressures Work demands Training demands Opening new stores Other priorities Submission not required	Unaware of requirement
16	To what extent have you stayed on schedule with your planned action?	Very well (2) Well (1) Average(1) Not well (1)	No response
17	What additional support do you believe could be provided by management that would encourage and help you?		

Only 24 percent of participants submitted action plans, and of these only 7 or 8 percent met the specified requirements. The reasons given for nondelivery in this area ranged from time pressures, work demands, and other priorities to a belief that the submissions were not required. The general response from line managers was that they were unaware of the requirement.

The poor response in terms of the submission and quality of the action plans necessitated that a revised process be adopted. A new template and submission process for the action plans was formulated with the vice president of operations. The outcome of this process will be reported under Section 5 of this report.

Again, the poor response to the action plan component of the workshop highlights the need for initiatives of this nature to be a well-integrated component of the training, with management support, commitment, and accountability in the process.

In terms of Question 17, both participants and line managers indicated a need for follow through to ensure implementation of learning and support in the process. Participants specifically highlighted that development needs identified by the coaches during the workshop be addressed. There was also a request for on-the-job assistance when required.

Barriers and Enablers to Application

As part of the Level 3 evaluation, data were captured regarding barriers and enablers to implementation. Participants and line managers were asked to select the items they believed to be barriers and enablers to applying their learnings. Table 9.6 summarizes the findings for these two issues.

There are significantly more factors that impact positively on the application of the learnings than detract from it. Of note with regard to the

TABLE 9.6   Barriers and Enablers

Question	Level 3: Application—Action Plans	Participant	Line Manager
18	**Barriers to implementation**		
	No opportunity to use the skills	1	1
	Lack of management support	2	0
	Lack of support from colleagues/peers	2	1
	Insufficient knowledge and understanding	0	1
	Lack of confidence to apply the knowledge/skills	0	1
	Systems and processes that do not support the application	5	1
	The material does not apply to my job situation	0	0
	Other	0	1
19	**Enablers to implementation**		
	Opportunity to use the skills	15	2
	Management support	12	2
	Support from colleagues/peers	8	0
	Sufficient knowledge and understanding	14	1
	Confidence to apply the knowledge/skills	17	0
	Systems and processes that support the application	7	2
	The material is very appropriate to my job situation	12	0

barriers is the perception on the part of the participants that the systems and processes within the business do not support the application of the learning. The need for continued coaching and guidance appears to be a critical factor in the transfer of learning.

Level 4 Evaluation: Impact

As a result of the action plans exercise that formed part of the initial SODW not having been seen as an integral part of the learning and evaluation process and because the template used was not designed to provide the necessary financial information, with the appropriate supporting evidence, it was decided by the vice president of operations to reinstitute this exercise. A new template was designed with input from members of the executive team. This was redistributed with a request that the initiatives be revisited and the information be provided in terms of the new template requirements (see Appendix 9.C). It was also requested that the submissions be checked and approved by the respective line managers. The distribution went out under the signature of a senior vice president. A follow-up note was sent a week later to ensure that responses were received timeously. Table 9.7 reflects the status of the returns received.

Action Plan Initiatives

Store managers (participants) were asked to complete two action plan initiatives, requiring them to put the knowledge and skills gained on the SODW into practice. Table 9.8 provides an indication of the various business areas in which initiatives were possible and where initiatives were undertaken. Also indicated in Table 9.8 are the initiatives that have been included or excluded from the ROI calculations.

TABLE 9.7   Action Plan Returns

Participant Response to Action Plans	Number
Total number of action plans returned	35
Number of action plans from which data was used	24
Number of action plans excluded because of extreme data items	1
Number of action plans with inadequate or unsupported data	10

TABLE 9.8   Action Plan Initiatives

Action Plan Initiative	Included	Excluded
Cost of sales	10	2
Stock control		1
Merchandising		1
Queue management		1
Stock loss	6	1
Increasing sales	1	3
Stockroom productivity	4	7
Service centre management		2
Managing people		1
Printing and stationery expenses	1	
Remuneration ratio management	5	
Performance agreements		1
360 MOT		1
Customer service	1	5
Replenishment process	1	2
Stock assortment	1	
Managing profitability	1	
Training/development/talent management		2
Opening new accounts		2
Operational efficiencies		1
Standards and disciplines		1
Process management		
Stock takes		
Other expenditure control		
Frauds and disputes		
Introduction of food		
Bad debt		
Staff planning and scheduling		

Isolating the Effects of Training and Verification of Data

Participant estimates were used to isolate the effects of the training. The action plan template included a process whereby store managers were asked to estimate the contribution attributable to the training and were also asked to provide a confidence level associated with this estimate. These two factors were combined and used to adjust the final monetary figures used in the calculations.

Two further approaches were taken to ensure the reasonableness and accuracy of the data. Firstly, the template used specifically requested that supporting evidence be provided and individuals were requested to ensure that their line managers approved the submissions. Secondly, each submission was reviewed with the vice president of operations for accuracy and verification against reported management accounting information. Only those submissions that met the above criteria were included in the ROI calculations. It must also be remembered that participants were asked to report on two initiatives that they planned to implement as a result of the SODW. Again, only those initiatives that met the criteria of "reasonableness" and where the source of the information could be confirmed have been included in the ROI calculations. As a consequence of this, submissions from 10 participants have been excluded from the ROI calculations in their entirety. One has been excluded as it represents an extreme data item (Guiding Principle 8 of the ROI Methodology states that "extreme data items and unsupported claims should not be used in the ROI calculations"). Table 9.9 provides a summary of the initiatives that have been included in the ROI calculations.

Level 5 Evaluation: ROI

Data Conversion

To convert the business data to monetary value, several issues needed to be addressed. Firstly, as indicated in Table 9.8, there was a choice from a list of 28 possible initiatives that could have been made by participants on the SODW. These ranged from directly increasing sales to managing the cost of sales, cost control, people management, productivity, and efficiency initiatives to stock loss, shrinkage control, and so forth. For each initiative chosen and submitted, an appropriate conversion formula was used. These ranged from simple direct cost saving to standard costing to standard formulae used in the business. Each initiative was vetted by senior management for appropriateness and accuracy.

TABLE 9.9   Summary: Action Plan Initiatives

Participant	Assignment	Planned Action	Rand Value	Period	% Attributable to Training	% Confidence Level	Final Value
1	Cost of selling	Analysing P & L	233606	Sept–Dec	70	75	0
		Expenses control		Sept–Dec	70	75	122643
2	Cost of sales	Cutting on remuneration	30000	Sept–Jan	50	100	15000
		Controlling expenses	50000	Oct–Dec	50	100	25000
3	Reducing stock loss	Analysing needs/action	98640	Aug–Jan	65	85	54499
4	Decrease stock loss		131160	Aug–Nov	60	80	62957
5	Stockroom productivity	Analyse/correct layout	220	August	80	80	141
		Train staff	6603	Aug–Oct	80	80	4226
	Cost of selling	Control expenses/increase sales	109520	Aug–Oct	80	80	70093
6	Cost of selling	Control expenses/increase sales	160000	Aug–Jan	60	80	76800
7	Cost of selling	Analyse P&L/control expenses/increase sales	150000	Aug–Nov	60	80	72000
8	Stock losses	Analyse stock master/hazard counts	88716	Aug–Feb	50	70	31051
9	Stock losses	Stock loss action	106814	Aug–Jan	85	100	90792
	Printing/stationery expenses	Analyse wastage	74572	1 year	85	100	63386
10	Stockroom productivity	Training in stockroom process	7488	Sep–Feb	50	80	2995
11	Remuneration ratio	Training/team involvement	502912	3 months	50	100	251456
12	Increase sales	Train 10 canvassers	235121	April–Sept	25	80	47024
	Remuneration ratio	Control casual wages	1500	April–Sept	70	90	945
13	Cost of sales	Control variable costs/training	280765	July–Jan	25	100	70191
14	Remuneration	Training staff/tasking	150000	Oct–Dec	70	100	105000
15	Stock losses	Stock action plan	120000	Aug–Jan	80	80	76800

Participant	Assignment	Planned Action	Rand Value	Period	% Attributable to Training	% Confidence Level	Final Value
16	Replenishment process	Training/setting targets/tasking	3480	Aug–Jan	40	100	1392
		Sales growth	141689	Aug–Jan	40	100	56676
		Casual wages	1596	Aug–Jan	40	100	638
	Cost of selling	Increase sales/control expenses	328674	Aug–Jan	45	100	147903
17	Managing productivity	Recruit and train casuals/tasking	15000	July–Sept	80	80	9600
18	Cost of selling	Scheduling tool/training/pipeline management	500000	May–July	75	85	318750
	Stock assortment	Manage out-of-stock items	700000	July–Sept	70	75	367500
19	Stock losses	Planned action	285000	6 months	90	100	256500
	Remuneration	Bring in line with budget	97500	3 months	100	100	97500
20	Cost of selling Managing profitability	Analyse P & L/focus on out of lines	53710	Sept–Nov	80	100	42968
21	Cost of sales	Reduce losses/reduce expenses	87047	July–Nov	90	100	78342
22	Save on REM line	Productivity norms/multiskilling	313823	Sept–Jan	80	100	251058
23	Improve MOT	Mystery shopper/staff training/recruit casuals	472557	Sept–Dec	60	90	255181
24	Stockroom productivity	Analyse/training/tasking	6000	July–Sept	60	90	3240
	Cost of selling	Control expenses/increase sales	50000	July–Sept	50	100	25000

						Accumulated benefits	3155247
						Fully loaded costs	2803594
						Cost benefit	351653
						Benefit-cost ratio	1.13
						ROI (net benefits divided by costs × 100)	12.54

Extreme Data Points—Not Included in ROI Calculations

Participant	Assignment	Planned Action	Rand Value	Period	% Attributable to Training	% Confidence Level	Final Value
25	Increase sales	Multiskilling/set targets/canvassers	1883304	Nov–Jan	60	90	1016984

Mention of 35 participants with only 24 initiative submissions that were included in the ROI calculations brings into focus Guiding Principle 6: "If no improvement data are available for a population or from a specific source, it is assumed that little or no improvement has occurred." As a consequence, the full cost of all delegates was included in the cost calculation, with the potential values of the excluded initiatives not included for contribution.

Program Costs

Table 9.10 provides an outline of the fully loaded costs for the SODW. Adhering to Guiding Principle 10, "Costs for the solution should be fully loaded for ROI analysis," the costs listed in Table 9.10 have been included. As can be seen from Table 9.11, the fully loaded costs for the workshops totaled R2,803,594.

Benefit-Cost and ROI Calculations

As shown in Table 9.12, a benefit-cost ratio of 1:1.125 and an ROI of 12.54 percent was achieved for the SODW workshops under review.

Intangible Benefits

Intangible benefits are those impact measures not converted to money. There was considerable anecdotal and reported evidence to support the intangible benefits of the SODW workshops. These are shown from the positions of both participants and line managers in Table 9.13.

COMMUNICATING RESULTS

Two feedback meetings were organised during which the results of the evaluation were presented. The first was to the operations executive team and senior members of the Supplier organisation. The second was to the regional managers. A decision was taken to convey the results to a broader

TABLE 9.10   Fully Loaded Costs

Needs assessment	Workshop development costs
Workshop material	Equipment
Travel and accommodation	Facilities
Office supplies	Personnel cost to company

audience including the store managers and their immediate line managers at a convenient opportunity. Unfortunately, the latter event did not materialise. An appropriate forum could not be found, and other organisational needs became more important priorities.

OVERALL ASSESSMENT

From an overall perspective, the SODW appears to have been a successful training intervention. Both the participant and line manager review of the process on evaluation Levels 1, 2, and 3 and the anecdotal evidence collected are positive and generally meet or exceed the Premier Retail standard. From the information provided in the action plan initiatives, the workshops have yielded a positive ROI.

The intangible benefits of the ODC workshops that have been captured at different phases of the evaluation are significant and lead to a better understanding of the dynamics associated with a business of this nature, improved teamwork, and potentially improved business performance.

The evaluation study has highlighted the need to ensure that an evaluation methodology be built into the training and development process at initiation and forms an integral part of the learning, performance, and delivery management cycle.

LESSONS LEARNED

The key lessons learned from this exercise can be summarized as follows:

- Evaluation is not an after-the-event exercise. Evaluation needs to be strategically positioned as an integral component of any training or development intervention. Critical data gets lost or is not collected systematically if evaluation is done on a *post facto* basis.
- Line management involvement in every step of the training process—from needs analysis through to evaluation—must be sought.
- Evaluation questionnaires must be carefully designed to provide high-value information that can be used by the program developers, facilitators, delegates, line managers, and executives alike.
- If an action learning component is included as part of the training process, the templates used to collect and report on the initiatives must be designed to provide financial data that can be easily used to measure business impact and ROI.

TABLE 9.11 Fully Loaded Cost Information for Store Operations Development Workshop: Premier Retail Learning Department

Store Operations Development Workshop	Costing	25–27 Jan Pilot	14–16 March Workshop	04–06 April Workshop	15–17 May Workshop	05–07 June Workshop	11–13 July Workshop
Needs assessment cost							
Development cost			R 98,125.00	R 98,125.00	R 98,125.00	R 98,125.00	R 98,125.00
Workshop materials (files)		R 1,233.75	R 1,233.75	R 1,233.75	R 1,233.75	R 1,233.75	R 1,233.75
Facilitator cost							
Workshop cost		R 110,000.00	R 110,000.00	R 110,000.00	R 110,000.00	R 110,000.00	R 110,000.00
Equipment (including phones)		R 650.00	R 650.00	R 650.00	R 650.00	R 650.00	R 650.00
Travel and accommodation		R 7,636.00	R 47,127.00	R 42,865.00	R 25,933.00	R 44,178.00	R 27,733.00
Facilities (venue on pro-rata basis)		R 5,250.00	R 5,250.00	R 5,250.00	R 5,250.00	R 5,250.00	R 5,250.00
Office supplies, printing and reproduction		R 820.00	R 820.00	R 820.00	R 820.00	R 820.00	R 820.00
Salaries and benefits (cost to company) for HR, admin, assessment centre personnel, executives involved, participants	12061	R 164,859.00	R 107,013.00	R 114,336.00	R 96,860.00	R 107,198.00	R 95,443.00

Store Operations Development Workshop	Costing	25–27 Jan Pilot	14–16 March Workshop	04–06 April Workshop	15–17 May Workshop	05–07 June Workshop	11–13 July Workshop
Assessment centre employees—always six (average 28 hours per workshop)	8615	R 8,615.00	R 8,615.00	R 8,615.00	R 8,615.00	R 8,615.00	R 8,615.00
Premier Retail facilitator @ 24 hours		R 2,584.00	R 2,584.00	R 2,584.00	R 2,584.00	R 2,584.00	R 2,584.00
HR administrator average 12 hours per centre							
Business coaches aveage of 24 hours per SODW	0	R 27,507.00	R 27,323.00	R 27,323.00	R 13,292.00	R 13,292.00	R 13,292.00
Average delegate cost to company @ 24 hours	3446	R 126,153.00	R 68,491.00	R 75,814.00	R 72,369.00	R 82,707.00	R 70,952.00
Delegates	25						
Totals		R 388,573.75	R 370,218.75	R 373,279.75	R 338,871.75	R 367,454.75	R 339,254.75
							(continued)

245

TABLE 9.11   Continued

Store Operations Development Workshop	15–17 Aug Workshop	12–14 Sept Workshop	Totals
Needs assessment cost			0
Development cost		R 98,125.00	R 785,000.00
Workshop materials (files)	R 1,233.75	R 1,233.75	R 9,870.00
Facilitator cost			R 0.00
Workshop cost	R 110,000.00	R 110,000.00	R 880,000.00
Equipment (including phones)	R 650.00	R 650.00	R 5,200.00
Travel and accommodation	R 33,204.00	R 32,152.00	R 260,828.00
Facilities (venue on pro-rata basis)	R 5,250.00	R 5,250.00	R 42,000.00
Office supplies, printing and reproduction	R 820.00	R 820.00	R 6,560.00
Salaries and benefits (cost to company) for HR, admin, assessment centre personnel, executives involved, participants	**R 76,860.00**	**R 51,567.00**	**R 814,136.00**
Assessment centre employees—always six (average 28 hours per workshop)	R 8,615.00	R 8,615.00	
Premier Retail facilitator @ 24 hours	R 2,584.00	R 2,584.00	
HR administrator average 12 hours per centre		R 13,292.00	
Business coaches aveage of 24 hours per SODW	R 13,292.00		
Average delegate cost to company @ 24 hours	R 52,369.00	R 27,076.00	
Delegates			
Totals	**R 339,254.75**	**R 299,797.75**	**R 2,803,594.00**

TABLE 9.12

Level 5: ROI	SODW
Costs (fully loaded):	R2 803 594
Benefit:	R3 155 247
Net benefit:	R351 653
Benefit-cost ratio:	1:1.125
$\text{ROI (\%)} = \dfrac{\text{Benefits} - \text{Costs}}{\text{Costs}} \times 100$	12.54%

- A senior corporate executive should be appointed as program sponsor and be held accountable for the effective implementation and execution of the program.

- A short introduction to the ROI Methodology to key stakeholders will provide a uniform framework in which the design and execution of a training program can occur.

- The results of an evaluation exercise of this nature must be communicated to all stakeholders, particularly those involved in the training and who have taken the time and trouble to complete the questionnaires and the action plan requirement.

RESOURCES

Phillips, J.J. (2003). *Return on Investment in Training and Performance Improvement Programs.* New York: Butterworth-Heinemann.

Phillips, P.P., J.J. Phillips, R.D. Stone, and H. Burkett. (2007). *The ROI Fieldbook: Strategies for Implementing ROI in HR and Training.* New York: Butterworth-Heinemann.

QUESTIONS FOR DISCUSSION

Bearing in mind that the evaluation of the SODW was conducted on a *post facto* basis, comment on the methodology adopted by the evaluators.

1. What is your view on including and reporting aggregated data collected using different questionnaires, administered at different times?

2. What do you think could have been done differently to get better responses to the original as well as the subsequent action plans?

3. Would you consider a 12.54 percent ROI adequate for a program of this nature?

TABLE 9.13 Anecdotal and Intangible Benefits

Participant/Store Manager	Line/Regional Manager
• The value of this intervention lies in the provision of a strategic viewpoint of the business as a whole, aiding understanding of the business in total and stimulating strategic thinking (nine responses).	• This intervention provided the bigger picture of the work of delegates, aiding understanding of the total business.
• The importance of a systems view was also stressed by these respondents—i.e., a change in one component affects one or more components, which influence performance.	• Enhanced focus on customer service.
• Understanding of every part of our business.	• Higher productivity.
• Maximum utilisation of resources.	• Greater understanding of productivity and scheduling.
• A better understanding and integrating of all of the departments (two responses).	• Training pitched at store management level and they will greatly benefit from this training.
• Focus orientation on specific goals.	• Better understanding of all Premier Retail processes.
• A better understanding of COS (two responses).	• More confidence in total business acumen.
• Attention to detail—not just completing tasks and go home.	• Improved productivity in stockrooms.
• Understanding how each line in the profit and loss affects our business either positively or negatively.	• Becoming a team player.
• Tasking improved.	• Training and development.
• Good on using scheduling tool.	• Stockroom productivity has increased.
• New accounts improved.	• People management.
• Level of productivity has increased in the store.	• Sales percentage growth.
• More ownership has been taken by individuals.	• Stock turn.
• Level of communication has also increased, staff now speaks more freely.	• Turnaround in performance in Botswana.
• Knowledge to run business.	• Improvement in MOT standards.
• Store standards improved.	• Understanding of process and the flows of stockroom and the productivity norms.
• Staff more positive.	
• Building good relationships with team members.	
• Staff are very positive and optimistic with training methods and changes of the day-to-day running of the business.	
• Better understanding of throughput and output of units and the effect on the business.	
• Scheduling as per productivity norms.	

Participant/Store Manager	Line/Regional Manager
• Teamwork (two responses). • Planning. • Higher performance people. • Self-confidence. • Better understanding of staff strength in order to determine the proper skills utilisation in correct areas. • Thinking out of the box. • Going an extra mile always. • More effective planning and scheduling. • Better understanding and effectively managing processes. • Understanding productivity. • Better understanding of stockroom productivity and scheduling correctly. • Lower staff turnover. • Increasing sales. • Reducing losses. • Understanding that I can achieve results through my people with the correct training and motivation and standards set. • Understanding the stockroom productivity more in detail and analysing the P & L. • Within the business unit, I, along with my management team, have attained a bonded team working our store.	• Enhanced focus on goal orientation. • Better understanding how COS can be minimised. • Importance of multiskilling • Corrective implementation of IDP.

ABOUT THE AUTHOR

J. H. (Jay) Owens is the Director for Africa for the ROI Institute. With careers in manufacturing, academia, and consulting, he brings a wealth of experience to the fields of organisational effectiveness, human resource development, training, and evaluation. Jay lives in Johannesburg, South Africa, and works extensively with local and international organisations operating on the continent.

Appendix 9.A   Participant Questionnaire

To: (Participant's Name) _____

Workshop: Store Operations Development Workshop

Date attended: (Date attended) _____

Dear _____ ,

The ROI Institute is an independent organisation specialising in the evaluation of training and human performance processes. We have been retained to conduct an independent evaluation of the Store Operations Development Workshop. The purpose is to provide all parties with information to ensure the effectiveness of the workshops. Your input in the process is essential, and we value the time you will spend completing this questionnaire. We guarantee that the information you provide will be held in the strictest confidence. All information will be presented in aggregated form only, with nothing being traced back to individuals.

Please spend some time reflecting on the workshop content and learning processes and answer the following questions:

	Strongly Agree			Strongly Disagree		
REACTION	5	4	3	2	1	N/A
1. The workshop was a worthwhile investment in my time and effort.						
2. The workshop was relevant to my work—I can use the skills in my job.						
3. The workshop is important to my job success.						
4. The workshop held my interest—I was engaged throughout.						
5. I have recommended the workshop to others.						

	Strongly Agree			Strongly Disagree		
LEARNING	5	4	3	2	1	N/A
6. I learned new knowledge and skill from this workshop.						
7. I am confident in my ability to apply the new knowledge/skills learned.						
	Very Valuable		Of Little Value		N/A	
8. I found the feedback and input provided by the business coaches during the workshop in adding to my learning to be						
	Low					High
	0%	20%	40%	60%	80%	100%
9. Rate your level of improvement in skill or knowledge derived from the workshop content in the following areas. Where **0%** = no improvement **100%** = significant improvement.						
a. Increasing sales volumes						
b. Understanding and managing the critical components of cost of selling in my business						
c. Understanding and managing the elements affecting Productivity in my business						
d. Understanding and managing the impact of customer satisfaction in my business						
e. Understanding and managing the factors influencing employee satisfaction						
	Frequently			Infrequently		
APPLICATION	5	4	3	2	1	N/A
10. To what extent have you applied the knowledge/ skills learned during the workshop.						

	Extremely	Not at all	N/A
11. How critical is applying the content of the workshop to your job success in terms of			
a. Increasing sales volumes			
b. Understanding and managing the critical components of cost of selling in my business			
c. Understanding and managing the elements affecting productivity in my business			
d. Understanding and managing the impact of customer satisfaction in my business			
e. Understanding and managing the factors influencing employee satisfaction			

	High	Low	N/A
12. How would you rate your level of effectiveness in applying the knowledge/skill learned during the workshop in terms of			
a. Increasing sales volumes			
b. Managing the critical components of cost of selling in my business			
c. Managing the elements affecting productivity in my business			
d. Managing the impact of customer satisfaction in my business			
e. Managing the factors influencing employee satisfaction in my business			

	Frequently				Infrequently
	5	4	3	2	1
13. Rank order the five components listed above in terms of your use as a strategy in managing the success of your business.					
a. Increasing sales volumes					
b. Managing the critical components of cost of selling in my business					
c. Managing the elements affecting productivity in my business					
d. Managing the impact of customer satisfaction in my business					
e. Managing the factors influencing employee satisfaction in my business					

	Yes	No
14. Have you submitted your Learning Implementation Action Plan?		

15. If you answered no to the above question, what has prevented you from doing so?

	Very well	Not well
16. If you answered yes to the above question, to what extent have you stayed on schedule with your planned action.		

17. What additional support could be provided by management that would help you apply the knowledge/skills learned at the workshop?

   a.

   b.

   c.

BARRIERS/ENABLERS TO APPLICATION	Check
18. Which of the following deterred or prevented you from applying the knowledge/skills learned at the workshop? (Check all that apply)	
No opportunity to use the skills	
Lack of management support	
Lack of support from colleagues/peers	
Insufficient knowledge and understanding	
Lack of confidence to apply the knowledge/skills	
Systems and processes within the business do not support the application	
The material does not apply to my job situation	
Other	
If you specified "other," please explain here:	

	Check
19. Which of the following supported you in applying the knowledge/skills learned at the workshop? (Check all that apply)	
Opportunity to use the skills	
Management support	
Support from colleagues/peers	
Sufficient knowledge and understanding	
Confidence to apply the knowledge/skills	
Systems and processes within the business actively support the application	
The material is very appropriate to my job situation	
Other	

If you specified "other," please explain here:

OTHER PERSONAL AND ORGANISATIONAL BENEFITS

20. Please list below some of the personal and organisational benefits you have experienced as a result of attending the workshop.

a.
b.
c.
d.
e.

FEEDBACK

21. What suggestions can you give to the developers of the workshop to make it more relevant to your job?

a.
b.
c.
d.
e.

THANKS   Thank you, we really value the time and effort you have taken to complete this questionnaire.

Appendix 9.B   Line Manager Questionnaire

To: <u>Line Manager</u>

Dear: <u>(Name)</u>

The ROI Institute is an independent organisation specialising in the evaluation of training and human performance processes. We have been retained to conduct an independent evaluation of the Store Operations Development Workshop created for Premier Retail. The purpose is to provide all parties with information to ensure the effectiveness of the workshops. Your input in the process is essential, and we value the time you will spend completing this questionnaire. We guarantee that the information you provide will be held in the strictest confidence. All information will be presented in aggregated form only, with nothing being traced back to individuals.

The records indicate that the following people reporting to you attended the SODW

Name: _____   Workshop Attended: _____

Participant name: _____   Date attended: _____

Participant name: _____   Date attended: _____

Please spend some time reflecting on the workshop content and learning processes and answer the following questions as you perceive the value of the SODW on their learning and performance. We know that individuals may have been influenced differently by the SODW experience, but we are seeking an overall and general response from you in this survey.

	Strongly Agree			Strongly Disagree		
REACTION	5	4	3	2	1	N/A
1. The workshop was a worthwhile investment in their time and effort.						
2. The workshop was relevant to their work—they can use the skills in their jobs.						
3. The workshop is important to their job success.						
4. They speak enthusiastically about the workshop.						
5. I have recommended the workshop to others.						

LEARNING	Strongly Agree			Strongly Disagree		
	5	4	3	2	1	N/A
6 They learned new knowledge and skill from this workshop.						
7. I am confident in their ability to apply the new knowledge/skills learned.						
8. I found the feedback and input provided by the business coaches during the workshop to have added value to their learning.						
	Low					High
	0%	20%	40%	60%	80%	100%
9. How would you rate their level of improvement in skill or knowledge derived from the workshop content in the following areas. Where: **0%** = no improvement **100%** = significant improvement.						
a. Increasing sales volumes						
b. Understanding and managing the critical components of cost of selling in their business						
c. Understanding and managing the elements affecting productivity in their business						
d. Understanding and managing the impact of customer satisfaction in their business						
e. Understanding and managing the factors influencing employee satisfaction in their business						
APPLICATION	Frequently			Infrequently		
	5	4	3	2	1	N/A
10. To what extent have they applied the knowledge/skills learned during the workshop.						

	Extremely	Not at all	N/A
11. How critical is applying the content of the workshop to their job success in terms of			
a. Increasing sales volumes			
b. Understanding and managing the critical components of cost of selling in their business			
c. Understanding and managing the elements affecting productivity in their business			
d. Understanding and managing the impact of customer satisfaction in their business			
e. Understanding and managing the factors influencing employee satisfaction in their business			
	High	**Low**	**N/A**
12. How would you rate their level of effectiveness in applying the knowledge/skill learned during the workshop in terms of			
a. Increasing sales volumes			
b. Managing the critical components of cost of selling in their business			
c. Managing the elements affecting productivity in their business			
d. Managing the impact of customer satisfaction in their business			
e. Managing the factors influencing employee satisfaction in their business			

	Frequently			Infrequently	
	5	4	3	2	1
13. Rank order the five components listed above in terms of how you have seen them used as a strategy by your staff in managing the success of their businesses.					
a. Increasing sales volumes					
b. Managing the critical components of cost of selling in their business					
c. Managing the elements affecting productivity in their business					
d. Managing the impact of customer satisfaction in their business					
e. Managing the factors influencing employee satisfaction in their business					

	Yes	No
14. Have you signed off and has a Learning Implementation action plan been submitted for each individual?		
15. If you answered no to the above question, what has prevented you/them from doing so?		

	Very well	Not well
16. If you answered yes to the above question, to what extent do you believe they have stayed on schedule with their planned actions.		
17. What additional support do you believe could be provided by management that would help them in applying the knowledge/skills learned at the workshop?		
a.		
b.		
c.		

BARRIERS/ENABLERS TO APPLICATION	Check
18. Which of the following do you believe may have deterred or prevented them from applying the knowledge/skills learned at the workshop? (Check all that apply)	
No opportunity to use the skills	
Lack of management support	
Lack of support from colleagues/peers	
Insufficient knowledge and understanding	
Lack of confidence to apply the knowledge/skills	
Systems and processes within the business do not support the application	
The material does not apply to their job situation	
Not enough time	
Other	
If you specified "other," please explain here:	

	Check
19. Which of the following do you believe may have supported them in applying the knowledge/skills learned at the workshop? (Check all that apply)	
Opportunity to use the skills	
Management support	
Support from colleagues/peers	
Sufficient knowledge and understanding	
Confidence to apply the knowledge/skills	
Systems and processes within the business actively support the application	
The material is very appropriate to their job situation	
Enough time to implement the new learnings	
Other	
If you specified "other," please explain here:	

OTHER PERSONAL AND ORGANISATIONAL BENEFITS
20. Please list below some of the personal and other organisational benefits you have seen from your staff as a result of attending the workshop.
a.
b.
c.
d.
e.

FEEDBACK
21. What suggestions can you give to the developers of the workshop to make it more relevant to the jobs of those working for you?
a.
b.
c.
d.
e.
THANKS   Thank you, we really value the time and effort you have taken to complete this survey.

Appendix 9.C   Store Operations Development Workshop: Evaluating the Impact of Learning

Name: _____

Position: _____

Workshop: _____

Date attended: _____

The purpose of this exercise is to evaluate the impact the Store Operations Development Workshops have had on the business and to determine the return on investment of the training. In order to do this, we need your help in revisiting the **Action Plan Initiatives** exercise you completed after attending the SODW and providing the information requested below.

This relates to the two initiatives you were asked to implement at the end of the workshop.

Your cooperation in this matter is greatly appreciated.

RESULTS: 1st Application
Please provide evidence to support your actions and results

1. Describe the opportunity in your business area you chose to address

Planned actions taken to address the opportunity

What specific business measures did these actions impact

Business measure before attending ODC
Business measure change
Rand value of change
Review period

Please provide evidence to support your actions and results

2. Will this action have an impact (positive or negative) on

a. Customer service:	Explain:
b. Employee satisfaction:	Explain:

3. In your view, were there any other factors that could have influenced (positively or negatively) the results during the period under review?

a.

b.

c.

4. Recognising that the other factors could have influenced the outcome, estimate the % of improvement that you can directly attribute to actions taken as a consequence of the training received at the workshop. Express as a percentage out of 100%—i.e. if only 60% of the change can be attributed to the new learning and action, then enter 60 here.

5. What confidence do you place in the estimate you have provided above? A **0%** is no confidence and a **100%** represents certainty

RESULTS: 2nd Application

Please provide evidence to support your actions and results

1. Describe the opportunity in your business area you chose to address

Planned actions taken to address the opportunity

What specific business measures will these actions impact

Business measure before attending ODC

Business measure change

Rand value of change

Review period

Please provide evidence to support your actions and results

2. Will this action have an impact (positive or negative) on

a. Customer service:	Explain:

b. Employee satisfaction:	Explain:

3. In your view, were there any other factors that could have influenced the results (positively or negatively) during the period under review?
a.
b.
c.
4. Recognising that the other factors could have influenced the outcome, estimate the **%** of improvement that you can directly attribute to actions taken as a consequence of the training received at the workshop. Express as a percentage out of **100%**—i.e. if only **60%** of the change can be attributed to the new learning and action, then enter 60 here.
5. Confidence level. What confidence do you place in the estimate you have provided above? A **0%** is no confidence and a **100%** represents certainty

RESULTS: Other Benefits
In addition to the above, are there any other results that have been achieved as a consequence of attending the Store Operations Development Workshop?
Describe the result
a.
b.
c.
Business measure impacted
a.
b.
c.

Estimated rand value of the impact (if possible)
a.
b.
c.
Confidence level %
a.
b.
c.
Sign-Off Delegate: _____ Date: _____ Region manager: _____ Date: _____

10

Measuring the ROI in Business Performance Management

Garanti Bank
Turkey

Esra Eseroğlu and Önder Korkmaz

This case was prepared to serve as a basis for discussion rather than an illustration of either effective or ineffective administrative and management practices. Names, dates, places, and data may have been disguised at the request of the author or organization.

Abstract

This case study describes the evaluation of Garanti Bank's Garanti Leadership Academy Business Performance Management Training. "Business Performance Management" (BPM) is one of the trainings in "Garanti Leadership Academy" (GLA1 in English; GYA1 in Turkish), which aims to improve the competencies of the target group related to their job specifically. GLA1 is a two-year modular program whose target group is talents in branches. The ROI is 921 percent, which is satisfactory for the program team, sponsors, and stakeholders alike. This shows that not only has participant performance increased, but also there are many intangible benefits. The main recommendation was to make the training design according to ROI Methodology before the training takes place. Moreover, there should be information concerning all stakeholders for a future ROI study to understand the targets, whether the tools are right, and whether the content of the training can meet the targets wanted.

PROGRAM BACKGROUND

As the talent programs gain importance around the world day by day, Garanti Bank is one of the entrepreneurs in this area. GLA1 is a banking and leadership program that is considerably long (two years) and expensive but strategically vital to the top management. The target group is branch manager candidates with three to five years' experience, which we call High Potentials (HI-POs). The program is mainly structured in three modules. The modules are shown in Figure 10.1.

All of the modules are centralized through competencies and aim to develop these competencies not only through training, but also through all the pre-work and follow-up. The design process of the training is carefully made because of several reasons:

- The program is a long and expensive process that needs attention.
- The target group works in branches that need quick data, solutions, and follow-up, as their business is located in a highly competitive structure and their work has a tight schedule.
- All the participants are evaluated as future leaders within the bank, which needs attention and follow-up during and after the program.

The methodology is structured around experiential learning within in-class trainings that are highly interactive and consist of cases, role play, and

FIGURE 10.1 Program Modules

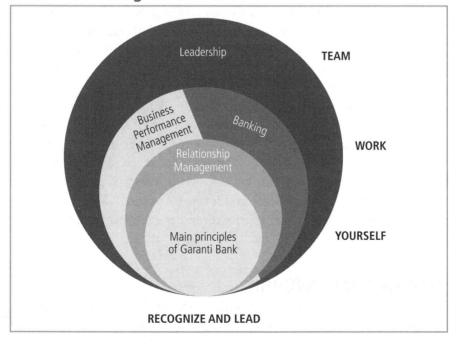

simulations. Nonetheless, the follow-ups are made through performance contracts that are monitored by the training department and the participants' branch managers. They found a complicated training process that allowed them to understand their competencies, especially the ones that needed attention and development.

The needs assessment was a complicated and long process that started from the strategic presentation of the Learning and Development (L&D) staff, clarified as a need from top management. After the request, we interviewed region and branch managers to specify the needs of the high performers in the branches. For a statistically significant analysis, we checked the Assessment Center results to understand which competencies were their weak ones. If we checked their needs in all five levels including the target group, stakeholders, and sponsors, in the first and second level, participants should have complex training as they are already talented. In the third level, they should have better management of themselves, their work, and possible teams. In the fourth level, the expectation is an increase in their performance and, specifically, sales volume.

Sponsors are mainly top management, regional managers, and branch managers, as they are mainly responsible for the target group's performance. Key stakeholders of the training program are L&D, various solution providers, branch managers, and Human Resources.

BPM is located in the second module, which is "managing your job." It is three days of training to develop main competencies related to managing our daily lives or work, mainly in branches. The target group consists of 45 people who are talented members of our branches.

Program Objectives

BPM is designed to develop four main competencies of the participants:

- analytical thinking
- decision making
- result orientation
- planning and time management.

  At the end of the training, participants can

- analyze quantitative, qualitative, and other data sources
- build causal links between data

- argue an analogy from data and information by making an analysis
- use the analysis to clarify business opportunities and create new ones
- prioritize the job to be done
- plan the to-do list in line with importance and urgency
- use SMART planning
- question risks, benefits, and costs in decision making
- make decisions in expected duration
- examine the possible results of the decisions on others
- follow the works until they are done
- use time planning effectively in finalizing the work.[1]

During the training, participants will learn all the tools effectively (such as SPIN, SWOT, etc.) by having theory and cases taken from both daily life and the branches. They have all these cases, games, and simulations during training to make adaptation to all of these tools easier. At the end of the training, they have a performance contract in line with these competencies and homework in which they should analyze their portfolios in the branches, according to the tools that they have just learned.

The objectives for the training at every level are summarized in Table 10.1.

Evaluation Purpose

BPM is especially chosen for the ROI study for the following reasons:

- The program and the training is strategically important for the sponsors and the stakeholders.[2]
- The target group is also strategically important for the bank as they are talents of the branches whom we can call future branch managers.[3]
- The cost of the program is considerably higher within the bank, which needs attention because it is one of the most expensive trainings.

---

[1] In Appendix 10.A, you can find the session plan of the BPM.

[2] The sponsors consist of the executive team and the line of businesses in the headquarters.

[3] At the end of the programme, if their performance is still good, they go into the assessment process and are promoted to branch managers.

TABLE 10.1   Objectives

Levels	Broad Objectives
1. Reaction	The evaluation of the training should be greater than 4,7.
2. Learning	Know SWOT, SPINA, GRID, PMI, and Urgency/Importance tools. Improve writing the SMART targets. Understand business performance management and its details in a micro way.
3. Application	Do not use assumptions. Analyze quantitative and qualitative data. Use casual links between data. Prioritize job. Plan according to the importance and urgency. Clarify smart targets in action planning. Use analysis for new job opportunities. Understand the possible results of decisions. Follow up works.
4. Impact	Increase sales and profitability by using the tools learned.

■ The content of the training consists of real-life situations such as preparing branch budgets and so forth, and all these situations are strategically important for the bank.

The ROI study of the training aims to

■ understand whether these tools are used effectively through their daily lives

■ challenge if the progress in specified competencies is positive

■ analyze whether they can turn this performance tool into numbers such as profitability and volume and if there is a positive ROI for the bank.

Our project was one of the ROI studies presented to the CEO and top management in a strategic meeting. They expressed their satisfaction with the results, which is highly favorable for us. You can find the general structure of our training program and what we measured in Figure 10.2.

FIGURE 10.2   GLA1 Program Structure

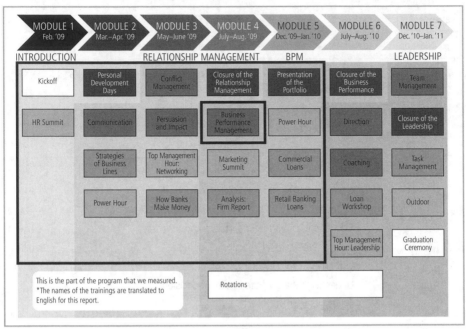

EVALUATION METHODOLOGY

The five-level evaluation framework and ROI Methodology were used as the basis for the evauation.

Data Collection and Assessment Tools

A variety of data collection and assessment tools allowed us to collect multiple types of data to measure the success of the BPM.

End-of-Program Questionnaire

This questionnaire is used for understanding the first reaction of the participants in terms of the training as a whole, the skills of the trainer, and the content of the training. It is a formal questionnaire that is used for every training program at the bank and evaluated in the online environment. You can find the general questionnaire in Appendix 10.A.

Assignment

After one month, we gave an assignment to find out if they had learned the reporting and assisting tools. In the assignment, all the participants were asked to make a SPIN (Situation-Problem-Implications-Needs), SWOT (Strength, Weakness, Opportunity, and Threat), and impact-effort and importance-urgency analysis of their portfolios by using the tools they learned during the training. We asked them to clarify which tools from among the ones they learned during training they used to make this analysis. After this analysis, they were asked to make an action plan using SMART objectives. For the whole task, they were prepared not only for analysis, but also for the presentation that they made via a webinar to the trainers and regional and branch managers. You can find the assignment in Appendix 10.B.

Simulation

After three months, we had a one-day workshop called "Closure of the BPM Training." In the simulation, the participants took roles in different cases related to the competencies and also evaluated by the trainers on a one-by-one basis. In the evaluation part, both the trainer and the participant were asked to evaluate the competencies.

Competency-Based Observation Form

After the program, the managers of the participants were asked to evaluate the competencies of their employees. The participants also completed an evaluation form for a self-assessment to demonstrate their progress in the competencies and in their subbehavioral indicators. The process was carried out by an external independent firm, which promises us an evaluation that is objective in all ways. You can find a sample form in Appendix 10.C.

Competency-Based Survey

The competency-based survey was created by a consulting firm and us to understand how participants can rate their ability in the competencies that GLA1 emphasized. It was sent online to make it objective and asked participants to rate themselves. You can find a part of it in Appendix 10.D.

Performance Record

To understand the impact of the BPM, the performance record form was used. Performance records are used for performance evaluations of the portfolio managers by having the numbers in profitability and target/realization at the end of the year. We customized the form according to our needs and let participants fill it in using figures located in the online system of the bank.

All the data collection methods generated the necessary data to help us understand through different perspectives what we had done. In Table 10.2, you can find which tools we used for each evaluation level.

Another vital issue is the timing of data collection. For leadership programs such as GLA1, the impact is generally a long-term investment, but the competencies of BPM are ones from which we can capture benefits in a considerably shorter time. The application and impact data is gathered through one year to understand the effects.

Data Collection and ROI Analysis Plans

The impact study is based on performance records and uses a standard form that the branch workers fill out. All the records are taken by them from an online system. For understanding the direct contribution of the training, it is left to the assessment of the participants, as they are considered the best source of this information in the ROI Methodology. We will give details on this in the section titled Isolating the Effect of Training. In Figure 10.3, you can find an overview of the ROI Methodology and where our study fits within it.

Tables 10.3 and 10.4 are the data collection and ROI analysis plans, respectively. These plans describe our approach to evaluating the project.

TABLE 10.2 Data Tools in Levels of Evaluation

	Level 1 Reaction to Program	Level 2 Learning	Level 3 Application	Level 4 Impact	Costs
End-of-program questionnaire	X				
Assignment		X			
Simulation		X			
Competency-based observation form			X		
Performance record				X	
Records of the bank					X

FIGURE 10.3 ROI Methodology

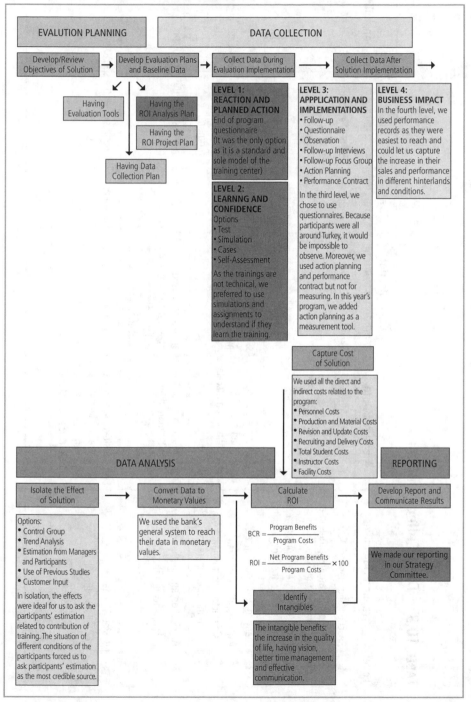

TABLE 10.3 Data Collection Plan

Level	Training Objectives	Measures/Data	Data Collection Method/Instrument	Data Sources	Timing	Responsibility
1	Reaction and Planned Action Participants rate the program as relevant to their jobs. Participants rate the program as important to their job success.	4,7 out of 5 on a 5-point rating scale	Questionnaires	Participants	End of the program	L&D staff
2	Learning and Confidence Participants demonstrate satisfactory performance on each major competency.	Average of the participant evaluation should be more than 70 on a scale of 100.	Assignment Simulation	Facilitator	1 month after the program 3 months after the program	Facilitator Facilitator and L&D staff
3	Application and Implementation Participants use the competencies daily in their jobs.	Scores of all competencies should be more than 4.	Competency-based observation form that includes all subbehavioral indicators	Participants Participants' managers	3 months after the program	L&D staff
4	Business Impact Portfolio profitability Efficiency ratio	Every positive performance measure should increase 3%; negative ones should decrease 3%.	Performance records	Participants	6 months after the program	L&D staff
5	ROI: 40%					

TABLE 10.4 ROI Analysis Plan

Data Items (Usually Level 4)	Methods for Isolating the Effects of the Program	Methods of Converting Data to Monetary Values	Cost Categories	Intangible Benefits	Communication Targets for Final Report	Comments
Portfolio profitability	Participant estimates	Standard value	Needs assessment	Improved employee job satisfaction	Participants	A high response rate is needed.
			Program development Facilitation fees Meals and refreshments	Improved communication	Participants' managers Senior executives	
			Facilities	Time savings	L&D staff	
			Participant travel Participant salaries Benefits		HR staff	
			Evaluation		Prospective participants Learning and development Strategy committee	

THE RESULTS

Reaction and Satisfaction

Data Collection

The first level of evaluation matters for us in redesigning our trainings. For that purpose, we use a standard end-of-program questionnaire. As we have mentioned, this will give us an idea about the overall training, the content, and the trainer.

The response profile of the first level was our participants in BPM, and they were the ones who could give the most credible data on the first level. There were 48 participants in the training. We decided to administer our questionnaire in a hard-copy version so we would have a 100 percent response rate.[4] As the participants had been involved in a lengthy program, they were not like usual participants who came only for one training session and did not give feedback. All the participants were motivated to give feedback, and there was not any barrier in the first level.

The end-of-program questionnaire can be found in Appendix 10.A. The questionnaire was given to all participants at the end of the class by L&D staff. Participants were given a reasonable amount of time to fill in the forms and were not required to give their names. Moreover, the participants were asked to give feedback by email if they wanted to. The questionnaire contains the following topics:

- training program: relevant information according to the needs, suitable content for the level of information that the participants have, the adequacy of the methods and instances, the attention of other participants to the training, the length of the training (short, long, or enough)
- the trainer's specialization in the topic, effective time usage, and presentation skills
- whether the trainer is suitable for the training and willing to promote the training to other employees.

Data Analysis and Results

In our training, we aimed for scores of at least 4,7 out of 5 in participants' reaction to the training overall and the trainer. The training score is 4,76

---

4 After the ROI training, we created an online version of the questionnaire.

out of 5, and the trainer score is 4,87 out of 5. The vital evaluation is related to whether the training contains topics relevant to the needs of the participants. They graded it as 4,82, which exceeded our objective.

We also asked if participants wanted to give feedback on the content and trainer. Their feedback included the following comments:

"Cases related to bank is really beneficial for me, it really worked in terms of understanding my portfolio."

"The content was productive and suitable for my needs."

"It really matters for me to be result oriented and plan again according to the changing conditions."

As we mentioned in the previous section, all of this reaction data matters for the designers of the training; it is a chance to understand how the participants perceive the content and if the trainer is successful in the training. It gives us the opportunity to redesign the inefficient parts and make it more suitable to the needs of the bank. The first level does not matter to the sponsors, especially top management. For us, the scores exceeded our expectations, so for the learning level measurement, we assumed that participants had enough tools to show satisfactory performance on each competency.

Learning
Data Collection

BPM is a training program for which it is hard to use traditional tests and other end-of-class materials to measure the learning. We used an assignment that would show us whether participants were clear enough to use all the tools, reporting methods, and analysis methods effectively. They were requested to use SPIN, SWOT, impact/effort, and importance/urgency analysis of their portfolios[5] and clarify the necessary actions in their action plans. To understand their learning level, we gave them a specific time and they made a presentation via webinar to the trainer and L&D personnel. Moreover, their managers were invited to attend. Another method to measure the learning was informal: We had closure training three months after the actual training, in which they had role plays and

---

[5] The templates and selection from participants' presentations are in Appendix 10.C.

had feedback from the trainer about the related competencies. We did not use it as an evaluation tool, as the competencies were mainly the ones that cannot be observed.

Data Analysis and Results

The evaluation criteria were mainly related to the content, presentation skills, and participants' ability to show effectiveness in the competencies and related tools. Forty-five out of 46[6] participants attended the presentation session. The average was 77,6, which also surpassed our objectives. In the assignment, the participants found the chance to apply the analysis tools, decided to take actions in necessary areas, made an action plan with timing, and kept in mind to be result oriented. The assignment and presentation were effective in terms of understanding their skills to capture what they had learned.

The results of Level 2 are still important for us, the L&D personnel, as we became sure about what the participants had learned and that they had the chance for application in their daily lives. If the scores had been lower than expected, we would have redesigned and changed our ROI plan according to that. All these results in Level 2 led us to believe that all the participants were competent about application if they would not meet any barriers.

Application and Implementation

Data Collection

All the trainings in GLA1 are competency based, so the best measure in the application level should be a model that is competency based. The measure in the third level was critical for us as it was the only way to understand if they applied the tools that can lead to an improvement in their performance.

Together with a consultancy firm, we formed a new competency-based survey, based on all the competencies that we include in our trainings. In every competency, there were the behaviors that we expect from that competency. In an online system, the participants were asked to fill in the form. A 5-point scale was used: 1 = "Completely disagree," 2 = "Disagree,"

---

[6] While the programme was going on, there were two participants from the bank who quit.

3 = "Neutral," 4 = "Agree," and 5 = "Completely agree." For us, the desirable level for each competency should be greater than 4. After two weeks, we got the results from the consulting firm.

Data Analysis and Results

The results were for every competency. The following scores represent the average of all participants:

- analytical thinking, 4,11
- conflict management, 4,02
- persuasion and impact, 4,17
- decision making, 4,20
- planning and time management, 4,20
- result orientation, 4,45.

In all levels, the results are at the desirable level, which shows us that participants applied the tools. It can be said that we can measure Level 4 in the next step, as we expect an increase in their performance because they applied all the tools.

Moreover, we asked participants to identify the enablers and barriers that influenced their implementing what they had learned from the training. The biggest barrier was their workload, as all of them were working in branches, which led them to manage their time ineffectively. Also, they pointed out that they sometimes had trouble getting help from their first-line managers. Besides, there were enablers that forced them to apply what they had learned. The talent program kept their motivation considerably high. They tried to apply their action plans, and we watched their progress closely, which led to many follow-ups.

Business Impact
Data Collection

The most important part of the evaluation for the top management started with Level 4, which was "Business Impact." For a participant who had the chance of implementing what he or she learned, we assumed that it would improve their performance in different areas. In that framework, we examined different tools that are used for measuring the performance of the portfolio managers. We had meetings with Human Resources personnel to understand the tools better and decided to use the performance form, which is used for measuring the performance of a portfolio in four main areas:

- profitability
- sales volume
- productivity
- risk management.

Then, we had meetings with financial planning personnel to discuss how we could evaluate the data and guide the portfolio managers. After developing the final form, we sent an email to participants, which explained all the details of the performance form, why it was needed, where they could get the data needed, and how we would use it. They had one week to complete it, and we had calls from those who had questions. In the form we wanted to complete the numbers in quarter 1 and quarter 2 of the year 2010. As the training took place in December 2009, we assumed that quarter 1 would see their usual performance, but after three months, we expected their performance to improve. For the scores in targets, the numbers are cumulative because the performance is apparent in that way. For profitability, we asked participants to take the independent numbers as they would be used in ROI. The last question was related to the participants' estimation of the contribution of the training to the increased performance. We clarified that there can be numerous effects such as campaigns, guidance from management, economic situations, and competition in the market. Moreover, we asked participants to be conservative in assigning a percentage to the training. You can find the template of the performance form and a selected form in Appendix 10.E.

Our objective in Level 4 was an increase of a minimum of 3 percent in every positive measure and 3 percent decrease in negative measures. The year 2010 was hard for the banking sector and that kind of an increase would be very favorable in the eyes of top management. All these measures can change by being competent in BPM training, and the performance of the portfolio managers directly reflects the numbers of the banks that have the most strategic importance, starting from profitability.

There were 46 participants; we excluded the participants from the headquarters and regional directorship who had no portfolio. So six participants were excluded. Of 40, there were 34 people who answered the form.

Isolating the Effect of Training

To isolate the effect of training, we preferred the estimation of the partici-pants. GLA1 is a talent program, so all participants are high potentials and come from different parts of Turkey. There are various reasons why we used the estimation of the participants instead of the other methods.

In trend-line analysis, it was hard to make it as all the participants come from different hinterlands, which leads to various dynamics that affect their performance. It was impossible to combine all of them in an analysis and achieve an effective result.

For the control groups, as our entire target group is high potentials, it was not possible to find a different but similar performance group with which to make the right comparison.

The best method was to take their estimation, because they could judge the contribution of the training by taking other conditions into con-sideration. It was also feasible for them to reach the data and send it by email. As was stated before, the most accurate answers could be from the participants for this case. There were no costs associated with this mea-surement, and it took less than 10 minutes of the participants' time. After choosing the method, we finalized the performance forms by adding the necessary part that asked their estimation. We then sent them a detailed email.

Data Analysis and Results

The results for the fourth level were as follows:

- a 5,35 percent increase in net profitability
- a 4,22 percent increase in deposits
- a 6,03 percent increase in loans
- a 13,4 percent increase in customer visits
- a 3,3 percent decrease in bad credit.

The method that we used is quite complicated. For finding the change in the numbers, we multiplied the increase in percentages by their estima-tion of the contribution by the training. The average of all the participants gave the numbers above.

It was clear that we reached our objective in all means, and they used their action plans effectively to increase their performance.

ROI and Its Meaning
Converting Data to Monetary Values

To convert improvement at Level 4 to a monetary value, we asked participants to send us their newly published profitability results as an amount.
There was a standard value that they could reach from the company's
records. All the profitability data were prepared by the financial planning
staff, so credibility was not questionable.

Because our unit of measure is profitability, there was no need for valu-
ation as it was a direct indicator of what we earned. Their change in two
quarters gave us their performance change. So for annualizing the data, we
multiplied by 4 as there are 4 quarters in the year. The calculations are
described in the following section titled ROI Calculation.

Program Costs

All the cost items of the program are shown in Table 10.5. In the table, all
the direct costs (such as personnel and material costs) and indirect costs
(such as total student costs) have been clarified. As BPM is part of a program, we took the number of days before BPM. We believe that there was
a high contribution of the previous trainings to the effectiveness in BPM.
Those trainings were: communication (two days), persuasion and impact
(two days), conflict management (two days), closure to the relationship
management (one day), and lastly, BPM (three days). The total was 10
days. These trainings occurred in one year. In all trainings, for the ones
who used travel, we used the value of 70 percent. In the personnel and
material costs, the costs were the ones that we paid to the firm and also to
the design process. Moreover, we added the evaluation costs because we
devoted quite a lot of time to the evaluation. The time of the L&D staff and
the cost of the surveys were added to the program costs.

For the revision, we did take 20 percent of the initial development
costs. In the student costs section, we took the standard measure of the
bank for the personnel, which equals 60.000 Turkish Liras for one personnel for a year on average. We divided the average annual salary by the
work days per year and multiplied with duration of the program and number of students. Also, the travel costs were added, with the average cost of
250 Turkish Liras. And lastly, the facility cost was added, with the total cost
multiplied by the percentage of allocation to BPM time. In the end, the total
cost was **201.414** Turkish Liras (125.962 USD).

TABLE 10.5 Program Costs

Class Demographics			RECURRING DELIVERY COSTS		
How long is the class (in days)					
How many classes per year			Revision & Updated Costs		
How many students per class			**Total revision costs**		**12.231,00**
% of students who must travel to class			Enter as a % of initial development costs	20	
Life expectancy of class/course (years)					
			Student Costs		
ONE-TIME DEVELOPMENTAL COSTS			**Total student costs**		
			Avg annual student compensation (salary + benefits)		
Personnel Costs			Work days per year (235 avereage)		
Total internal labor costs for developing the course			Avg student per diem		
	Hours	Rate	Avg travel costs per students		
Trainer 1			Cost of course materials per student		
Trainer 2					
Trainer 3			Instructor Costs		
Total outside costs for developing the course			**Total instructor costs**		
Contractor/Consultant #1			Avg instructor compensation		
Contractor/Consultant #2			Work day per year (235 average)		
Contractor/Consultant #3			Avg instructor per diem		
Production & Material Costs			Avg travel costs per instructor		
Books and Articles			Cost of course materials per instructor per class		
Insights					
Describe Here			Facility/Hosting Costs		
			Total facility/hosting costs		
Evaluation Costs			What is the cost of facilities/hosting per year		
			What % can be allocated to this course/class		
Total evaluation costs			**TOTAL COST**		**201.414,35**
Surveys (314 TL per week)					
Staff Time (1 week)					
Describe Here					
*The costs are hidden because of privacy.					

ROI Calculation

For reaching ROI, we used the net profitability of our participants. As we clarified in the previous sections, we took their profitability for the first and second quarter of 2010 and wanted them to clarify the contribution of the training as a percentage. We subtracted the first quarter profitability from the second quarter and multiplied it by the percentage of the contribution of the training. For omitting the errors, we excluded the high numbers, which were marginal compared with others. Then we reached the result of **642.755**. To compute the annual benefits, we multiplied this amount by 4 and reached **2.571.022** as annual total benefits. For the error rate, we did not take the estimation of the participants, for various reasons. If the complexity of the form increases, then there would be more mistakes regarding to the numbers. Even so it was hard for them to understand how to clarify the percentage of the contribution. We asked the financial planning department the percentage of their error estimation in the reporting and they told us 20 percent, so we took **20 percent** estimation of error. The program benefits became **2.056.817**. The total annual cost was 201.414. By subtracting the costs from the net profitability coming from the training and then dividing by the cost, we reached ROI as **921 percent.** This is a sign of the success of the program. The details are given in Table 10.6.

For the benefit-cost ratio, the benefits are divided by the cost, which was 10,2. That means that for every 1 Turkish Lira we spent, we earned 10,2 Turkish Liras in the end.

If we check the guiding principles, we see that our participants are the most credible sources of data who can see and evaluate all the conditions that can affect them (Guiding Principle 3). For the most conservative way, we asked participants to be conservative both in communicating with them and also in the performance form that they filled out. Moreover, we excluded the numbers that were too high in a marginal way (Guiding Principles 4–8). For the isolation, we used the participants' estimation (Guiding Principle 5). For the ones who did not send the performance form to us, we took their performance as zero (Guiding Principle 6). We took a 20 percent potential error of estimate (Guiding Principle 7).

Intangible Benefits

GLA1 was designed for developing the competencies of our portfolio managers as they were selected as talent and candidates for branch manager

TABLE 10.6   ROI Calculation

	ROI: NET PROFITABILITY			
	Net Profitability		**Contribution of the Training**	**(Q2 Net Profitability − Q1 Net Profitability)* Contribution of the Training**
Participants	**2010 1st Quarter**	**2010 2nd Quarter**		
Participant 1	169.080	216.397	25%	11.829
Participant 2	842.174	692.413	20%	−29.952
Participant 3	702.458	767.882	30%	19.627
Participant 4	15.403	258.860	50%	121.729
Participant 5	265.332	264.726	15%	−91
Participant 6	337.000	479.000	46%	65.320
Participant 7	1.704.174	1.796.893	15%	13.908
Participant 8	465.422	447.492	55%	−9.862
Participant 9	1.026.442	1.837.829	5%	40.569
Participant 10	2.793.991	3.373.362	70%	405.560
Participant 11	845.198	547.520	46%	−136.932
Participant 12	310.523	304.203	10%	−632
Participant 13	374.091	386.650	70%	8.791
Participant 14	225.376	163.974	10%	−6.140
Participant 15	144.753	100.989	40%	−17.506
Participant 16	297.091	279.147	35%	−6.280
Participant 17	436.314	509.700	25%	18.347
Participant 18	188.543	194.745	20%	1.240
Participant 19	175.000	151.000	30%	−7.200
Participant 20	605.291	652.166	15%	7.031
Participant 21	295.904	285.814	15%	−1.514
Participant 22	218.430	217.315	20%	−223
				(continued)

TABLE 10.6   Continued

ROI: NET PROFITABILITY			
Participants	**Net Profitability**	**Contribution of the Training**	**(Q2 Net Profitability – Q1 Net Profitability)* Contribution of the Training**
	2010 1st Quarter	**2010 2nd Quarter**	
Participant 23	398.631	421.419	20%	4.558
Participant 24	342.400	308.488	60%	−20.347
Participant 25	228.587	471.233	20%	48.529
Participant 26	66.736	215.211	50%	74.238
Participant 27	247.787	164.582	10%	−8.321
Participant 28	188.909	195.638	30%	2.019
Participant 29	165.000	148.000	30%	−5.100
Participant 30	180.059	179.359	20%	−140
Participant 31	146.000	288.000	35%	49.700
			Total	642.755 TL
			Costs	201.414 TL
			Annual Total Benefits	2.571.022 TL
			Error Estimation	20%
			Annual Total Benefits (except error)	2.056.817 TL
			ROI annual	921%

Note: Costs measured in Turkish Liras (TL).

positions. For all competencies, it is valid that if they become better in those areas, this fact will be reflected in their performance records.

Moreover, our participants emphasized the intangible benefits that they had been experiencing in both their private and work lives. These benefits could not be turned into a monetary value for ROI calculation, as there are no sources for putting a value on them. But still, all the intangible benefits were vital for the bank.

The intangible benefits of the program were

- an increase in the quality of life
- having vision
- better time management
- effective communication.

All of these were vital in terms of having better personnel both in private and on their jobs. They could not turn into numbers because they were all hard to assign a value to, and in the end, if they were better in these areas, all of them could be observed in their performance, which we chose to measure.

RECOMMENDATIONS AND SUGGESTIONS FOR IMPROVEMENT

GLA1 is a good example of a program for various reasons. First of all, the program is a talent program and evaluated as strategically important. There is strong support from top management, and the investment is proportionally high compared with most of the programs. Another vital thing concerns participants. They are mostly motivated to participate actively and contribute to possible discussions.

The measurement was made on the first program, so for the second program we had some improvements in the content and in the follow-up. In BPM, the participants have a chance to learn different reporting methods, but by the change in reporting system of our bank, we adapted the content to the new system and aligned it more with their daily life. Moreover, we added videos and best practice sharing to strengthen the content of the training. For the follow-up, their action plans will be followed more closely, by making meetings regularly, to understand whether they can apply what they have learned from the training. We will encourage all participants to share their experiences with one another to learn from each other.

There are many lessons that we have learned during the evaluation process. To start with, we are clear on the necessity of explaining the details of the evaluations to the participants. This is needed to ensure that participants are clear on why there is an evaluation, what they should do, and which data they need to find if they are the data sources. Moreover, it is better to understand the dynamics of the organization by having the meetings with departments such as financial planning. Before collecting data, the big picture of the organization should be known by the L&D staff. Besides, the motivation of the participants and assistance of people in other departments really helped us to gather the data we needed to complete the application. In the future, we will maintain close cooperation with financial planning and human resources.

Also, we observed that some managers of the participants' were not so active in giving feedback, so we made a webinar for all managers explaining how the program would take place, how they could follow up with their employees, and what our expectations were. That was intended to improve the managers' involvement to the program, which is desirable for us.

In the measurement part, we started to rate people in the closure trainings. We used to have feedback only, but now we have an idea of where people succeed in the second level.

The recommendations for future programs start with the support of top management; if they are available and aware of what is going on, they will give the necessary support. Also, the managers should follow the participants closely, understand their barriers, and reinforce their enablers. For us, it is important to be in cooperation with other departments in headquarters to understand the inner dynamics and adapt our program as soon as possible with the changes.

For our team, the ROI process is totally new, and we need some more experiences. We learned various lessons during the process. Also, it helped us to develop stronger relations with various departments, understand the dynamics of the bank more deeply, examine the design of BPM and the program in a more detailed way, and go with the evaluation process. As our evaluation process is among the first ones, we shared all our experiences with our colleagues, and we will continue to measure our other leadership programs for our talents.

CONCLUSION

BPM is a vital part of the GLA1, and all the participants are talents of Garanti Bank. The program is strategically important as there is strong support from top management, the investment is high, and performance of the talents is strategically vital for the bank.

By our complex content, we succeed in having nearly 921 percent ROI annually even though we had a conservative approach to measurement. The participants had the chance to change their perspective, working style, and attitudes in their business life, which had a direct effect on their performance. We had the chance to find proof of their success in learning, application, and impact level.

DISCUSSION QUESTIONS

1. How credible is the process? Explain.
2. How could the evaluation process be improved?
3. Would it be possible to convert intangible benefits to a monetary value?
4. Critique the data collection plan. How could it be improved?
5. Would you prefer any other methods in isolating the effects of training.

ABOUT THE AUTHORS

Esra Eseroğlu has been working as a performance consultant in the Learning and Development Center of Garanti Bank since 2008. She is responsible for talent management and leadership development and highly skilled in project management. She is also a professional in ROI studies and recently became a Certified ROI Professional (CRP).

Esra earned her undergraduate degree in the international relations and economics as a double major student at Istanbul Bilgi University and her graduate degree in international relations at Koc University. She had scholarships in both universities.

Önder Korkmaz has more then seven years' experience in the banking industry. During his career, he has held various positions in Learning and Development. He is now the Talent Development Vice President of the Training and Development Department of Garanti Bank.

Önder has extensive, firsthand experience in talent management and leadership development, and he also is a Certified ROI Professional (CRP). Önder has led a number of significant initiatives to improve the Learning & Development organization, design talent management programs, and establish ROI culture.

Önder earned his undergraduate degree in business administration and economics from Marmara University and his MBA degree from the Fordham University Graduate School of Business Administration.

He is married and lives with his wife in Istanbul.

Appendix 10.A   The End-of-Program Questionnaire

EĞİTİM PROGRAMI DEĞERLENDİRME ANKETİ

Eğitimin Adı: _____   Tarih: _____

Eğitici Adı- Soyadı: _____

Katılımcı Adı - Soyadı: _____
(İsteğe Bağlı)

Anketin amacı, katıldığınız eğitimin başarısını ölçmek ve geliştirilmesini sağlamaktır. Değerlendirmenin amacına ulaşabilmesi için formda yer alan soruları dikkatli bir şekilde cevaplayınız.

5- Kesinlikle katılıyorum
4- Katılıyorum
3- Kararsızım
2- Katılmıyorum
1- Kesinlikle katılmıyorum.

CEVAPLAR İÇİN ÖRNEK KODLAMA			
Yanlış	Yanlış	Yanlış	Doğru
⊗	✓	○	●

EĞİTİM:	5	4	3	2	1	■
Eğitim iş hayatıma katkı sağlayacak nitelikteydi.	○	○	○	○	○	■
Eğitim iş hayatım için önemliydi.	○	○	○	○	○	■
Eğitim harcadığım zamana değdi.	○	○	○	○	○	■
Eğitim içeriği bilgi ve beceri düzeyime uygundu.	○	○	○	○	○	■
Uygulamalar ve metaryaller eğitimi (varsa kitap, sunum, video, örnekler vs) daha iyi anlamamı sağladı.	○	○	○	○	○	■
Eğitimi çalışma arkadaşlarıma tavsiye ederim.	○	○	○	○	○	■

Questions related to the training

EĞİTİCİ:	5	4	3	2	1	■
Eğitici konuya hakimdi ve sorulara tatmin edici yanıtlar verdi.	○	○	○	○	○	■
Eğitici eğitimi etkin şekilde aktardı.	○	○	○	○	○	■
Eğiticiyi çalışma arkadaşlarıma tavsiye ederim.	○	○	○	○	○	■

Questions related to the trainer

Sizce bu eğitimin...

Olumlu Yönleri	Geliştirilmesi Gereken Yönleri

Sizce bu eğiticinin...

Olumlu Yönleri	Geliştirilmesi Gereken Yönleri

Appendix 10.B   The End-of-Program Assignment

GARANTi
LEADERSHIP ACADAMY
1.CLASS
BUSINESS PERFORMANCE MANAGEMENT

❊ Garanti

S — Situation
- ☐ Competition A.
- ☐ SWOT
- ☐ Pareto A.

P — Problems
- ☐ Risk A.
- ☐ SWO
- ☐ Imp./Urgency

I — Impact
- ☐ P.M.I.
- ☐ GRID
- ☐ Result orient

N — Needs
- ☐ Impact/Effort
- ☐ Result orient
- ☐ Analytic Think

A — Action Planning
- ☐ Active Planning
- ☐ SMART targets
- ☐ Imp./Urgency

Appendix 10.C   Competency Survey

← This is the competency that is measured.

This is the clarification of who
→ evaluated and the average

The expected behaviors
→ of the competency

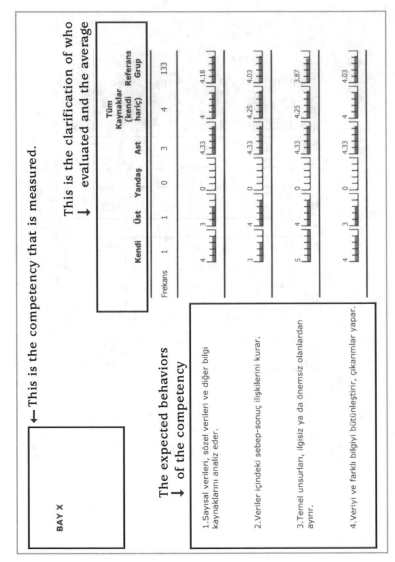

BAY X

	Kendi	Üst	Yandaş	Ast	Tüm Kaynaklar (kendi hariç)	Referans Grup
Frekans	1	1	0	3	4	133

1. Sayısal verileri, sözel verileri ve diğer bilgi kaynaklarını analiz eder.

4   3   0   4.33   4   4.18

2. Veriler içindeki sebep-sonuç ilişkilerini kurar.

3   4   0   4.33   4.25   4.03

3. Temel unsurları, ilgisiz ya da önemsiz olanlardan ayırır.

5   4   0   4.33   4.25   3.87

4. Veriyi ve farklı bilgiyi bütünleştirir, çıkarımlar yapar.

4   3   0   4.33   4   4.03

11

Developing the ROI of an Online English-as-a-Second-Language Program

Wyeth Pharmaceuticals
USA

Edward P. Nathan

T his case was prepared to serve as a basis for discussion rather than
an illustration of either effective or ineffective administrative practices. Names, dates, places, and data may have been disguised at the
request of the author or the organization.

Abstract

This case study examines the methodology used to determine the return on
investment (ROI) of an online English-as-a-second-language (ESL) program.
The online ESL program was implemented in more than 20 countries, and
the scope of the analysis includes data from all participating countries. A
form of ROI analysis had been conducted annually prior to the addition of
the Phillips Methodology in 2008. The latest analysis follows the Phillips
approach step by step and has provided greater credibility as a result.

ORGANIZATIONAL BACKGROUND

The organization evaluated is a multinational research-based genetic engineering company. In order to respect the privacy of the client company and
for purposes of this project, the company will be called "Performance
Genetica." The return-on-investment (ROI) evaluation described here represents the sixth year of evaluating the online English-as-a-second-language
(ESL) course from a company called GlobalEnglish (GE). Due to its previous
history as a holding company for many different types of businesses,

Note: This case study previously appeared as a journal article in Nathan, E. P. (July
2009). Determining the ROI of an online English as a second language program.
Performance Improvement, 40(6), 39–48. Used with permission.

Performance Genetica has an HR function that does not include technical skills training but focuses more on senior management and leadership skills. While the company has shed many of those other businesses and now focuses exclusively on health care, technical training still resides in the various business units that currently exist in the organization. As a result, the GE program was originally sponsored and rolled out by the largest training organization in the company. This group, which is called the Learning & Performance (L&P) department, is responsible for training (directly and indirectly through global affiliates) more than 8,000 employees in the commercial organization (sales and marketing).

THE TRAINING NEED

Due to the size of the organization and the scope of the initiative, good metrics are very important to this project. In 2007, after exposure to the Phillips ROI Methodology (Phillips 2003, p. 52), the existing training evaluation methods that had been previously employed were enhanced by the 12 Guiding Principles of that methodology. As the process is described, this case study will reference the related guiding principles. For the company to meet its succession planning and career ladder goals, it needs to move a number of high-talent and high-potential people from country to country with an expected rotation in the United States. Succession planning is a stated business objective whereby the company is committed to developing and promoting highly talented people. These are the people who are identified as tomorrow's company leaders. As a U.S.-based multinational corporation, the lingua franca of the company is English. Developing the English language skills for nonnative speakers is a major concern of the company, but one that has been left up to the local affiliates to resolve on their own.

Historically, the affiliates would try to hire high-potential employees who already had suitable English language skills, although no standard for "suitable" was ever established. When employees' ESL skills were less than "proficient," it was up to the local affiliates to offer local ESL solutions to their staff. As a result, the outcomes of ESL training have been mixed since each affiliate has taken its own independent approach. In early 2001, a number of affiliates suggested it would be more effective if the company would consider leveraging its global economies of scale to drive a global ESL learning initiative (if possible), since at that time there was no global coordination of this effort.

KEY STAKEHOLDERS

There were a number of stakeholders in this effort. However, it is a complex set of relationships. While the HR group (a key stakeholder) is responsible for the succession planning process, that group offers no ESL training to support that effort. A significant number of succession planning candidates in the affiliates come from their sales and marketing departments; therefore, it was felt the global L&P department (another key stakeholder) should be tasked with supporting the ESL training. In addition, the affiliate HR managers are also key stakeholders responsible for implementing the local succession planning process. These affiliate HR managers will also be critical decision makers in terms of both funding any ESL solution and enrolling affiliate learners in the ESL program.

ADDRESSING THE NEED: ONE FAILURE—ONE SUCCESS

Because succession planning was the driving factor in developing English language skills in high-potential affiliate personnel, the solution had to be one that would be cost-effective, minimize time away from work, and accommodate students at various levels of English capability. After repeated requests from the overseas affiliates for support of this activity, several global ESL training companies were located and reviewed. Ultimately, a global contract meant to leverage global buying efficiencies was negotiated with Berlitz language services. However, after the first year, the approach was abandoned for the following reasons:

1. Despite global pricing, many affiliates were able to find local classroom training at lower prices, usually from a local university.
2. Classroom training sponsored within the company's local offices presented a challenge in scheduling.
3. To keep costs reasonable by essentially limiting the number of classes available, classes had a wide range of learners at various skill levels. There were beginning, intermediate, and advanced learners in the same classroom, which created a lot of challenges.

After the first year, when the affiliates refused to participate in the Berlitz program any longer, the Berlitz contract was allowed to expire without renewal. An alternate solution needed to be identified—one that would address the problems experienced with the Berlitz program, and one that the markets would be willing to participate in and pay for. A new service was located that could potentially meet this need. The service,

GlobalEnglish, was a one-year-old online ESL training system that had been started by a venture capital company. GE's premise was simple:

1. English is the global language of business.

2. All resources would be put into developing interactive learning tools to support just one language—English.

3. There would be 11 levels of business English covered in the GE program.

4. There would be different course tracks for different English language skills such as grammar, writing, speaking, and listening.

5. The approach would allow a learner with Level 10 skills in writing to take the Level 10 writing track. However, if the learner had Level 5 English grammar skills, the learner would be placed in the Level 5 grammar track. This would allow for unprecedented customization not possible in a group classroom setting.

6. Instructions on using the system in the first five levels would be provided in local languages until the learner had sufficient English language skills to follow both lesson instructions and lesson content completely in English.

During the second half of 2002, a pilot program for GE was commenced for 50 people in several affiliates. The ROI Methodology was not applied to the pilot. What was used was a simple measure of Levels 1 through 3 results (Kirkpatrick 1998). Specifically, learners provided feedback on their experience using the GE system (Level 1). Their improvement (or lack therefore) in English test scores from their original placement to when they completed the pilot were measured through assessment in the GE system (Level 2). Simulated application exercises, also within the GE system, were measured from the benchmark placement process at the beginning of the pilot to the learner's final performance at the end of the pilot (Level 3). Based on the results of the pilot, which were favorable, the GE system was adopted.

MEASURING RESULTS FROM 2003 TO 2007

As a result of the pilot, in 2003 the GE program sponsor (the L&P department) was tasked with organizing the global rollout of the program. Since then, a limited ROI analysis was added to the original pilot measures and conducted in the fourth quarter every year. The original ROI method simply asked the learners to provide an estimate of how much time was saved due to the learner's new English language skills. Once an "hour" value was established, conducting an ROI was relatively easy.

On average, the company has seen an 800 percent ROI in each of the five years the program has been employed. However, many stakeholders were skeptical about the results of those earlier ROI analyses. Therefore, in 2008, elements of the Phillips (2003) Methodology were added, and for the first time, learners and their managers were asked to report, in addition to how much time was saved due to the learners' improved English language skills, how confident learners and their managers were in their estimates, and how certain learners (and their managers) were that the GE program was the reason for the results. Using this approach, the ROI methodology employed was enhanced to create a more defensible and credible ROI analysis. The balance of this chapter will focus on this improved process made by using the Phillips (2003) ROI Methodology. In 2008, the last full year for which learner data exists, there were 426 users on the system, an all-time high. Therefore, developing a more credible and rigorous ROI analysis methodology was a very helpful and important activity to measure the value of the program.

EVALUATION APPROACH

As part of the evaluation planning process, objectives were developed at each of the five levels of evaluation. In addition, a data collection plan was developed and agreed on, as were techniques for converting data to monetary values and isolating the effects of the program.

Evaluation Objectives

Following are the objectives established for each level of evaluation.

Level 1: Reaction Objectives

1. Determine learner satisfaction with the GE learning methodologies using a five-point Likert scale from "dissatisfied" to "extremely satisfied."

2. Determine learner self-satisfaction with progress improving English skills using a five-point Likert scale from "dissatisfied" to "extremely satisfied." This last point can be correlated to actual Level 2 and 3 assessment results to see if learner perception matches reality.

Level 2: Learning Objectives

1. Objective test scores for knowledge based on placement assessment and progress assessment in order to progress through the 11 levels.

An assessment score of 80 percent or higher is required to move to the next level in a particular skill set.

2. Learning objectives will focus on knowledge of vocabulary and rules of grammar.

Level 3: Application Objectives

1. Objective test scores for skill application based on placement assessment and progress assessment in order to progress through the 11 levels. An assessment score of 70 percent or higher is required to move to the next level in a particular skill set.

2. Application objectives that focus on reading, writing, listening, and speaking skills as applied to specific, real job tasks as differentiated from simulated tasks or assignments for reading, writing, listening, and speaking skills within GE. It is important to note that reading, writing, listening, and speaking skills, whether applied to a simulated task, as within a course lesson, or applied to a real job task or activity, will be evaluated by similar methods. The difference in this case is that the simulated Level 3 situations within GE can be automatically assessed by the administration module within the GE system. The real-world job application will need to be evaluated by qualified assessors on the job.

3. Assessment by the learners and their managers (or qualified assessors) using an on-the-job checklist of 12 business situations will be conducted. Ratings will be ranked on a measure of five levels of improvement.

Levels 4 and 5: Business Impact and ROI Objectives

1. Determine the level of importance of English skills to the learner's job and career aspirations.

2. Determine the learner's estimate of time saved due to improved English language skills.

3. Determine the learner's confidence estimate of how much time was saved due to improved English skills.

4. Determine the learner's percentage estimate of GE's contribution to the improvement in the learner's English language skills.

5. Achieve monetary benefits exceeding costs.

Data Collection Plan

Table 11.1 provides a detailed look at the data collection plan. It is important to note that the Level 2 and 3 data (Kirkpatrick 1998) are actually collected through placement and progress assessments within the GE program administrative module and are not extraneous data collection tools. As an integral part of the GE program, these assessments meet the recognized generally accepted standards and criteria of ESL assessment methodology.

Converting Data to Monetary Values

Based on the data collected, the Levels 1 through 3 objectives contribute to the development of a positive case for the use of GE in delivering ESL learning. Translating that learning into a monetary value will come from the Levels 4 and 5 assessments, which will ask the learners how much time they (and their managers) believe was saved due to improved English language skills. To add to the credibility of this estimate, the respondents' level of confidence in that estimate will be captured, and ultimately the respondents' level of confidence in GE's contribution to that result will be combined to develop a conservative and credible estimate of the time saved due to the learners' new ESL skills. Once a time saved value is determined (for instance, 1 hour per week), a financial value will be associated with that time (such as a fully loaded labor cost) and an ROI cost determined by taking into account the annual estimate of the value of the time saved, less the annual value of the time spent studying divided by the annual cost per learner for the GE program. This approach will provide a very solid ROI case for the program.

Isolating the Impact of Training

As pointed out by Phillips (2003), a chain of evidence is an essential component of demonstrating the impact and ROI of a training solution used as a performance improvement intervention. Specifically, conducting Levels 1, 2, 3, and 4 evaluations (Kirkpatrick 1998) in addition to the Phillips (2003) Level 5 evaluation is critical to developing a supportable and credible foundation for the overall ROI analysis.

It is important to note that the learners using the GE system are scattered around the globe—along with their supervisors. With 426 users (and associated supervisors) around the world, the most efficient method to gather both learner reaction (Level 1) and business impact (Level 4) and ROI

TABLE 11.1 Data Collection Plan

Purpose of the Evaluation: Determine the personal and business impact, including ROI, of employee use of the online ESL training program known as GlobalEnglish.

Program/Project: GlobalEnglish online ESL program

Level	Broad Program Objective(s)	Measures	Data Collection Method/Instruments	Data Sources	Timing	Responsibilities
1	**Reaction and Usage** • Positive reaction to program • Usage pattern	• Feedback on a five-point Likert scale • Number of hours of use	• Annual survey • Compare satisfaction levels with previous years. • GE user data	• Participants • Participants' supervisors • GE admin. software	October every year	• GE support services
2	**Learning and Confidence** • Vocabulary and grammar for placement and progress.	• There are 11 levels of vocabulary and grammar in GE. To progress from one level to the next, learners will need exam scores of 70% or higher in vocabulary and grammar.	• Online assessments (11 levels for vocabulary and grammar)	• Participants through GE assessments	For placement to begin using the GE program; also for progress as each course is completed to continue to the next level	• GE online program
3	**Application and Implementation (Simulated)** • Listening, reading, writing, and speaking for placement and progress	• There are 11 levels of listening, reading, writing, and speaking in GE. To progress from one level to the next, learners will need exam scores of 70% or higher in each of these areas (listening, reading, writing, and speaking).	• Online assessments (11 levels for listening, reading, writing, and speaking)	• Participants through GE assessments	For placement to begin using the GE program; also for progress as each course is completed to continue to the next level	• GE online program

Level	Broad Program Objective(s)	Measures	Data Collection Method/Instruments	Data Sources	Timing	Responsibilities
4	**Application and Implementation (on the Job)** • Listening, reading, writing, and speaking for placement and progress	• Observed usage of English skills for emails, telephone conversations, meetings, and presentations	• Checklist using a five-point scale significantly improved, improved, somewhat improved, not yet improved, and not used at work	• Learners and their supervisors (or trained assessors)	15–45 days following the completion of Level 4, Level 8, and Level 11 of the GE curriculum, which has a total of 11 levels	• Local affiliate administrators and the managers of learner managers; checklist to be conducted by the learners and their managers
5	**Business Impact** • Estimated time savings due to improved English skills	• Estimated time savings per month, convert time saved to dollar value	• Annual survey	• Participants • Participants and participants' supervisors	October every year	• GE support services
6	**ROI** • ROI to exceed costs of GE program	Comments: The plan is to take the estimated monthly time saved as determined by the Level 4 data collection and subtract the time spent in class to determine the "net time saved." Multiply by the average confidence factor and multiply again by average belief that GE was responsible for the time saved. Annualize that number and divide by the annual cost per learner for GE.				

Source: Copyright © 2004 ROI Institute, Inc. All rights reserved.

Note: GE = GlobalEnglish.

(Level 5) data was in a single survey. The critical element is that the survey had to be crafted in such a way that learner (and supervisor) reactions and expectations are aligned with a perception of the metrics that are important and relevant to the measure of success and impact used by these learners and supervisors and their organization. By linking Levels 1, 4, and 5 data questions into a single survey, collating the data from potentially more than 850 people (426 learners and the same number of managers) from around the globe, the data collection became a much more manageable task. It is also important to keep in mind that in addition to this annual survey, which captures Levels 1, 4, and 5, the learners are constantly taking Level 2 and Level 3 assessments as they progress through the GE program.

Another factor that was considered in planning to conduct a global ROI study for an online English language program was the quality of English of both the beginning learners and the supervisors. Just because a learner is learning English language skills does not mean all the skills to answer a survey will be mastered or that the learner's supervisor(s) will have mastered English as well. In addition, there are no resources to translate the survey into all the languages that might be required. As a result, it is important to keep the survey as short as possible, using as simple a form of English as possible, and to leave enough time for respondents to complete the survey. These factors were treated as prerequisite issues and potential constraints that had an impact on the design of the evaluation tools.

Consistent with Guiding Principle 5, "at least one method must be used to isolate the effects of the solution" (Phillips 2003, p. 52), to isolate the contribution of training to improved job performance as a result of better English language skills, a number of the Phillips methods (2003, pp. 111–145) were employed. Two of the nine methods of data isolation techniques cited by Phillips were used in this ROI analysis.

Guiding Principle 7 states that "estimates of improvements should be adjusted (discounted) for the potential error of the estimate" (Phillips 2003, p. 52). To accomplish this, a questionnaire to gather data from learners was developed. The three key questions for the learners in order to capture data for the ROI analysis were these:

1. How much time has been saved due to improved English language skills? _____ hours have been saved each week.
2. On a percentage basis, what is the confidence level concerning the number of hours saved each week? _____ %

3. On a percentage basis, what is the confidence level that GE is the reason this time has been saved? _____ %

Again, consistent with Guiding Principle 7, a second questionnaire was developed to gather data from the learners' supervisors (Phillips 2003, p. 52). The key questions for the supervisors were these:

1. If one were to assume that improved English language skills allow an employee to work more effectively due to the ability to read and respond to English language emails, telephone calls, teleconferences, and meetings with greater skill and confidence, what would an estimate be of how many minutes or hours per week the learner(s) would save due to a perceived improvement in English language skills? _____

2. On a percentage basis, what is the confidence level concerning the number of hours saved each week? _____ %

3. On a percentage basis, what is the confidence level that GE is the reason this time has been saved? _____ %

With the data that resulted from these questions, a unit of measure, that is, time saved, was established that was converted into a dollar value and ultimately generated an ROI and a benefit-to-cost ratio (BCR). This is an approach that, while not terribly sophisticated, is simple to measure, is very defensible to management, and fits within the constraints that exist in conducting a global ROI analysis that were discussed earlier.

EVALUATION RESULTS

Determining the Benefits

As mentioned earlier, for the company to meet its succession planning and career ladder goals, it needs to move a number of high-talent and high-potential people from country to country with an expected rotation in the United States. No financial analysis of the value of such a program has been conducted by the company, and such an analysis is beyond the scope of this chapter. Succession planning is, however, a stated business objective whereby the company is committed to developing and promoting highly talented people. The assumed and accepted benefit of such a program is key to the company's growth, and effective English language skills are required for the succession planning process to be successful. That said, the financial benefit of the GE ESL program can be found in Table 11.2.

TABLE 11.2   Calculation of Dollar Benefits of the GlobalEnglish Online ESL Program

Item	Measure	Objective	Source	Value
1	Average number of hours per month each learner spends on the GE system	To determine how much time each learner spends using the GE system	Administrative report from the GE system	3.06 hours online per month per learner in 2008
2	Not all hours spent using the GE system are while the learners are at work	To determine how many work hours are lost due to learners using GE while at work	Learners (from survey)	Learners used GE at work only 26% of the time.
3	Time spent using the GE system while at work	To determine the average actual monthly study hours used by learners when they are at work	Calculated	3.06 hours online per month per learner × 26% while at work = 0.80 hours per month online at work per learner
4	Estimated work hours saved per week due to improved English skills	To determine how many work hours are saved each week due to improved English language skills	Learners and supervisors (from survey)	1.68 hours per week
5	Total estimated work hours saved per month due to improved English skills	To determine how many work hours are saved each month due to improved English language skills	Calculated	1.68 hours per week × 4.3 weeks per month = 7.2 hours saved per month per learner
6	Net estimated work hours saved per month due to improved English skills (total saved less time consumed online at work)	To determine the number of hours saved each week due to improved English language skills less time online using GE while at work	Calculated	7.2 hours saved per month – 0.80 hours spent online using GE = 6.4 hours net savings per month per learner
7	Confidence level of estimated work hours saved	To determine the confidence level in the estimate of how many work hours are saved each month due to improved English language skills	Learners and supervisors (from survey)	Respondents indicated only a 37% confidence level in their estimate of the time saved by the learner per week.

Item	Measure	Objective	Source	Value
8	Confidence level that the GE training contributed to the estimated work hours saved	To determine the confidence level in how much the GE training program contributed to the estimated number of work hours saved each month due to improved English language skills	Learners and supervisors (from survey)	Respondents indicated only a 49% confidence level that GE was the reason the learners' English skills improved.
9	Calculation of work hours saved per month per learner	Taking an estimate of work hours saved and applying the two confidence evel estimates to the value to determine a best estimate of work time saved due to participation in GE	Calculated	Item 6 × Item 7 × Item 8 = Item 9 6.4 hours × 0.37 × 0.49 = 1.17 hours saved per month per learner
10	Calculation of hours saved per year	Taking the monthly hours estimated saved and converting the number to an annual value	Calculated	Item 9 × 12 months = annual hours saved per learner 1.17 hours saved per month × 12 months per year = 14.04 hours savings per learner per year
11	Calculation of dollar value of work hours saved per year per learner	Taking the estimated time saved per year per learner and multiplying it by the fully loaded labor cost	Calculated	Item 10 × $ of fully loaded labor cost 14.04 hours × $50.00 = $702 saved per learner per year
12	Total dollar value of hours saved per year by 426 GE learners	Calculating the annual dollar benefit of the GE program for 426 learners	Calculated	Item 11 × 426 learners $702 per learner per year × 426 learners = $299,052

Note: GE = GlobalEnglish.

Calculating the Costs

For the five years since the GE program was introduced, an annual ROI analysis has been conducted. Each previous year in which the older ROI analysis was conducted, the analysis was applied to just that year, as in the 2008 study. This is consistent with Guiding Principle 9, which states that "only the first year of benefits (annual) should be used in the ROI analysis of short-term solutions" (Phillips 2003, p. 52). Since most learners are only in the system for 12 to 15 months, each year can be considered the "first year" for that audience. That is why the survey is conducted annually. Its ongoing value to each year's audience needs to be established. By adding the concepts offered by the Phillips Methodology (2006), the quality and credibility of these annual ROI analyses will be enhanced. In fact, the costs that need to be captured for this project are quite easy to calculate. In the previous ROI calculations, a fully loaded labor cost per hour was provided by Human Resources and includes opportunity cost; that is, what work the employee could be doing if he or she was not taking the GE program. This aligns with Guiding Principle 10, which states that "costs for the solution should be fully loaded for the ROI analysis" (Phillips 2003, p. 52). Additional costs include the per user license fee for one year of access to GE as well as the cost of broadband access for GE users. The cost of broadband access to GE turned out to be minuscule. Therefore, that measure, while having been calculated, turned out to be inconsequential in the final analysis. The details of that calculation can be found in Table 11.3.

The actual survey for 2008 was conducted between September 1 and September 24, 2008. The entire calculation of all costs for the GE program implementation can be found in Table 11.4.

Using the data from Tables 11.2, 11.3, and 11.4, the final ROI cost calculation is provided below:

$$\frac{\$299,052 - \$153,601}{\$153,601} = 0.9469 \times 100\ \% = 94.7\%\ \text{ROI}$$

The BCR is calculated as follows:

$$\frac{\$299,052}{\$153,601} = 1.95{:}1\ \text{or approximately 2:1}$$

COMMUNICATION PLAN

Guiding Principle 12 states that "the results from the ROI Methodology must be communicated to all the key stakeholders" (Phillips 2003, p. 52).

TABLE 11.3 Annual Cost of T1 Broadband Access for 450 GE Learners

Item	Measure	Objective	Source	Value
1	Cost of broadband connectivity	To determine the cost of company T1 broadband per person	SBC communications (a broadband supplier)	1. $23/month/1,000 users or $0.023 per user per month 2. The cost for the 426 GE learners for an entire month (450 × $0.023) is $9.80
2	Percentage and number of hours per month learners spend online with GE	To determine monthly broadband usage per GE learner	GE	1. 4,821 hours online through April 30, 2008 2. 4,821 hours/4 months = 1,205.25 hours for all GE learners per month
3	Cost of broadband usage by GE learners	To determine how much of the overall cost of broadband is utilized by GE learners	Calculated	1. Hours per month per person = 730 2. Total hours available for 426 GE learners = 730 × 426 = 310,980 hours available 3. Percentage of monthly hours used by GE learners: 1,205/310,980 = 0.39% 4. Cost of 426 GE learners' use of broadband per month = 0.39% × $9.80 = $0.0382 $0.0382 × 12 months = $0.46/year
4	Total cost per year of T1 broadband access for 450 GE learners	Determine the annual cost of T1 broadband access for all GE learners	Calculated	$0.46 per year

Note: GlobalEnglish.

309

TABLE 11.4 Annual Cost of GlobalEnglish Usage for 426 Learners

Item	Measure	Objective	Source	Value
1	GE cost per learner	To measure the cost of the actual training program	GE	$350/learner/year
2	Number of learners	To determine how many learners require an annual license	Performance Genetica (client)	426 learners
3	Administration	To determine the cost of administering the GE program	GE	GE handles its own administration as part of the user fee. Performance Pharmaceuticals' administration costs come to $4,500 per year ($150/year/affiliate × 30 affiliates)
4	Materials	To determine if there are any material costs	GE	$0. Since the entire program is online and using computers already assigned to learners, there are no material costs. The $350/learner/year fee covers all materials and support costs.
5	Cost of broadband connectivity	To determine the cost of company T1 broadband per person	Calculated in Table 11.3	Less than $1.00 per year.
6	Total annual cost of GE	Total cost of implementing GE for 450 users for 1 year	Calculated (Items 1 × 2) plus Items 3, 4, and 5	Total cost of GE for 426 learners for one year = $153,601

Note: GE = GlobalEnglish.

Therefore, after determining the ROI and BCR for the GE learning initiative, it was critical to communicate those results to key stakeholders who influence the availability of resources to continue the program. Without communicating the results of the study, there would be a very high risk that in a budgetary downturn, the program could be cut simply because key stakeholders were unaware of the impact of the program. Putting together an effective communication plan required the following elements:

1. Communication must be timely.
2. Communication should be targeted to specific audiences.
3. Media used must be carefully selected.
4. Communication must be unbiased and modest.
5. Communication must be consistent.
6. Testimonials are more effective coming from individuals the audience respects.
7. The audience's opinion of the learning and development staff (and their function) will influence the communication strategy.

CONCLUSIONS

This case study demonstrates that by using a disciplined, comprehensive approach to evaluating the GE online ESL program, it is quite possible to make a strong qualitative and quantitative case for investing in this learning intervention. The Phillips (2006) approach has provided valid and persuasive tools and methods to tease out the financial impact, specifically the ROI, of implementing the GE online learning program. The added rigor, discipline, and operating standards brought to the evaluation process help to insulate the program and the study from critics who use subjective criteria to attack the value of the program. This process moves the entire evaluation methodology for learning programs from a soft, subjective assessment to a concrete, comprehensive, and objective analysis of the impact of the program on learner performance and company business results. These are very powerful tools for training and performance improvement organizations to master and will help training and HPT (Human Performance Technology) professionals support their recommendations for investments in future learning interventions.

REFERENCES

Kirkpatrick, D.L. (1998). *Evaluating Training Programs,* 2nd edition. San Francisco, CA: Berrett-Koehler.

Phillips, J.J. (2003). *Return on Investment in Training and Performance Improvement Programs*. Oxford, UK: Butterworth-Heinemann.

Phillips, J.J. (2006). Return on Investment Measures Success [Electronic version]. *Industrial Management 48*(6): 39–48.

DISCUSSION QUESTIONS

1. Although trainers are guided to think of program evaluation as including five distinct levels, for reasons of practicality, this study clearly combined the qualitative aspects of Levels 1, 3, 4, and 5 into one survey tool. Is this acceptable? If so, why? If not, why not?

2. Why is the "chain of evidence" so important in a study such as this one?

3. An important part of this ROI case study was the ability to determine an increase in workplace application of improved English-as-a-second-language (ESL) skills by using percentages of time and converting those percentages to dollar values. Were there other methods one could use to determine the financial impact of new ESL skills? Please explain your response.

4. How might the ROI process in this case study be improved?

ABOUT THE AUTHOR

Edward (Ed) Nathan, PhD, CRV, holds a PhD in education from Capella University with a specialization in training and performance improvement. He holds a BS in animal science from the University of Delaware and an MBA from SUNY at Albany, New York. He is also a Certified ROI Professional (CRP) from the Phillips ROI Institute. Ed began his career in the pharmaceutical industry more than 25 years ago, having held a number of positions within sales, sales management, and international training and performance improvement. At the time that this case study was originally developed, Ed was Director, Institutional Sales Training, at Wyeth Pharmaceuticals. He then joined Pfizer and has recently left and is currently Managing Director for Global Performance Consulting. Ed served for 10 years as a board member of the Society of Pharmaceutical and Biotech Trainers, and he now makes his home in West Chester, Pennsylvania, USA. Ed can be contacted at his email address, **EPNathan1@gmail.com.**

12

Consultative Sales Program in a Telecommunications Company

Telecommunications Company—
Corporate Division
Chile

Rodrigo Lara Fernández, César Mendoza Díaz,
Ana María Pérez Carmona

Abstract

This case study describes the evaluation of a consultative sales program in a telecommunications company in Chile. The program was developed in the Corporate Division, part of the commercial area. The company wanted to evaluate this experience because they invested a lot of time and money in the program. The evaluation implied interesting learnings for the training and commercial areas, which decided to continue with the program in the next year.

BACKGROUND

The Corporate Division is a business unit of a large telecommunications company, offering fixed and mobile telecommunications products and services to enterprises and corporate customers throughout Chile. The Corporate Division has a total staff of 350 in back office and technical and commercial areas; the latter is made up at present of 150 key account managers, nine assistant managers, and three commercial managers. At the time of program implementation, there were only 92 account managers handling a portfolio of 2,300 business customers. The commercial team's main activity is selling technology and telecommunications solutions.

As a business unit, the division's main concerns are

- budget compliance, based on new projects and renewals
- customer loyalty and satisfaction to build long-term relationships (customer satisfaction index)

- billing for new projects in the period
- increase in volume of high present value business.

The same concerns were passed down from the division's general management to the human resources and training teams in order to implement a program to leverage certain commercial conditions. As a result, the development of a training program in consultative sales was proposed (Sales Process Standardization and Management Program). The program was implemented by an external consultant with a multidisciplinary team, including representatives from commercial planning, human resources, and business processes.

Program Objective

The overarching objective of the program was to develop division account managers' commercial competencies in order to boost the management of strategic and high present value business opportunities.

Program Methodology

The program provides theoretical and practical training, including overseeing account managers' daily activities. The program uses the Individual Work Methodology, which mainly aims to reconcile individual differences in the task of getting new business. During program execution, the facilitator may provide guidance in class.

Participants

The program targets the sales force of the Corporate Division, which is made up of 92 account managers. The average participant profile is that of a high-performing individual with undergraduate studies and with selling practices deeply rooted in everyday life and involving a routine three-month sales cycle.

Duration

Program duration was three months, although this was part of a cyclical training process that took place between May and December 2009. The methodology was presented in a 16-hour training workshop (two working days) and the training took place at a neutral location, specially adapted for the experience.

EVALUATION METHODOLOGY

The evaluation process followed the Phillips ROI Methodology. This process calls for the collection and analysis of five levels of data. These levels are Level 1 Reaction; Level 2 Learning; Level 3 Application, Level 4 Business Impact, and Level 5 ROI. It also calls for the step to isolate the effects of the program. Calculating ROI requires that Level 4 Impact measures are converted to money, and then compared to the cost of the program.

Data Collection

The following methodologies were used to gather data at Levels 1–4:

Level 1 Reaction

- Survey (with a Likert scale from 1 to 5 points) to evaluate usefulness of and satisfaction with the course, facilitator, and training organization and the potential of action plans to be developed.

Level 2 Learning

- Cognitive test to evaluate pre- and post-program learning of the Miller Heiman Consultative Selling methodology. Sales case studies were used also.

Level 3 Application

- Field observation by the direct leader.
- Ongoing coaching and feedback meetings regarding application of the methodology to the current business.
- Self-reports prepared by the account manager using the tools learned (these carry less validity and specific weight in the final analysis).

Level 4 Business Impact

- The percentage variation of the Win Rate (an indicator of opportunities won, over current opportunities in the period prior to measurement), obtained from the Enterprise Work Flow for Customer Projects, called Business Opportunities Follow-up System (SISON).
- The contribution in Present Value (PV) of Opportunities followed up and won under the Consultative Selling model.

315

- The percentage variation in the Customer Satisfaction Indicator, obtained from the Customer Satisfaction Survey Report.
- The percentage variation of the Organizational Climate Survey, in the training section, obtained from the Work Climate Survey Reports.

Table 12.1 shows the data collection plan, and Table 12.2 shows the ROI analysis plan. These plans provide more detail about the data collection approach and the analysis of Level 4 business impact data.

Observations of the Analysis Plan

1. The Corporate Division presents an Average Opportunity Development Time (T) of two months, so it is not feasible to measure ROI of opportunities at the funnel stage (the stage prior to close), as this is a prospecting and creation process. The real Present Value can only be measured once it has been gained; this is why it is better to measure Level 5 only using Win Rate converted to Present Value.

2. Items that cannot be tangibly measured are indicated in the Data Analysis Plan. These are considered intangible benefits and include:
   - improvements in training issues in the Work Climate Survey
   - improvements regarding customer satisfaction
   - relational improvement with internal clients and support areas.

3. The isolation of program effects is done using trend analysis and is based on the following precedents:
   - academic preparation and training of account managers
   - differences in customer portfolio type
   - year-on-year comparison of the average opportunities created, won, and present for each manager
   - year-on-year comparison of the Present Value accumulated by each manager
   - year-on-year comparison of the Win Rate in the group of opportunities to be measured, considering certain ratio seasonalities
   - the percentage impact of commercial or other campaigns that affect sales positively or negatively.

4. To permit specific follow-up of opportunities dealt with by the Consultative Selling model, during the second quarter of 2009 a workflow module system was implemented, into which the account manager enters opportunities to follow up and each of their impacts are measured.

TABLE 12.1   Data Collection Plan

L	General Training Goals	Indicator/Goal	Methods and Instruments	Data Sources	Time of Measurement	Leader
1	• Evaluate usefulness of and satisfaction with course, instructor and organization	• Score between 4 and the items indicated in 80% of cases	• Survey (with Likert evaluation scale between 1 and 5)	• Participant	• At end of activity (workshop)	• Consultant • Training unit
2	• Learn Miller Heiman sales methodology • Note: 1 Module is effective PPT (PBP) and 3 Modules of MH sales planning	• Comparison of pre and post course evaluations with minimum score of 80	• Knowledge test	• Participant	• At start and end of activity	• Consultant • Training unit • Business process (validator)
3	• Use of sales planning tools	• Implementation of 80% of tools learned • 80% of Sales Force applies tools	• Leader's field observation • Self-report • Prospecting methodology evaluation (via Accounts Plan module)	• Direct leader • Participant • Internal consultant	• Period May–December 2009 (quarterly periods)	• Direct leader • Internal consultant • Project manager
4	• Δ+ of Win Rate indicator business > US $ 500.000 (Q projects) • Δ+ Q opportunities < US $ 1000.000 (funnel) • Increase in climate indicator • Increase in customer satisfaction	• Δ+ 3% Win rate • ΔΔ+ 10% Funnel • Δ+ 10pp climate survey (training item) • Δ+ 0.5pp in customer satisfaction item	• Reports from internal systems and tools • Climate survey • Customer Service Survey report	• Work Flow SISON • CMI Commercial • Accounts Plan • Module Climate • Survey ISC Survey	• Monthly between May–December 2009 with information on 31st of each month	• Business process Quality Commercial Planning Training Unit
5	ROI	• Incomes: Values in (revenues and/or value gained) from consultative selling opportunities > US $500.000 / PV which generate the increase in Win Rate • Costs: Direct program costs + indirect MH costs per participant + indirect incremental costs per drop-out concept in the application of learned methodology				

317

TABLE 12.2   Data Analysis Plan

Data Items (Level 4)	Methods for Isolating the Effects of Training / Process	Methods for Converting to Monetary Values	Cost Categories	Intangible Benefits	Communications Target for Final Report	Other Influences or Issues During Application	Comments
• Δ+ 3% Win Rate (Q) in business > US$500.000	Trend analysis	• Proportional value in US$ (revenues and/or value earned) of Consultative Selling opportunities that impact on Win Rate increase	**Direct Cost** (course and transfer in case of regions) + **Indirect Costs** (participants' MHs) 72 account managers + **Indirect Incremental Costs** Course MH value proportional to application level of participants who did not use methodology	• Improvement in work climate quality • Improvement in work satisfaction • Relational improvement with internal clients and support areas	• General management • PMO • Account managers • HR	• Economic crisis • Close of enterprises' 2008 budget • Sales campaigns • Sales convention • Integration of commercial fixed-mobile force	• Business cycle for Corporate Division, average 3 months
• Δ+ gradual period in Customer Satisfaction Survey (6.47 to 6.97)	Trend analysis	• Not applicable (only Level 4)					
• Δ+ 10pp in Climate Survey for training items	Trend analysis	• Not applicable (only Level 4)					
• Δ+ 10% Q of opportunities in funnel (≤ US$100.000)	Trend analysis	• Not applicable (only Level 4)					

Isolation of Variables

The isolation methodology for the analysis of this program is the *trend line,* given the possibility of analyzing business behavior monthly. The business condition presented by the Corporate Division is based on the selling of fixed-mobile solutions and projects; to measure this commercial activity, Win Rate analysis is mainly used, which measures the number of sales opportunities:

$$\text{Win Rate} = \frac{\text{Opportunities won}}{\text{Present opportunities at end of period}} \times 100$$

This ratio can also be analyzed according to the Present Value (PV) range of the business opportunities. So, we can calculate Win Rate for businesses < US$100.000; between US$100.000 and US$500.000; between US$500.000 and US$2.500.000; and greater than US$2.500.000. For the purposes of the analysis of this program, the measures considered at the impact level is the trend in Q (which is the number of opportunities) for sales ranging greater than US$500.000 of Present Value (PV).

The trend analysis is done by comparing the average Win Rate from the 2008 period (May–December) and the Win Rate generated over the same period in 2009.

This ratio will also make it possible to evaluate the proportionality of the contribution of business followed up under the consultative sales modality.

The precedent for measuring the trend is the following:

- Average Win Rate (Q) for the period May–December 2008: 9%

  Comparison of these trends is shown in Figure 12.1.

Converting Data to Monetary Values

Data are converted to monetary contribution, as standard values; these results correspond to proportional values (Revenues and/or Value Won in the period) of opportunities greater than US$500.000 in Present Value, which generate the increase in Win Rate in the period measured. For the analysis to be objective, the only proportional value contributed by business opportunities considered is that which has been dealt with and registered under the consultative selling modality.

For the purposes of control, management, and follow-up of this program and other initiatives of the Corporate Division, an application was implemented (the Accounts Plan) to make it possible to register

Figure 12.1   Isolation Variables: Trend Line Analysis

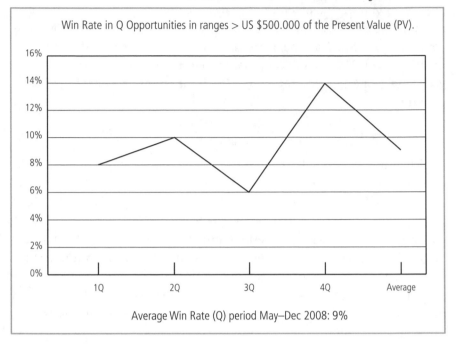

Win Rate in Q Opportunities in ranges > US $500.000 of the Present Value (PV).

Average Win Rate (Q) period May–Dec 2008: 9%

those businesses implemented under the methodology learned; from the information entered into this system, it is possible to analyze data and convert them into monetary values.

The other Level 4 indicators, corresponding to the Customer Satisfaction and Work Climate Index, were not converted into monetary values, as they are qualitative and of little objective consistency. In turn, the Opportunities Funnel Increase indicator < US$100.000 at Present Value was not converted into monetary values.

Program Costs

The evaluation and structure of program costs are generated around three items:

■ **Direct program costs:** These correspond to program implementation and consultant hiring costs; as this is a closed program, all costs are billed by the same supplier and include rental and food logistics during the working day. Added to this direct cost is the transfer of the account managers from other regions.

■ **Indirect program costs:** These correspond to man-hour costs of program participants; the total places available for the program is 72, including account managers and assistant managers. Table 12.3 shows a breakdown of the cost structure.

RESULTS

The general results of the program are "accepted" in consensus with the managers, the program leaders, and the validation team working with the ROI Methodology. However, the Level 3 indicator in regard to 80 percent of the sales force applied to the consultative selling methodology includes observations by this team and is taken as a gap that will increase indirect program costs, affecting in turn the profitability of this team. Table 12.4 shows the objectives proposed at the start of the evaluation and the results obtained from each of the measurements.

Reaction

After completing the two workshops over two working days (16 hours), participants were surveyed for their reactions. These survey questions, shown in Table 12.5, yielded the following results:

■ Course/objectives/modality and applicability to work: 4.37

■ Instructor/level of presentation/time for cases: 4.44

■ Organization/attendance/logistics: 4.28

■ **Overall program evaluation: 4.38**

The final score for Level 1 fulfills the objectives proposed for a score of 4 or 5 for 80 percent of participants.

TABLE 12.3   Cost Structure

Direct Cost	Cost
Miller Heiman Consultative Selling Program, including delivery and evaluation	Total Direct Cost
Indirect Cost	**Cost**
Participants time (MH)	Total Indirect Cost
Supervisors and support team time (MH)	
Total Cost	**Direct + Indirect**

TABLE 12.4   Results Summary

L	General Training Goals	Indicator / Goal	Result	Compliance
1	• Evaluate usefulness of and satisfaction with course, instructor, and organization	Score from 4 to 5 in the items indicated in 80% cases	Overall evaluation 4,38 Course 4,37 Instructor 4,44 Organization 4,28	Accepted
2	• Learn Miller Heiman sales methodology	Comparison of evaluations pre- and post-course with minimum score of 80	65% of participants (88) with evaluation > 80 on maxim 100-point scale, average score 79 points	Accepted
3	• Use of sales planning tools	Implementation of 80% of the tools learned 80% of sales force applies tools	11 coaching actions 220 Account Plans entered 206 opportunities using methodology 35 managers using model (49% sales force)	With observations
4	• Δ+ of Win Rate indicator business > US$ 500.000	Δ+ 3% Win Rate	8% increase in Win Rate average range > US$500.000	Accepted
	• Δ+ Q of opportunities < US$ 100.000 (funnel)	Δ+ 10% funnel	Average increase of 41% in opportunities funnel < US$100.000	Accepted
	• Increased in Climate Indicator	Δ+ 10pp climate survey (training item)	Increase of 11pp (80% to 91%) in the group in which the methodology was applied	Accepted
	• Increased in customer satisfaction	Δ+ 0,5pp in customer satisfaction item	Close of CSI Corporate 2009 score 7,15; 1,4 pp on close 2008	Accepted
5	• ROI	ROI >= 15% at 2009 close as effect of compliance of Win Rate item	ROI 19% for Consultative Sales Program Corporate Division BCR = 1,19 Payback: 10 months	Accepted

TABLE 12.5   Results Level 1

	Code	Score						X
		1	2	3	4	5		
Course	The aims of the workshop were explained . . .	0	0	6	55	44		4.39
	By the end of the workshop, the aims had been achieved . . .	0	1	10	50	46		4.39
	The proposed work modality was . . .	1	0	14	53	39		4.25
	The usefulness of the teaching resources used was . . .	1	1	18	39	49		4.33
	The content worked with contributed to my performance in my role . . .	1	1	7	35	55		4.50
								4.37
Instructor	The instructor's degree of knowledge shown was . . .	0	0	11	48	49		4.39
	The clarity of the explanation of content was	0	0	10	48	50		4.38
	The instructor encouraged those attending to participate	0	1	13	31	63		4.48
	The instructor's time management was	0	0	9	39	60		4.49
								4.44
Organization	I was invited to the meeting in advance	4	4	17	28	54		4.27
	The prior information I received (program, schedule) was . . .	1	5	26	35	40		4.11
	The provision of support materials for the classroom work was	0	2	8	37	61		4.50
	The classroom was . . .	1	1	14	48	43		4.22
	General Average							**4.28**
	Overall Evaluation	0	0	1	39	23		**4.36**
		0	0	1	39	23		**4.38**

5 = Excellent / High / Highly Satisfactory
4 = Very Good / Medium High / Very Satisfactory
3 = Good / Medium / Satisfactory
2 = Regular / Medium Low / Less-Then-Satisfactory
1 = Bad / Low / Unsatisfactory

The survey included qualitative and observation questions, which were taken by the program planning and development team to show a trend of higher scores from participants in each of the training sessions held.

Learning

To measure participants' learning level, a pre- and post-workshop evaluation test was taken on participants' theoretical knowledge of the Miller Heiman Consultative Selling methodology.

Although the proposed objective was that 80 percent of account managers would get a score of 80 points or higher, the indicator was accepted with observations and a program was created to formally improve those managers with a score lower than expected. This activity was not a deviation from the official program, as it was held for the same previously trained group and not a different control group. Table 12.6 presents the learning level results.

Application

The application level of the methodology learned was generated with blue sheets (written instructions) given to the account managers as part of the training process. In addition, a module was made available in the workflow of the Enterprise Division in which managers entered business opportunities to be followed under consultative sales; the information entered was

TABLE 12.6   Results Level 2

Summary 2009 Miller Heiman Methodology Workshops	
Participants	72
Average Score	79
Average Participant Positive Score (>80)	65%
Indicator	
Pre- and post-course evaluation with minimal score of 80 on a maximum scale of 100 points	
• The indicator will agree with observations. • Generates a formal strengthening program for executives with a rating lower than expected. • Is not assumed as a deviation to the official program.	

an integral part of the Customer Account Plans, and it also was integrated to quantitative business information to obtain precedents of Present Value, Revenue, and others.

In addition to this, once the blue sheets had been created, every assistant manager had the responsibility to coach his or her managers in order to adapt the information and provide more precedents to strategic selling. For each of the items that make up Level 3 of the application, clear compliance rules and metrics were established with which the proposed objectives would then be measured.

In accordance with the above, four objectives were set, which on average would provide the real level fulfillment indicator. The objectives include the following:

- **Coaching actions:** The same or higher number of coaching actions as the number of opportunities to follow up under the consultative selling model.

- **Accounts Plans:** Seven Accounts Plan information modules were set to be completed, with precedents from the influencers, buyers, technicians, and administrators of the client, to comply with 100 percent of the 2009 Accounts Plan.

- **Consultative selling opportunities:** Managers had to enter into the Accounts Plan module the opportunities for which they would follow up during the year in the consultative selling modality, establishing opportunity progress percentage parameters depending on the milestones to be met and the maturity stage of the opportunity (funnel concept). If the opportunity is abandoned or the manager does not continue with the consultative selling model and with the formality of the system implemented, this is considered outside of the model and is therefore not counted in the final indicator.

- **Use of methodology:** This was fixed as a minimum parameter for all account managers participating in the program. Managers had to have a minimum of one opportunity under the model taught.

The final results of Level 3 are shown in Table 12.7. The average fulfillment percentage for Level 3 fell short by 46 percent of the proposed objective. Given this condition, this shortfall and drop-out in methodology use was analyzed according to what was seen in the Program Costs item of the same document.

TABLE 12.7   Results Level 3

Results	Indicator / Goal	Objective	Compliance (Real %)
11 Coaching Actions		411 (Q opportunities committed to follow-up in consultative selling)	3%
220 Account Plans entered with 100% information validated to 100% of those solicited	Implementation of 80% of the tools learned

80% sales force applies tools | 357 (Q Account Plans entered into the system) | 62% |
206 opportunities using methodology in different Present Value ranges		411 (Q opportunities committed to follow-up in consultative selling)	50%
35 opportunities to follow-up continuously, under Consultative Sales Model		411 (Q opportunities committed to follow-up in consultative selling)	9%
35 managers trained using the methodology		100% of sales force trained using the methodology	49%
Average Percentage of Level 3 Compliance			34%

Note: The average compliance Level 3 was in deficit by 46% in this target.

Business Impact

The level of impact on business was measured considering four indicator. Two of these (Funnel and Win Rate) were associated with the commercial activity of the Corporate Division and the other two were associated with Customer Satisfaction and Work Climate in training aspects. Just the Win Rate was converted to monetary values.

The results were as follows:

- **A 3 percent increase in Win Rate (Q) in business > US$500.000:** In isolating the business opportunities addressed under the Consultative Selling model, the average 2009 Win Rate of the range of opportunities ≥ US$500.000 was 17 percent; we compare it with the average 2008 (9 percent); so, the difference was 8 percent. Figure 12.2 shows the comparison. It is important to note that we are considering just the opportunities dealt under the Consultative Sales model. And we are just considering the marginal contribution to the sales comparing with the period before.

- **A gradual increase in Customer Satisfaction Survey results (5.77 to 5.97) for items associated with the Commercial Area:** With regard to this objective, there was a positive variation of 0.9 percentage points over the established goal, as shown in Table 12.8. These items are not converted into monetary values because they are qualitative.

- **A 10 percent increase in Opportunities Funnel < US$100.000 of Present Value:** The low present value opportunities funnel was positively affected: projects using the consultative selling methodology in the range < US$100.000 contributed 17 percent to the effective variation of 41 percent of opportunities, as shown in Table 12.9.

- **An increase of 10 percent in training items, from the Work Climate Survey:** Global satisfaction and work climate indicators of the division were positively impacted, attaining their expected objectives; the specific training indicator for the Corporate Division increased 15 percent; the account managers trained in the

FIGURE 12.2   Results Level 4

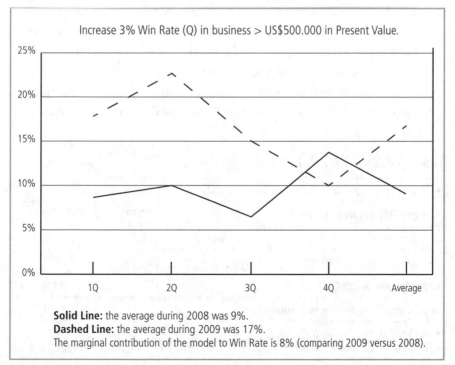

Increase 3% Win Rate (Q) in business > US$500.000 in Present Value.

Solid Line: the average during 2008 was 9%.
Dashed Line: the average during 2009 was 17%.
The marginal contribution of the model to Win Rate is 8% (comparing 2009 versus 2008).

TABLE 12.8   Results Level 4

• Goal: increase in 0.5 points in Clients Satisfaction Survey.		
ISC Corporate Segment	**2008**	**2009**
Period Jan–Dec	5.77%	7.15%
Var % 2008 / 2009		**1.4%**
• Positive variation of 0.9 percentage points over the established goal. • These items are not converted to monetary values because they are qualitative.		

consultative selling methodology gave an increase of 11 percent in their satisfaction with training items. Improvement in the work climate survey is shown in Table 12.10.

ROI Calculation

This program's ROI analysis consists of three key elements:

- management's concern and mandate regarding budget compliance and the increase in high present value business
- the way in which the Corporate Division's commercial activity is measured (Win Rate in number of opportunities and present value)
- the focus of analysis on only those projects and business opportunities that have been addressed with the consultative selling methodology.

In accordance with the above, the ROI analysis will be made around the Win Rate converted to monetary value (present value, value earned) at

TABLE 12.9   Results Level 4

• Goal: increase 10% in Opportunities Funnel < US$100.000 of Present Value.			
Present Opportunity (Funnel)	**2008**	**2009**	**Var %**
Q Opportunities < US$100.00	1,082	1,612	40%
PV Opportunities < US$100.00	189,042	262,914	42%
Var effective % 2008 / 2009			**41%**
% of Consultive Selling in a Funnel			**17%**
• This indicator exceeds its objective. • Funnel data will not be converted to monetary values, being considered an intangible benefit.			

TABLE 12.10 Results Level 4

• Goal: increase of 10% in training items from Work Climate Survey.			
Satisfaction Training Items	**2008**	**2009**	**Var pp**
General Satisfaction (Corporate Division)	80%	95%	15
Trained Account Managers	80%	91%	11
Average Variation (pp)			**13%**

• Global satisfaction and work climate indicators of the Division were positively impacted. • The specific training indicator in the Account Managers group (trained in the Consultative Selling Methodology) gave an increase of 11% in their satisfaction level.

the end of the period to be measured (May–December 2009), considering just the projects addressed under the consultative selling methodology.

$$ROI = \frac{\text{Present Value in Consultative Selling Projects} - (\text{Total Program Costs})}{\text{Total Program Costs}} \times 100$$

*Proportion of Contribution in Present Value of Opportunities in consultative selling at the Win Rate of the Range > US$500.000 at Present Value.

The calculation of the program costs has already been indicated in the respective item in this document.

- **Step 1:** Analysis of Opportunities to be considered is shown in Table 12.11.

TABLE 12.11 Results Level 5: ROI Calculation

Step 1: Analysis of opportunities to be considered.	
Opportunities	**PV**
Client A	592,235
Client B	2,839,343
Client C	501,678
Client D	1,211,883
Sales Contribution	**5,145,139**

TABLE **12.12**   Results Level 5: ROI Calculation

Step 2:
Analysis of proportion contribution of business opportunities in consultative selling at Win Rate range > US$500.000 of Present Value; because of the isolation process, we are going to consider that this sub-group of opportunities contributes 8%.
Step 3:
Calculation in money of business opportunities analyzed.

8% × US$5.145.139 = US$411.611

- **Step 2:** Analysis of proportion contribution of Business Opportunities in consultative selling at Win Rate range > US$500.000 Present Value; this subgroup of opportunities contributes 8 percent, as shown in Table 12.12.

- **Step 3:** Calculation in money of business opportunities analyzed:

$$8\% \times US\$5.145.139 = US\$411.611$$

- **Step 4:** Calculation of direct and indirect costs. Costs are shown in Table 12.13.

- **Step 5:** ROI calculation and RCB calculation:

$$ROI = \frac{411.611 - (345.250)}{345.250} \times 100$$

$$ROI = 19\%$$

$$BCR = 1.9$$

TABLE **12.13**   Results Level 5: ROI Calculation

Step 4:	
Calculation of direct and indirect costs.	
Direct Cost	**Cost**
Miller Heiman Consultative Selling Program, including design, delivery, and evaluation	50.000
Indirect Cost	**Cost**
Participants' time (MH)	44.250
Supervisors' and support team's time (MH)	51.000
Total Cost	**345.250**

Intangible Benefits

The Miller Heiman Consultative Selling Program is part of the Corporate Division Quality Project, whose main aim is to increase customer satisfaction in different areas—specifically this program—in account managers' understanding of customers' needs and the possibility of gaining customer loyalty in long-term accounts during the negotiation and selling processes. From this perspective, some intangible benefits can be identified. Specifically, the program

- is an integral part of the commercial certification process of the sales force
- leads to an increase in the professional and work value of the commercial area
- promotes greater closeness to customer needs
- generates consultative ties in the customer relationship
- inserts systematic work methodologies under quality norms
- allows team leaders to identify best practices in their teams
- brings team leaders closer to their managers' "day-to-day" experiences
- contributes in commercial areas to attack key accounts
- detects gaps in the competencies of the organization's sales teams
- projects new HR evaluation programs and methodologies.

CONCLUSIONS AND LESSONS LEARNED

The objective and quantifiable analysis of the Consultative Selling program helped to identify gaps that should be addressed in the continuity and/or repetition of this program. The investment return obtained from this program is a positive condition (19 percent). Despite this, the results obtained at Level 3 indicate that there are additional efforts to be made to attain the objectives proposed.

The first thing to be analyzed is that consultative selling as a model should respond to a culture and/or way of carrying out daily sales work and not only to a condition imposed that would achieve the goals merely by being implemented; programs should also be developed together that give team leaders competencies that allow them to evaluate the fulfillment and implementation of each one of the tasks to be done by the sales managers when applying this model.

In general, the conclusions of this program are positive and open up possibilities for continuing the objective measurement of other initiatives. The program also enables the development and implementation of a methodology to visualize projects and is a cultural opportunity (for the company) to assess internal needs.

One reflection that should be evaluated mainly by training and development departments jointly with management and/or administration control regards installing a profitability model for the company for nonfinancial projects, specifically staff development projects, which would boost a more continuous measurement of projects under the ROI methodology in the medium term.

DISCUSSION QUESTIONS

1. What is the real validity and importance of measuring Level 1 in programs of this type, especially when the main contribution should come from Levels 3 and 4?

2. How should organizational cultural gaps be approached in programs of this type, in which knowledge of customer accounts is mainly in the hands of the business manager who must share it with the organization?

3. What is the contribution of including qualitative indicators and objectives in an analysis such as this (Level 4)?

ABOUT THE AUTHORS

Rodrigo Lara Fernández has obtained a bachelor's degree in both psychology and business administration and a master's degree in human resources. He has enjoyed 18 years of experience in training and development and has worked as a consultant for the last 16 years with MAS Consultores, a Chilean company in which he is a partner. With Jack Phillips, he created Instituto ROI, a company to deliver ROI Methodology workshops and consultancy in Latin America, and has built the first ROI Network in South America. He holds the ROI Methodology Certification from the ROI Institute and is a member of ASTD, where he also has participated as an adviser for the Evaluation and ROI Network. He received the Practitioner of the Year Award from the ROI Institute in 2007 and the Measurement and Evaluation Award from ASTD in 2008.

César Mendoza Díaz has a bachelor in economy and administration and a diploma in marketing, with a specialization in business intelligence and commercial planning. He has worked as a business consultant for a couple of companies and currently is in the same position at a telecommunications firm. He received certification in Project Management from the Project Management Institute and he is also certified in ROI Methodology by the ROI Institute.

Ana María Pérez Carmona is an industrial psychologist with three years' experience in training and organizational development, specializing in measurement and evaluation and needs assessment. She works at MAS Consultores–Instituto ROI Chile as Project Director. Ana María is currently finishing a case study to obtain certification in ROI Methodology by the ROI Institute.

13

Determining Impact and ROI for Knowledge Management

Global Consulting, Inc.
USA

Bruce C. Aaron

T his case was prepared to serve as a basis for discussion rather than an illustration of either effective or ineffective administrative and management practices. All names, dates, places, and data may have been disguised at the request of the author or organization.

Abstract

This case study is an evaluation of business impact and return on investment (ROI) for a knowledge management (KM) system within Global Consulting, Inc. The evaluation used a longitudinal design to measure impact and ROI across time and groups. Results showed a significant positive impact on productivity, based largely on the effect of time savings realized by leveraging a cost-effective KM system across a large population of employees.

PROGRAM BACKGROUND

As our global economy has been transformed by information technology, organizations have struggled to maximize the value of the vast amounts of information available to them. Competitive advantage has become increasingly dependent on harvesting and applying information from systems, employees, and customers. The goal of this process is knowledge, and the practice of knowledge management (KM) has arisen to accomplish it.

Global Consulting's strategy is to align both KM and training with the capability development needs of the business. In general, the role of training is to build long-term skills in the workforce, and the role of KM is to provide point-of-need knowledge. Both functions serve the organization by enabling the workforce with the knowledge and skills needed to perform their roles and deliver value to customers.

Training evaluation, including the measurement of return on investment (ROI), has evolved over several decades, generating relatively established approaches. Evaluation of KM, however, lags in addressing many of the issues that have a longer history of debate and application in the practice of training evaluation. For example, Cohen notes in the December 2006 issue of *Harvard Business Review* that over the preceding decade, companies had largely failed to calculate ROI for KM, often relying on transactional data (e.g., the number documents created in, or downloaded from, information repositories) to evaluate the success of KM. This is not unlike the discussion within the training industry about using course attendance data and "lower level" metrics to evaluate courses. In the training industry, however, this discussion has now generally evolved into acceptance of the feasibility of ROI evaluation, with debate shifting to consideration of the most appropriate approaches and applications.

This case study describes how Global Consulting approached the measurement of business impact and ROI for KM. Pseudonymous Global Consulting has more than 200,000 employees in more than 50 countries. The company offers management consulting, technology services, and outsourcing services to businesses and governments. Global Consulting's business model requires attention to KM and the need to access and leverage the experience and knowledge of employees globally, as recognized by Global Consulting's chairman and CEO:

> "The question is how to bring out the best ideas, the best technologies, and the best expertise wherever they are in the world. . . . to be organized in such a way that we are constantly learning and bringing our new ideas, innovations, and expertise to our clients. . . . "

Many changes followed an organizational restructuring within the company, and the subsequent implications for the company's KM organization included consolidation of more than 1,000 separate KM databases into a central KM technical infrastructure. In addition, a KM strategy and planning group was created within the central training organization to provide global KM and work with the KM deployed (line-facing) teams. After replatforming the global technical architecture and stabilizing operations, attention turned quickly to metrics and evaluation. An evaluator was enlisted to develop a measurement framework and reporting for the KMX (the company's primary global KM repository) and to help determine business impact and ROI. This case study focuses on the results of that effort to measure KM impact and ROI.

EVALUATION METHODOLOGY

Evaluation should begin with a model that describes the targets of measurement and the logical relationship between them. Kirkpatrick's (1994) and Phillips's (1997) familiar framework, for example, models a process in which learner reaction, learning, application of learning, and business impact resulting from application are joined in a logical model of what is expected if the training solution succeeds. Each of these levels suggests a set of metrics against which the solution can be evaluated.

The measurement models traditionally used for training are an imperfect fit for KM evaluation due to the differences in the nature and intent of training and KM. Unlike courses, for example, knowledge assets do not imply learning objectives and other outcomes that apply commonly across the diverse group of users. We can expect that a knowledge asset might be of great value to one particular user or in one context, but of little use to another user or in a different situation. The KM evaluation model developed to guide the project is shown in Figure 13.1. It comprises six levels (0–5); Levels 3 through 5 are familiar and align with the models presented by Kirkpatrick (1994) and Phillips (1997; 2003). Levels 0 through 2 are focused on KM solutions and guide the metrics that need to be defined. The right side of the model guides evaluation design. Definitions of each level of evaluation are provided in Figure 13.2.

The first year of the KM evaluation study was spent developing and improving the reporting systems necessary to provide data at Levels 1 and 2. These consist of the web usage and transactional reports that help determine the extent to which employees are interacting with the KM system and finding needed information within it. Subsequently, effort focused on obtaining application and business results measures, converting Level 4 metrics to monetary values, developing the cost model, and determining ROI. The strategy for evaluating these application and business impact outcomes is the topic of this case study.

Figure **13.1** KM Measurement Model

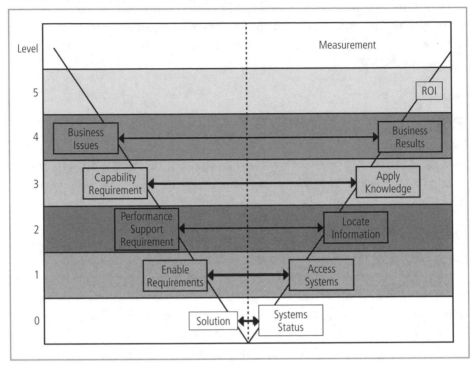

Value of the Model

Specifying the model is an essential step in the evaluation process, from both a methodological and a political perspective. Development of the model serves the evaluation in two important ways. When business results (Level 4 metrics) are *less* than expected, specifying levels that are logically connected and directly related to the phases of the solution (see Figure 13.1), and collecting data across all levels, are the means for identifying where the problems exist. Building systems to collect Level 1 and 2 data was prerequisite to developing the system for measuring business impact in the Global Consulting KM impact study. The systems that collect these transactional metrics were developed to filter by KM content areas as well as by demographic variables within the company. These data dimensions are also built into the collection of Level 3 through 5 (ROI) data, which is a powerful tool for isolating the factors that ultimately are responsible for the overall ROI for KM.

FIGURE 13.2   KM Measurement Model Level Defenitions

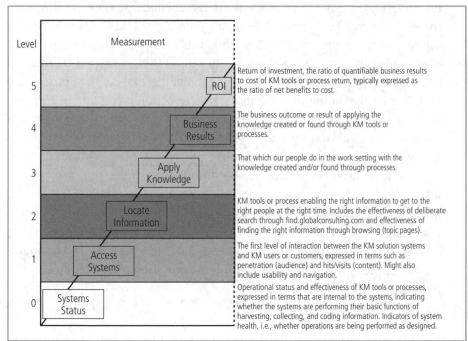

When business results are positive, in applied organizational settings in which many dynamic internal and external forces influence results, one of the greatest challenges in ROI evaluation is demonstrating the portion of documented results that can be directly attributed to the evaluated program (versus other competing factors). Techniques for isolating the effects of the initiative are required, but simply collecting data across all levels of evaluation strengthens the claim for program effects by establishing the "chain of impact" (Phillips and Aaron 2008). By demonstrating the relationship among metrics across levels, the program can support its claim that results were impacted as predicted because the solution met its objectives as intended across each level of implementation. This is "necessary but not sufficient" evidence of direct program impact, but it typically provides a convincing argument not available unless the measurement model is thoughtfully planned and executed.

In addition, the model helps communicate the approach to stakeholders and gain the buy-in necessary for the study and approach. In this case, the evaluator worked with a KM steering committee and KM Metrics Working Group representing the deployed KM organizations, whose support and input were critical to the success of the project. The measurement model provides the foundation to which all aspects of the evaluation approach are tied. It is easily communicated and serves to continually reorient the governance groups to the measurement plan and reenlist their support, which is critical for evaluation initiatives that must be maintained over months and years.

The measurement model defines the data elements that are needed across levels. After developing and implementing the systems for Level 1 and 2 data and reporting, and examining options for collecting the data necessary for Levels 3 and 4, it became apparent that end-user input would deliver the most information at these levels (see Figure 13.3) and that a survey strategy would be the most efficient method of obtaining the required metrics.

Scope of the Study

The KM impact study data collection began in July 2007 and continued through 2008. Level 0 through 5 measures were reported on an ongoing basis, and reported by group as the sample grew with continuing data collection. The case examined a single central component of the overall KM program at Global Consulting, the KM Exchange (KMX), which is the primary global KM repository. The purpose of the KMX is to harvest, categorize, and disseminate on demand the knowledge assets of the company. The evaluation design could also accommodate other KM initiatives of an organization, which could be subsumed within the evaluation as shown in the example in Figure 13.4, which suggests how result summaries at each level of the model can be organized across a range of other initiatives within a global KM program, with the results then aggregated into a more holistic evaluation of KM within a company.

Sampling

Global Consulting's central training and development organization strives to make survey research as efficient as possible in order to respect the many demands on employees' time and attention, and to maintain the highest possible response rates for survey efforts. Implications of this

FIGURE **13.3** General Data Requirements for Levels 3 Through 5

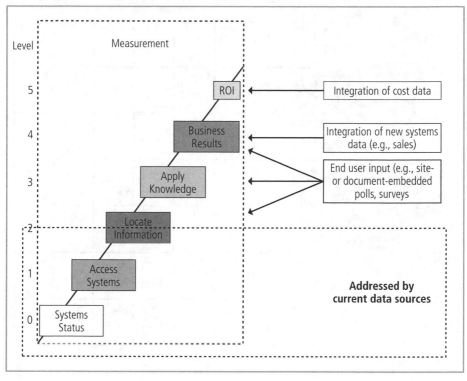

approach include that surveys must be as concise as possible, and that sampling strategies must be employed unless there is a strong business reason for collecting data from entire groups. Based on the sampling requirement, a central feature of this impact study is the strategic sampling plan employed, and an important characteristic of this case is the generalization of results from representative random samples of the population, with no extrapolation of benefits data beyond those actually reported. The latter requirement is aligned with the set of conservative assumptions adopted for ROI evaluation in the ROI Methodology (Phillips 2003).

In this study, repeated random samples were drawn such that reports could be generated for each of the groups of interest, and these results were aggregated to produce the enterprise-level results. The groups of interest are essentially industry groups (e.g., financial services, government, resources, and others) and specialized capability groups (e.g., human performance, supply chain management, and others) that define the

FIGURE 13.4 Global KM Evaluation Scorecard

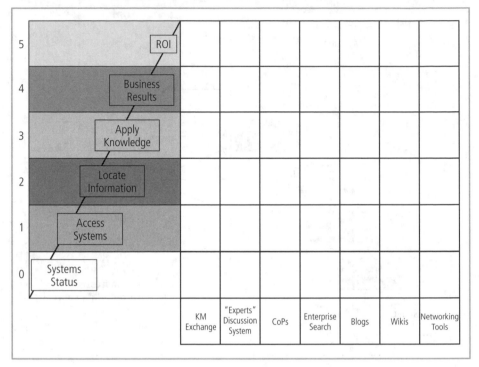

company's client service model. Therefore, the plan randomly sampled across people and time. Sampling was without replacement (so no one was surveyed twice).

The size of a survey effort using random samples (necessary to generalize to the population of interest) is determined by the confidence level one adopts (traditionally 95 percent), the size of the group from which the sample is drawn, and the response rate. Because this study sampled across time as well as people, samples were drawn for a group until the number of returns reached the threshold at which results could be generalized with an acceptable margin of error. Results were interpreted as generalizable, i.e., representative of the population from which the samples were drawn, within a known level of confidence. At a minimum, each group was sampled three times over the course of a quarter (but no person provided survey data twice).

Leveraging Penetration Statistics

At each sampling point in time, KMX transactional reports were run to indicate who within each target group had accessed the system within the preceding week. A random sample was drawn from each of these groups of KMX users. Nonusers were not sampled because (1) they had no application or benefit data to provide and (2) the sampling plan had to be highly efficient (minimizing survey administrations). These nonusers, however, were included in cost calculations for ROI and must be considered part of the sample. For every 100 users randomly identified in a group, there is a known percentage and number of nonusers for the same group and time period. This percentage is reflected as "penetration," a key Level 2 KMX metric available out of the web usage reporting system. If, for example, penetration is 50 percent (one-half of a target group has used the system at least once in a given time period), then for every 100 users randomly selected for study, there are 100 "random" nonusers. Level 4 benefits data used to calculate ROI are based only on the actual benefits reported by the portion of the user sample group that experienced business results, while costs would be based on the entire sampling frame ($n = 200$ in this example).

This approach is accurate since random sampling provides confidence that the entire group is represented by the data within an acceptable margin of error, and because the penetration statistic is an accurate representation of the ratio of users to nonusers for a given time period. No Level 4 benefits data are extrapolated beyond those actually reported, so no assumptions are made (other than the known margin of error for random samples) about nonusers and nonrespondents. Benefits data come from those surveyed users who responded and reported positive results. Zero Level 4 benefits are recorded for (1) nonusers, who were not surveyed, (2) nonrespondents to the survey, or (3) respondents who report no Level 4 benefits.

Impact Survey Strategy

The evaluation questionnaire was carefully designed to provide maximum information about Level 3 and 4 metrics as efficiently as possible. This required multiple response item formats ("check all that apply") and logical branching within the questionnaire (such that the instrument asks additional relevant questions based on previous answers). The questionnaire design used during the evaluation is summarized in Table 13.1.

TABLE 13.1 Questionnaire Design and Branching

Question (Abridged)	Responses (Abridged)	Metrics	Branching
1. Which of the following are true about your use of the KMX during the last two weeks? (check all that apply)	**(a)** Found useful information AND applied directly in work.	Percentage applying information from KMX directly to work (Level 3: Application)	GO TO item 2
	(b) Found useful information but NOT applied directly to work.	Percentage finding useful information as a result of KMX (Level 2: Locate). [(a) or (b)]	**GO TO item 8 (if b, NOT a)**
	(c) Strengthened business network.	Percentage increasing network as a result of KMX (Level 1: Access)	**GO TO item 8 (if c, NOT a)**
	(d) None of the above		GO TO item 8
2. The information I obtained from the KMX . . . (check all that apply)	**(a)** . . . helped close a deal or contract.	Percentage applying KMX info [for this purpose]. (Level 3: Application)	
	(b) . . . was included in a proposal or sales presentation.	Percentage applying KMX info [for this purpose]. (Level 3: Application)	
	(c) . . . helped analyze a client's need.	Percentage applying KMX info [for this purpose]. (Level 3: Application)	
	(d) . . . helped to design and build a client solution.	Percentage applying KMX info [for this purpose]. (Level 3: Application)	

Question (Abridged)	Responses (Abridged)	Metrics	Branching
	(e) . . . was used to better manage a project or program.	Percentage applying KMX info [for this purpose]. (Level 3: Application)	
	(f) . . . helped improve operations.	Percentage applying KMX info [for this purpose]. (Level 3: Application)	
	(g) . . . helped with strategy and planning (including due diligence).	Percentage applying KMX info [for this purpose]. (Level 3: Application)	
	(h) . . . helped prepare an internal presentation (e.g., for a community of practice, community meeting, etc.).	Percentage applying KMX info [for this purpose]. (Level 3: Application)	
	(i) Other (please describe in the space below):	Percentage applying KMX info [for this purpose]. (Level 3: Application)	
3. Without the KMX, it would have taken more time to do the same work or get the same results.	**(a)** Certainly true	Percentage saving time as a result of KMX (a) OR (b). (Level 4: Business Results)	
	(b) Probably true	Percentage saving time as a result of KMX (a) OR (b). (Level 4: Business Results)	
	(c) Probably not true		GO TO item 6

(continued)

345

TABLE 13.1   Continued

Question (Abridged)	Responses (Abridged)	Metrics	Branching
	(d) Certainly not true		GO TO item 6
4. During last two weeks, information from the KMX saved AT LEAST: (time estimate):	Open numeric field	Total and average time saved as a result of KMX. (Level 4: Business Results) (Level 5: ROI, converting to dollars and comparing with KMX cost)	
5. During last two weeks, information from the KMX saved AT MOST: (time estimate):	Open numeric field		
6. The information I obtained by using the KMX enhanced the quality of my work on these tasks.	**(a)** Certainly true		
	(b) Probably true		
	(c) Probably not true		GO TO item 8
	(d) Certainly not true		GO TO item 8
7. Describe how quality or success was enhanced by information obtained through the KMX:	Open text field	Qualitative	

Question (Abridged)	Responses (Abridged)	Metrics	Branching
8. Overall, how satisfied are you with the KMX?	**(a)** Extremely satisfied	KMX satisfaction mean rating, (a)–(e), KMX satisfaction (%) (a) OR (b) (Level 1: Reaction)	
	(b) Satisfied		
	(c) Neither satisfied nor dissatisfied		
	(d) Dissatisfied		
	(e) Extremely dissatisfied		
9. Other suggestions for improving KMX:	Open text field	Qualitative	
10. Would you like a copy of the results?	**(a)** Yes **(b)** No		
11. May we contact you directly?	**(a)** Yes **(b)** No		

Evaluation Requirements

The following is a summary of the guiding principles and requirements for the questionnaire and evaluation strategy:

1. Use a concise, efficient design with minimal impact on employees.
   a. Minimum items shown = 5, maximum = 11 (based on branching logic and participant responses).
   b. Average response time was less than 4 minutes for the questionnaire.
   c. Employ strategic random sampling:
      i.   Sampling across people and time
      ii. Sample without replacement (no one is sampled twice)
2. The evaluation design must be generalizable to other KM initiatives (e.g., CoPs, KM Client Services, other KM tools or systems).
3. Use a credible ROI process and metrics.
   a. Use conservative assumptions for ROI:
      i.   Use fully loaded costs of the KM solution.
      ii. Nonrespondents are assumed to have zero business impact.
   b. Use the lower bound on time savings estimates used for ROI.
4. Collect qualitative data and facilitate participant follow-up to obtain detailed continuous improvement information.
5. The process must be scalable.
   a. Minimize manual processes for administration and data analysis.
   b. Provide standardized reporting for the enterprise and by group.

The electronic questionnaires were administered through a URL link provided in a cover memo, distributed to the random samples and signed by Global Consulting's global KM director. The instrument was designed in Questionmark™, a web-enabled assessment and survey application. Individual employee identification was embedded, which enabled merging with internal systems data for reporting (by group, career level, and other demographic variables) and ensured that employees were included in only one wave of survey administration. Respondents were asked about their experience using any information they might have obtained from their visits to the KMX during the previous two weeks only; the short time period facilitated recall, making the data more reliable. Any benefits data were therefore annualized. As described above, the sampling strategy assumes random sampling across time, as well as people, and drew multiple samples throughout the year from each group to support this assumption.

As shown in Table 13.1, a number of useful key "tracking" metrics were provided at Levels 3 and 4, which had been previously unavailable. The Level 4 measure used in calculation of ROI was time savings, for which an upper and lower bound were collected to provide an error interval for each respondent's estimate. The lower bound (most conservative) estimate was used in ROI calculation (although leadership was also provided a sensitivity analysis to examine the range of ROI values across varying levels of conservatism).

It is important to realize that time savings is only one component of the likely benefits of KMX use, as suggested in Figure 13.5, and this was communicated clearly to stakeholders. Increase in quality was collected and reported as a Level 4 metric but was not quantified for conversion to dollars. Since the survey solicited permission to follow up (item 11), those reporting benefits and agreeing to follow-up are candidates for continued study in these areas.

FIGURE 13.5   Time Savings as a Portion of KM Benefits

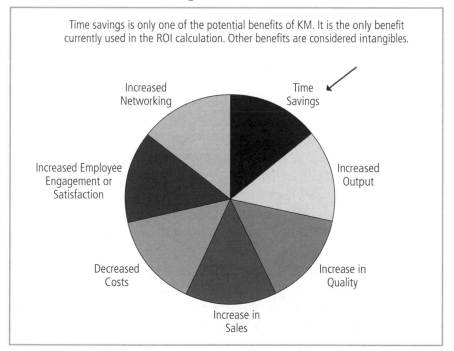

Time savings is only one of the potential benefits of KM. It is the only benefit currently used in the ROI calculation. Other benefits are considered intangibles.

Isolating the Effects of the Program

The unique impact of the initiative on benefits data has to be demonstrated. While challenging in most cases, isolating the effects of the program was straightforward in this study as a result of the survey strategy. As shown in Table 13.1, users who experienced time savings in general were identified by response to the item "Without the KMX, it would have taken more time to do the same work or get the same results." This selects persons who have time savings benefits that can be attributed directly and only to the program. These respondents are routed to core questions that quantify the time saved with the prompts and items shown in Table 13.1 as items 4 and 5. As a result, these time savings data can be attributed directly to the program; that is, they result uniquely from information derived from the KM tool.

RESULTS

The questionnaire was distributed to 2,668 randomly selected employees who had used the system across a 10-month period and was answered by 764—a 29 percent response rate (not atypical for this type of survey). The electronic survey was distributed by email, with no preceding communication. No significant item response differences were found between earlier and later respondents or in the distribution of key demographic variables for respondents and nonrespondents. The overall penetration rate for KMX use was 81 percent during the evaluation period, indicating that for the 2,668 KMX users surveyed, there were 626 "random nonusers" for whom the KMX logically could have had no effect. These nonusers are included in the analysis of ROI (providing a total sample frame of 3,294), with ascribed business benefits of zero.

Key Impact Tracking Metrics

The KM Impact Study is designed to fill several measurement gaps, particularly at Levels 3 through 5. Several of these needs are met by key impact tracking metrics, which provide simple, standard measures across groups and time capturing the essence of Levels 2, 3, and 4. These metrics are ideal for high-level scorecard report categories (as would appear, for example, in the first column of the scorecard template shown in Figure 13.4), comparisons between groups, and tracking across time. Results for these measures are displayed in Table 13.2.

TABLE 13.2 Key Impact Metrics, Pilot

Basic Impact Metrics	
FIND useful information as a result of KMX	60.7%
APPLY information found through KMX to work	44.0%
Build business NETWORK through KMX	5.4%
SAVE TIME as a result of KMX	41.0%
Increased QUALITY of work as a result of KMX	41.0%
Overall SATISFACTION with KMX	60.6%

Similar metrics are reported for the other items shown in Table 13.1, which are only summarized here for brevity. For example, 44 percent applied the information directly to work tasks (see Table 13.2), but additional metrics are provided across nine specific areas of application (see item 2, Table 13.1). Of these areas, the most frequently reported applications were in helping prepare a sales proposal or presentation (18 percent) and analyzing clients' needs (14 percent).

Return on Investment

As described previously, the benefit identified for conversion to dollars is time savings attributable to information obtained through the KMX. The instrument used for data collection guides users who report time savings through questions that ask them to reflect on their experience over the previous two weeks in applying the information obtained as a result of using the KMX. Two estimates are collected, providing a minimum estimate of time saved as a result of this application and a maximum estimate of time savings. The lower bound (i.e., the most conservative estimate) is used and reported in the ROI calculation. The series of questions is shown in Figure 13.6. The average salary plus fringe benefits for employees in the sample frame is used to value their time, and a cost model is developed to calculate the investment in delivering the KMX annually. These time savings attributable to the KMX are compared with the cost of delivering the tool to calculate ROI by the following formula:

$$\text{ROI} = \frac{\text{Benefits} - \text{Cost}}{\text{Cost}}$$

FIGURE 13.6   Quantifying the Range of Time Savings

Please estimate the amount of your time that you saved during the last two weeks as a result of this information.

First, enter your most conservative (lowest) estimate (for example, the information obtained saved "at least" this much time).

Then, enter the highest reasonable estimate for your time saved (for example, it saved "at most" this much time).

Enter time saved in hours, using numerals. You may use a decimal if needed (for example, .25 is 1/4 of an hour, or 15 minutes). Estimate only your own time savings, not time saved for others or for the project overall.

Lowest time savings estimate:
"During the last 2 weeks, this information saved me AT LEAST:" (in HOURS):

Highest time savings estimate:
"During the last 2 weeks, this information saved me AT MOST:" (in HOURS):

Since time saved is based on user input, the data were screened for outliers based on z scores and examination of the distribution of reported time savings, and extreme scores were not included in the analysis. This is shown in Figure 13.7. One case, in which a 40-hour minimum biweekly time savings was reported, was excluded from the analysis.

FIGURE 13.7   Outliers

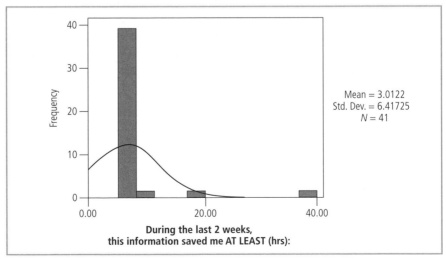

Mean = 3.0122
Std. Dev. = 6.41725
$N = 41$

**During the last 2 weeks,
this information saved me AT LEAST (hrs):**

The result of the ROI analysis indicated a 1,014 percent return on annual investment in the KMX, based on time savings attributable to use of the application (about $11 in savings resulting from each dollar invested in the KMX). Details on each of the elements of cost and time value for the study are provided in Table 13.3. The ROI summary data are show in Table 13.4.

TABLE 13.3 Investment and Benefits Data Used to Calculate ROI

Category	Item	Value
Annual investment in KMX content delivery	KMX design and development	$1,000,000
	Global KM salary and benefits (KMX only)	$500,000
	Outsourced salary and benefits (KMX only)	$1,500,000
	Deployed KM teams salary and benefits	$5,000,000
	Global training and development administration	$25,000
	Evaluation	$20,000
	KMX annual costs	$8,045,000
Annual investment in employees	KMX target audience	100,000
	Cost per person to deliver KMX	$80
	Average salary plus benefits per person per hour	$100
KMX survey impact data	Total hours saved per week attributable to KMX (lower bound, minimum estimate)	615
	Annual value of KMX, time savings	$2,951,966
	Surveyed count	2,668
	Penetration rate for sample group	81%
	Sample n	3,294
	Annual cost of delivering KMX to sample	$264,988
	ROI (of the KMX, based on time savings)	1014%

Note: Data are representative but transformed to protect confidential information.

TABLE 13.4   ROI Summary Table

Annual cost of KMX	$8,045,000
Cost of KMX per person (*n* = 100,000)	$80
Study random sample size	3,294
Annualized value (time savings) attributed to KMX	$2,951,966
Cost of KMX, study sample frame	$264,988
Benefit to cost ratio (BCR)	11.14:1
ROI	1014%

Qualitative Results

The survey solicited comments regarding areas of improvement for the KMX application. Sixteen percent of respondents provided suggestions. The predominant area for improvement related to the search engine for the repository, reflected by both general and specific suggestions.

CONCLUSIONS

This impact study provided continuous measurement, sampling across groups and across time. The ROI and other KM impact metrics were used to provide summary and tracking information, both for groups and for the enterprise. In addition to the quantitative analysis, qualitative data were tracked for continuous improvement, and a proportion of respondents self-identified for detailed follow-up.

The particular features of this case, which have contributed to its success and which might be effectively implemented in other studies of the value of KM, include the following:

1. A strategic random sampling plan that helps minimize "survey fatigue," which is an issue for Global Consulting and many other organizations
2. Use of penetration statistics to further minimize the footprint of the study while providing a credible basis for ROI calculations
3. Carefully designed electronic surveys that take advantage of branching logic to minimize the number of questions presented and

collect the most relevant information from respondents, resulting in an average time demand of less than four minutes per respondent

4. Identification of, and support for, a KM measurement framework to which evaluation projects can be anchored

5. Partnerships with key KM governance and working groups within the organization in developing and supporting the approach

6. A continuous measurement model, with a consistently updated ROI and impact metrics

7. A set of key impact metrics amenable to use in scorecards and trend charts, linked directly to the measurement framework, in addition to ROI calculations

Identification of respondents who can be followed up based on their individual response patterns to obtain more detailed qualitative information, as well as quantification and conversion to currency of Level 4 metrics currently classified as intangibles

LIMITATIONS

Time Savings Is a Limited Representation of Total KM Benefits

Because it is the most easily and credibly quantified benefits measure and can be directly converted to currency, time savings was the first target for this continuous measurement design. Subsequent metric targets for conversion could include increases in quality and contribution to sales. Increased quality is captured as a key impact tracking metric in the current design and treated as a Level 4 intangible because it could not be credibly converted. The individuals reporting these results could be selected for follow-up study to determine the specific nature and value of the contribution to quality. These follow-up studies should result in data about quality that could be converted to currency and included in the ROI calculation. A similar strategy can be pursued to convert the program's contribution to sales. Increased networking, another benefit of successful KM, is also tracked in the current study as a Level 4 intangible.

Assumptions About the Value of Time Saved

Some authors (see, e.g., Cohen 2006) suggest that ROI calculations based on time saved are flawed without evidence of how the saved time is actually spent. Although this might be a valid concern in some specific contexts, the deliberate approach of current study is to make no assumptions about variations in employee productivity; that is, that time saved can be valued at the same average rates of productivity and cost (salary plus fringe benefits) that are used to represent the value of an employee's total annual working time. These rates are adjusted according to factors such as career level, based on the distribution of these factors in the random sample.

RESOURCES

Cohen, D. (2006). What's Your Return on Knowledge? *Harvard Business Review*. Retrieved August 2011, from http://hbr.org/2006/12/whats-your-return-on-knowledge/ar/1

Kirkpatrick, D.L. (1994). *Evaluating Training Programs: The Four Levels*. San Francisco: Berrett-Koehler.

Phillips, J.J. (1997). *Handbook of Training Evaluation and Measurement Methods* (3rd ed.). Houston, TX: Gulf Publishing.

Phillips, J.J. (2003). *Return on Investment in Training and Performance Improvement Programs,* 2nd ed. New York: Butterworth-Heinemann.

Phillips, J.J., & B.C. Aaron. (2008). *Isolation of Results: Defining the Impact of the Program*. San Francisco: Pfeiffer.

DISCUSSION QUESTIONS

1. What are some business impact metrics that might be used to measure the effect of KM? Which metric was selected as the basis for the ROI calculation in this study, and why? What other approaches might you take to calculating ROI in this case?

2. Is it important to develop a logic model of the program in designing an evaluation? Why? What was the approach in this case?

3. What is "survey fatigue"? Is it an issue in the organization(s) in which you work? What can you do to address it? What were some of the strategies used to address survey fatigue in this case?

4. What is meant by "fully loaded costs"? Why are these costs important in calculating ROI? What were some of the costs used in this case? Are there others that should have been included?

5. In this case, why was the ROI percentage presented as a range, anchored by three points? Do you think this might be useful in reporting ROI?

ABOUT THE AUTHOR

Bruce Aaron, PhD. With more than 20 years of experience providing measurement and evaluation solutions to a wide array of global companies and organizations, Bruce Aaron is the author of dozens of publications and a frequent presenter at conferences of professional organizations such as ASTD, ISPI, SALT, AERA, AEA, and the Psychometric Society. He received ASTD's 2004 ROI Impact Study award and the ROI Institute's Impact Study of the Year award in 2007. Bruce holds an MA in school psychology and a PhD in educational measurement and evaluation from the University of South Florida and is the founder of Ametrico.

14

Winning Every Walk-in

TataSky Ltd
India

Capt. Charanjit S. Lehal

This case was prepared to serve as a basis for discussion rather than an illustration of either effective or ineffective administrative practices. Names, dates, places, and data may have been disguised at the request of the author or the organization.

Abstract

This was a training intervention that was critical and at the same time very costly in planning, implementation, and follow-through. The intervention was designed to teach three sales impacting skills to employees, and the business objective was to impact sales and monthly recharges. It was a pan-India rollout involving approximately 290 employees and 35 supervisors. The program was launched in the third quarter, and the impact was traced in the last quarter of financial year 2009–2010. The project was impacted by certain environmental factors, but an outstanding ROI of more than 300 percent was achieved.

PROGRAM BACKGROUND

TataSky is a satellite television provider that has redefined the television viewing experience for thousands of families across India. The service aims to empower the Indian viewer with choice, control, and convenience. The company is a joint venture between the Tata group and BSkyB (the News Corp group). In a short time span of three years after launch (2006), it acquired more than five million customers. It created a niche as a world-class service provider.

In order to increase distribution reach as well as serve customers from within their own vicinity, the company launched a new business vertical called retail operations. This was achieved by launching small retail stores called Experience Zone, whose aim was to provide the customer and the prospects with a unique experience. These were the key objectives for this vertical:

- to get closer to customers, both existing and potential
- to ensure consistency of business in a highly competitive landscape
- to service and retain TataSky's existing high-quality subscriber base
- to increase ARPU (average revenue per user)
- to reduce service costs.

The stores that were initially opened did not do well. The conversion ratio was low, sales were low, and so were the subscription recharges from these stores. The main challenges were the following:

- focus on sales transactions only and hardly any focus on relationship management
- failure to leverage presence near the customer
- lack of skills needed to manage customer interactions
- low service orientation.

Needs Assessment

In August 2009, the vertical head interfaced with the training team. After consultations, the following needs emerged:

1. Payoff needs:
   a. The revenues to be increased by
      i. Increasing sales
      ii. Increasing subscription recharges (electronic prepaid recharge service; EPRS)
2. Business needs: The following business parameters needed to be impacted:
   a. The hard data:
      i. To increase the conversion ratio of the walk-ins
      ii. To increase sales
      iii. To increase the subscription recharge
   b. The soft data: Nothing concrete was analyzed or felt.
3. Job performance needs:
   a. To handle the customer transaction in a standardized manner
   b. To do customer profiling by asking relevant questions

    c. To give demonstrations in a standardized manner

4. Learning needs: To impart three skills:

    a. Meeting and greeting

    b. Understanding what the walk-in wants and needs

    c. Influencing the customer to want to buy

5. Preference needs:

    a. The intervention to be initiated by 1st October 2009

    b. All regions to be covered simultaneously

    c. To conduct classroom training and preferably use company training facilities

    d. Training to be done based on role plays

Training Solution: "Winning Every Walk-in"

Based on the above-mentioned needs, it was decided that a two-day instructor-led classroom workshop should be developed. The training would be provided to all the employees of the Experience Zones. An external training company would provide the training content and train the trainer for a set of internal trainers. An important decision was made to train all the retail operations managers (ROMs) as well all the retail operations incharges (ROIs). This decision was based on past experience in which the biggest challenge to any training program was the transfer of learned skills to the workplace. It was decided that the ROIs would ensure the transfer of skills through on-the-job coaching. It was also decided that since this would be an intervention, which is very critical for the vertical and would require a huge investment, this intervention should be tracked for return on investment. Captain Charanjit Lehal, AGM Training and Development, was appointed coordinator for the project.

EVALUATION METHODOLOGY

It was necessary that all key stakeholders, along with the training team, were clear about the present reality and what was being targeted in terms of levels on which the project would be evaluated. Everybody was confident of the levels of evaluation that had been documented in the past (Level 1, 2, and 3), so the evaluation methodology dashboard was an excellent tool to keep the focus on all levels of evaluation. Table 14.1 presents the dashboard. As mentioned in Table 14.1, Winning Every Walk-in would be the first project for which a return on investment was calculated.

TABLE 14.1   Evaluation Dashboard

Level	Measurement Category	Current Status In TataSky	Evaluation Targets	Comments
0	**Inputs and indicators:** Measures inputs into program—includes the number of workshops, participants, costs	Done for less than 25% of the programs.	100% tracking of workshops, number of participants attending, and the total costs incurred	This is to be done with the help of tracking of the attendance sheets and loading all direct and indirect costs.
1	**Reaction and planned action:** To measure reaction to and satisfaction with the facilitator, content, training environment, and overall satisfaction with the program	Done for 100% of the workshops conducted.	100%	This is to be done with the help of a questionnaire to be administered to the participants at the end of the program.
2	**Application and implementation:** To measure what the participants have learned in the program, namely three skills: (1) meeting and greeting, (2) understanding what the walk-in wants and needs by asking relevant questions, and (3) influencing the customer to want to buy by giving a demonstration of the product	Done for more than 60–70% of the training programs by way of tests and role plays.	100%	This is to be tested by way of participants doing the role plays. The facilitator is to judge the learning by observation.
3	**Application and implementation:** To measure the progress after the program—the use of the skills learnt during the program	Done for less than 10% of the training programs.	30–40%	This is to be done by way of an action plan sheet. The survey would be conducted for all the ROMs so as to cover all the stores.
4	**Impact and consequences:** To measure the change in the following business parameters: (a) to increase the conversion ratio of the walk-ins, (b) to increase sales, and (c) to increase the subscription recharge	Not done for any training program previously.	To track these parameters for two to three months	This is to be done by tracking the business data for the months of January, February, and March 2010.
5	**Return on investment:** To compare the monetary benefits of the business impact measures to the cost of program	Not done for any training program previously.	To have a positive ROI	

Note: ROM = retail operations manager; ROI = retail operations incharge.

Chapter 14

Response Profile

The various participants for Winning Every Walk-in were as follows:

1. Employees of the Experience Zone stores: The person manning the store. He or she could be an employee or the owner of the store. The previous experience of this person was from the field of consumer electronics, telecommunications, or any other retail outlet. Initially the plan was to cover approximately 190 stores. Later, approximately 100 more stores were added. Thus, a total of 291 people were trained. These participants provided data for the end-of-program reaction questionnaire.

2. ROIs: The first-level supervisors (nonmanager level) of the company responsible for a number of Experience Zone stores in a particular territory. They report in to the ROMs. They were the first level of the channel managers. Their main responsibilities include opening new stores, smooth functioning of the stores, customer acquisition, and subscription management. There are 30 ROIs in the system. These participants provided data for the end-of-program reaction questionnaire. They also were responsible for the action planning sheet, as well as for responding to the application and impact survey.

3. ROMs: The first-level managerial employees. These are the supervisors of the ROIs. The ROM is responsible for the stores in his or her territory. Three to six ROIs report in to one ROM. The main responsibilities of the ROM are similar to those of the ROIs. There are nine ROMs. These participants provided data for the end-of-program reaction questionnaire. They also were responsible for the action planning sheet and for responding to the application and impact survey.

4. Regional manager for retail operations: There are two regional managers, one responsible for North and East India and the other responsible for West and South India. They were responsible for responding to the application and impact survey.

5. Vice president retail operations: This individual is number two in the retail operations hierarchy.

6. Executive vice president, retail operations: This individual heads the retail operations vertical. He was responsible for providing the business data and is the main sponsor for the training program.

Data Collection Procedures

A variety of data collection instruments were employed during the evaluation. These included questionnaires, observation of skill practice, action plan sheets, and business performance monitoring.

Satisfaction and Planned Action

The Level 1 feedback was collected through the feedback form. This was to be administered at the end of the workshop. The response target was 100 percent of the participants.

Learning

The training objectives were as follows:

- meeting and greeting
- understanding what the walk-in wants and needs
- influencing the customer to want to buy.

These were to be learned by role plays in the training. The facilitator was responsible for judging the ability of the participants to demonstrate all the skills at a satisfactory level. To help the participants do this, a standard script was used. The participants were to follow the script, from welcoming the walk-in to giving a demo.

For the ROIs and ROMs, an additional skill taught was on-the-job coaching. For this, there was also a standard "coaching document" that was created. The participants practiced with this document, and the same document was used in the field.

Application of Skills

The application of the skills learned during the workshop was planned to be captured through the action plan sheet. The ROMs were responsible for capturing this, and they were to compile the respective sheets for their territories. Initially, this was to be done after 45 days of training.

The action planning sheet, shown in Figure 14.1, documented the activities done by the ROIs in order to get the skills implemented by the training participants. The ROIs were supposed to coach the store employees for the three skills they had acquired during the training. Each skill was calibrated for three levels:

1. Level 1—no display of skill
2. Level 2—inconsistent display of skill

3. Level 3—consistent display of skill

This tool made the ROIs focus on the activities also in order to achieve the end result, which was ensuring that all store employees displayed the three skills consistently. It also captured the intangible benefits that they might observe.

Business Impact

The business impact measures were intended to be captured through the Winning Every Walk-in training ROI survey form, shown in Figure 14.2. This questionnaire was administered to a total of 30 participants via email. All but one responded. The following were the main items appearing on the questionnaire:

- What percentage of sales increase is attributable to training?
- What is the confidence level for the response?
- What percentage of recharge increase is attributable to training?
- What is the confidence level for the response?
- What are the other factors that have impacted sales and the recharge?
- What barriers, if any, did the ROM/ROI encounter that prevented this program from being more successful?
- What helped this program be successful?

The two business parameters that were targeted for impact were monthly sales as a result of improving conversion ratio of walk-ins and monthly subscription recharge. Table 14.2 presents the data collection plan, summarizing the procedures used to collect data for the Winning Every Walk-in training evaluation.

Data Analysis

Data analysis included the critical steps to isolate training effects from other influences, convert impact measures to money, and include fully loaded program costs.

Method of Isolation of Training Effect

While two impact measures were targeted by the program, monthly sales and monthly subscription recharges, it was important to account for other factors that influenced improvement in these measures. As the training was rolled out simultaneously in all regions, it was not possible to use the

FIGURE **14.1** Action Plan

Action Plan

Name _____ Instructor's Signature _____ Follow-up Date _____

Objective _____ Evaluation Period _____ to _____

Improvement   Current   Target
Measure _____   Performance _____   Performance _____

ACTION STEPS: I will do this	END RESULT: So that
1.	
2.	
3.	
4.	
5.	
6.	
7.	
EXPECTED INTANGIBLE BENEFITS:	

Figure 14.2 Winning Every Walk-in Training ROI Survey Form

Winning Every Walk-in Training ROI Survey		
1. What is your current role in retail operations?	ROI/ROM/Regional manager/any other	

Use the following scale:

1 = No change (the ROI has not been able to do the activity)
2 = Limited change (the ROI has been able to cover less than 30% of the stores)
3 = Moderate change (the ROI has been able to cover more than 50% of the stores)
4 = Much change (the ROI has been able to cover more than 80% of the stores)
5 = Very much change (the ROI has been able to cover more than 90% of the stores)

	1	2	3	4	5	No opportunity to observe
2. Please indicate the change in the application of skills of ROIs as a result of their participation in the Winning Every Walk-in workshops. The ROI were to coach for three skills: (a) greeting, (b) questioning for customer profiling, (c) giving demonstration and closing the sale. Please don't leave any item blank.						
a. Has been able to visit the stores that are under you?						
b. Has been able to do the coaching activity at the stores?						
c. Has been able to assess the performance level of employees at stores?						
d. Has been able to give appropriate feedback to the EZ employee after seeing the employee interacting with the customer or through a role play?						
e. Has been able to get an appropriate action plan from the EZ employee after the coaching session?						

3. Taking into consideration the different factors that can influence sales, how much do you feel the Winning Every Walk-in workshop has contributed to improving the sales at the EZ? (Please provide percentage between 0–100% where 0% = none and 100% = completely.) Please consider the period of Jan and Feb 2010 only.	%
4. What other factors have affected sales? Please consider the period of Jan and Feb 2010 only and provide specific information (e.g., promotional scheme, etc.) and the percentage of improvement associated with the factor (0% = none and 100% = completely).	%
Factor 1:	
Factor 2:	
Factor 3:	

(Continued)

FIGURE 14.2 Continued

5. What level of confidence do you place in the above estimation (0% = no confidence, 100% = certainly)? Please explain.	**%**
6. Taking into consideration the different factors that can influence recharge, how much do you feel the Winning Every Walk-in workshop has contributed to improving the recharges from the EZ? (Please provide percentage between 0–100% where 0% = none and 100% = completely.) Please consider the period of Jan and Feb 2010 only.	**%**
7. What other factors have affected recharge? Please consider the period of Jan and Feb 2010 only and provide specific information (e.g., promotional scheme, etc.) and the percentage of improvement associated with the factor (0% = none and 100% = completely).	**%**
Factor 1:	
Factor 2:	
Factor 3:	
8. What level of confidence do you place in the above estimation (0% = no confidence, 100% = certainly)? Please explain.	**%**
9. What barriers, if any, have you or your ROI encountered that prevented this program from being more successful? Please explain if possible.	
10. What has helped this program be successful? Please explain.	
11. Any other comments or suggestions about the program that you would like to give?	

Note: ROM = retail operations manager; ROI = retail operations incharge.

TABLE 14.2 Data Collection Plan

Level	Objectives	Measures/Data	Data Collection Method	Data Source	Timings	Responsibilities
1	Positive reaction	An overall average rating of 4 (on a scale of 1 to 5)	Questionnaire	Participants of the program	At the end of each workshop	Facilitator
2	Will be able to demonstrate all three skills during the role play	Facilitator's rating	Observation of skill practice by facilitator	Facilitator	During the workshop	Facilitator
3	1. Will be able to assess all the EZs for adherence to the taught processes 2. Will be able to bring all the employees to a consistent level of display of learned skills.	Completion of action plan	Action plan sheet	Retail operations incharges (ROIs) Retail operations managers (ROMs)	30–45 days after the workshop (31 December 2009)	Regional managers Retail operations
4	1. The walk-in conversion ratio will increase 2. The sales will increase 3. The customer retention will increase	Monthly data from the retail operation vertical of the Experience Zones	Business performance monitoring	Office of the executive vice president, retail operations	45–90 days after the workshop (15 February)	Regional managers Retail operations
5	ROI	No objective was set for this level in the beginning. The expectation was to have a positive ROI.				

Note: ROM = retail operations manager; ROI = retail operations incharge.

control group method. Also, since there were other factors contributing to growth, the trend line analysis method could not be used.

The method used for isolating the training effect was estimation done by way of a mail-in survey. This was done for the following reasons:

- Timing: The data were to be collected in the month of March. All the ROMs and ROIs were busy because it was the end of the financial year.
- Cost effectiveness: Since it was not possible to get all the participants to one location, this was a very cost-effective method. All the participants were covered through email. The responses were received within five days.
- Respondents' profiles: Since the respondents to the survey were the managers who were managing the retail operations channel, they could be trusted with their estimates, as they were the ones who were involved with the concerned business.
- Correction applied: Since the estimation method incorporates the correction to the estimate, required corrections were applied for all the impacted business parameters.

Method of Data Conversion

The data were converted into monetary values as described below.

Sales

- This value was worked out by the finance department. The average revenue earned from one customer is Rs.80/- (after taking into account all the costs involved). The average life for a customer is five years. Hence, the additional revenue that a new customer will bring is Rs.4,800/- (Rs.80 for 60 months).
- The company pays a subsidy of Rs.4,500/- on the set top box at the time of sale. Hence, the actual money value for one additional set top box sold is Rs.300/- (Rs.4,800 – Rs.4,500).
- These values were accepted by the retail operations vertical (the sponsoring department).

Subscription Recharge

This value was achieved by deducting the standard costs involved with the recharges. These are standard values given by the retail operations vertical.

The total costs were 70 percent. Hence, 70 percent of the value of subscription recharge was deducted to get the value.

Program Costs

The training involved buying content from an external training partner as well as getting a set of intern trainers trained for delivery. In addition, approximately 30 workshops were conducted all across India. All the indirect costs also were taken into consideration. Salaries of the company employees who participated were taken as indirect costs. These values were based on the average value as per the grades of the company employee. These values were taken from the HR department and shared with the sponsor vertical. Costs for the internal venues also were included.

A major barrier for the application and impact was reported as the churn of the trained employee. Hence, a provision for six batches for the employees who would be joining in place of churned employees was taken into consideration. Planning, collection, analyzing, and reporting on the evaluation was done by the coordinator, so his time loss of 26 working days on all activities was included in the program cost.

Table 14.3 presents the Return on Investment Analysis Plan summarizing the approach taken to evaluate Winning Every Walk-in.

Assumptions (Guiding Principles/Return on Investment Interpretations)

The following assumptions were made and followed during the project to have a consistency of approach:

1. Since the training was being conducted for a new channel, the impact of the training would be visible within two to three months.

2. The time for the project was estimated to be five to six months—that is, from training to impact on the business parameters.

3. The skills learned during the training would be applied on the job for 45 to 60 days.

4. The reports of the ROIs regarding the application of the skills in the store would be proof enough.

5. January 2010 would be the month for baselining, after which the data would be collected for the months of February and March 2010.

All the evaluation steps were in line with the 12 Guiding Principles of the ROI Methodology model described in the resources cited at the end of

TABLE 14.3   Return on Investment Analysis Plan

Data Items (Usually Level 4)	Method for Isolation	Methods of Converting Data to Monetary Values	Cost Categories	Intangible Benefits	Communication Targets for Final Report	Other Influences/ Issues During Application
Monthly conversion ratio	Participant estimate (ROMs and ROIs)	Standard value	1. Facilitation fees 2. Program materials 3. Market survey fees 4. Facility costs 5. Participant salaries 6. Cost of evaluation	Customer satisfaction Employee satisfaction	ROMs ROIs Exec. VP Retail operations	Any change in market factors
Monthly sales						
Monthly subscription recharges						

Note: ROM = retail operations manager; ROI = retail operations incharge.

this case study. The following are the examples in which one or more of the Guiding Principles were followed:

1. Evaluation at Levels 1 and 2 (reaction and learning) was not very comprehensive, as evaluations at Levels 3 and 4 were being planned (Guiding Principle 2).

2. The most credible source of data was used for data collection. The life term value of one customer (after accounting for all subsidies and expenses) was taken from the finance department and agreed to by the retail department (for whom the training was being organized). Similarly, the net profit percentage for the electronic prepaid recharge service (subscription recharge) value was also taken from the finance department (Guiding Principle 3).

3. The business data were taken from the retail department, considered the most credible source (Guiding Principle 3).

4. While analyzing data, the most conservative estimate was taken (Guiding Principle 4).

5. The participant and manager's estimate method were used to isolate the effects of training (Guiding Principle 5).

6. Estimates of improvement were adjusted for the potential error of estimate (Guiding Principle 7).

7. Only the first year of benefits (annual) were used in the ROI analysis (Guiding Principle 9).

8. The cost of the training intervention was fully loaded. All the direct as well as indirect costs were taken into account (Guiding Principle 10).

9. All the benefits that could not be converted into monetary values were reported as intangible benefits. Examples include increased franchisee commitment and increased customer satisfaction (Guiding Principle 11).

10. The results were shared with all the key stakeholders (Guiding Principle 12).

EVALUATION RESULTS

Level 1: Reaction

The target response rate for the Level 1 evaluation questionnaire was 100 percent. This was achieved. All the participants had a favorable reaction to the program. The average feedback score for all the training workshops received through the end of the workshop feedback was 4.53 on a scale of 1 to 5. Some of the feedback was as follows:

- The idea of a script will help us to standardize practices all across.
- Content is tailor-made for the store.
- Received good tips on coaching.
- Learned the demonstration for selling effectively.
- The trainer made the training more relevant by giving appropriate examples.

Level 2: Learning

Learning data were collected during the training. All the participants learned the skills by doing role plays. The three major skills practiced were

1. Meeting and greeting the walk-in to welcome the customer
2. Understanding what the walk-in wants and needs by asking questions
3. Influencing the customer to want to buy by giving a demonstration of the product

The skills learned were important for the success of the training, as these were the vital behaviors that had been identified as critical for the success of the Experience Zone. As one of the objectives of the training was to bring standardization of practices across India, it was important that all participants learn to use the same scripts.

Similarly, for the ROIs and ROMs, it was important that they follow the same coaching document. The coaching document helped the participants learn the coaching skills needed in the classroom. The script-based learning during the training sessions helped. It was also clear to all participants what they should do after the training to achieve the business objectives.

The channel managers (ROIs and ROMs) were also clear as to what skills were required to be displayed at the stores. The scripts allowed for standardization as everyone (the Experience Zone employee, the ROI, and the ROM) was clear as to what needed to be done.

Level 3: Application and Implementation

The objectives at Level 3 were for the participant to be able to assess all the Experience Zones for adherence to the taught processes and bring all of them to a level at which they were using the skills consistently. This was to be documented by the ROIs and ROMs by way of the action plan activity sheet.

The responsibility for ensuring that the skills learned during the training were being transferred to the workplace and used consistently was given to the ROIs and ROMs. They were supposed to observe the Experience Zone employees and coach them. They were given 45 days to bring about the change. In this time period, each ROI was supposed to visit each store in his or her territory at least four or five times. Each ROI was supposed to submit an action plan to his ROM. The ROMs were to compile action plans of their territories to document the "on-the-job transfer of skills."

The ROMs started doing that. The target for this level was a response rate of 30 to 40 percent from the managers. Seven managers out of 10 responded with their action plan sheets. Their response showed that approximately 60 to 65 percent of the Experience Zone employees had started displaying the skills at the workplace.

The application and implementation were also captured during the Winning Every Walk-in ROI survey. The ROIs were able to perform coaching at more than 80 percent of the stores. Ninety-five percent of the population of ROIs, ROMs, and regional managers responded. They reported the following:

- The ROIs were able to visit and coach more than 80 percent of the stores identified for coaching.
- The ROIs were able to give feedback to approximately 80 percent of the stores.
- The ROIs were able to get appropriate action plans after coaching from approximately 70 percent of the store employees.

  The successes of the implementation phase included the following:

- The skills learned during the training.
- The coaching done by the ROIs at the stores, which helped the store employees to overcome a very big hurdle—their old way of doing business.
- The use of standard scripts and steps, which also helped in quicker transfer of skills at the workplace.

  The enablers reported through the action plan included the following:

- Effective probing led to more recharges.
- Standardized scripts helped in other aspects, such as field sales activities.

- The confidence of the franchisees increased when they saw success due to the skills learned.

The major barriers during the implementation phase included:

- The initial hesitation on the part of the employees to follow a script. They felt that this made the whole deal very bookish.
- The addition of approximately 100 stores. The ROIs had to focus on the opening of the new stores and were thus unable to give sufficient time to coaching for some time.
- The churn of employees at the store. This is still a major concern.

These recommendations are based on the experiences of the implementation phase:

- The churn of employees needs to be controlled.
- For every region, some selected ROIs can be trained to conduct a shorter version of the training. This needs to be done to take care of the employee churn problem.
- Batches for the new joinees should be held at regular intervals.
- The span of control of the ROI should be kept manageable (depending upon the territory).
- Sufficient time should be given for the implementation phase. Any addition (significant numbers) should be done when consistency of operations has been achieved.

Level 4: Business Impact and Consequences

The following business objectives were targeted to be impacted:

- increase monthly sales
- increase the monthly subscription recharge.

The above parameters were to be tracked from the business dashboards of the retail operations vertical. These data were to be taken from the executive vice president's office. The impact data were collected through the Winning Every Walk-in training ROI survey.

Table 14.4 shows the number of boxes sold in January, February, and March and the average improvement.

The training was conducted in the months of October, November, and December 2009. Table 14.5 shows the percentage of incremental change for sales and subscription recharges attributable to training. This was done through the Winning Every Walk-in training ROI survey. Table 14.6 is the

TABLE 14.4   Number of Boxes Sold in January, February, and March

Month	January	February	March	Average Increment	Remark
Boxes sold	7,558	8,827	14,128	1,269	Although the average is greater, we have taken the lower value (increment of February over January).

TABLE 14.5   Reported Improvements

Business Parameter	January 2010	February 2010	Increment (February over January)	March 2010	Increment (March over January)	Average Increment (Keeping the Lowest Figure)
Boxes sold	7,558	8,827	1,269	14,128	6,570	1,269 boxes
Subscription recharge	48,308,569.00	55,401,497.00	7,092,928	59,236,679	10,928,110	Rs.7,092,928

compilation of the survey done of the various role holders in the company. A brief profile of each role holder is given in the response profile paragraph. In this survey, each responder was asked to attribute what percentage of the business parameter growth was attributable to training (survey items 2 and 5). After that, each participant was asked to tell how confident he or she was in attributing a percentage of growth to training (survey items 4 and 7). The same survey also asked the participants to list other factors that affected the growth of the two business parameters. The following factors also affected sales and subscription recharge:

1. A promotional scheme was implemented that waived the installation fee.
2. A new incentive scheme was launched that was focused on facilitating subscription recharge.
3. The Experience Zone owners started using Tele Callers. The tele-calling helped the subscription recharge as well as sales.
4. The Experience Zone also started doing outdoor activities. This included doing demonstrations at customers' homes or at shopping malls.

TABLE 14.6   Survey Compilation

Name	Sales Attributable to Training (%)	Confidence Level (%)	EPRS Attributable to Training (%)	Confidence Level (%)
Sudhir (ROI)	40	80	70	100
Sathish (ROI)	40	80	20	50
Kalyan (ROM)	20	100	20	100
Chellapathy (ROI)	50	75	60	80
Sanjay Jadon (ROM)	50	85	40	95
Tirumal (ROI)	35	80	70	100
JitendarAhuja (ROI)	35	80	30	90
D. P. Sharma (ROI)	20	80	20	80
Anant Londhe (ROI)	38	75	30	85
Dinesh G. (ROI)	50	100	35	100
Kalyan S. (ROI)	50	100	40	100
Manas B. (ROI)	40	100	50	100
Mani G. (ROI)	40	100	45	100
Khushnud (ROM)	40	100	35	100
Mansing (ROM)	30	100	50	100
Vinod S. (ROI)	10	100	30	100
Milind P. (ROI)	30	100	40	100
Pravin G. (ROI)	30	100	40	100
Arun Upadhyay (ROI)	50	80	100	100
Suresh Goyal (ROI)	100	100	100	100
Harpreet (ROM)	70	100	50	90
Balwant Vaghela (ROI)	40	70	30	70
Anup Lobo (ROI)	35	80	40	100
Shilpi (ROM)	15	95	20	100

Name	Sales Attributable to Training (%)	Confidence Level (%)	EPRS Attributable to Training (%)	Confidence Level (%)
K. P. Singh (ROI)	100	100	60	100
Bharat Parmar (ROI)	40	100	30	100
Kamaldeep (ROI)	70	90	50	90
Ankur Jain (ROM)	70	100	60	75
Rejo F. (Regional Manager)	10	100	10	100
Krishan Kansal (Regional Manager)	10	80	10	90
Jitander Sharma (ROI)	30	40	40	40
Pawan Kumar (ROI)	100	100	60	100
Anurag Agrawal (Vertical Head)	0	0	0	0
Total average for the group	**42**	**86**	**42**	**88**
Corrected group average for sales	**36% of the increase in sales of boxes**			
Corrected group average for subscription recharge (EPRS)	**37% of the increase in monthly recharge (EPRS)**			

Note: ROM = retail operations manager; ROI = retail operations incharge; EPRS = electronic prepaid recharge service.

Level 5: Return on Investment

The return on investment was calculated as detailed in the ROI model. The most appropriate formula to evaluate training and performance improvement investments uses net benefits divided by cost. The ratio is usually expressed as a percentage when the fractionalized values are multiplied by 100. In formula form, the return on investment becomes

$$\text{ROI} = \frac{\text{Net Training Benefits}}{\text{Training Costs}} \times 100$$

Net benefits are training benefits minus training costs.

Monetary Benefits

The monetary benefit for the project was determined by calculating values on improvement in sales and recharge subscriptions. A step-by-step process was used to calculate the annual benefit for each measure. For example, the details of converting sales to annual monetary benefits is shown below.

1. The number of boxes sold in the months of January, February, and March are shown in Table 14.4.

2. The average increase in sales (number of boxes) after the training was 1,269.

3. There was a 20 percent churn of the customer (in the first month). Hence, the number of boxes sold after deducting the churn is

$$\frac{(1,269 \times 20)}{100} = 1,016$$

4. The percentage increase in sales attributable to the training is 36 percent. Hence, additional boxes sold due to training will be

$$\frac{(1,016 \times 36)}{100} = 365$$

5. The monetary value of one new connection (one additional box sold) is calculated as follows:

   a. The lifetime value of one connection is calculated for average revenue of Rs.80 for five years. Hence, the value for one box is
   $$80 \times 12 \times 5 = Rs.4,800$$

   b. On each box, at the time of sale, the company gives a subsidy of
   $$Rs.4,500/-$$

   c. Hence, the adjusted value for one new customer acquired or one new box sold is
   $$Rs.4,800 - Rs.4,500 = Rs.300/-$$

6. Therefore, the total value of the additional 365 boxes sold is
   $$365 \times 300 = Rs.109,500/- \text{ per month}$$

7. The annualized value of increased sales =
   $$Rs.109,500 \times 12 = Rs.1,314,000/-$$

Similar steps were used to calculate the value of improvement in subscription recharges. In summary, the monetary benefits of the two measures are as follows:

1. The value of increased sales of boxes was calculated as
   $$Rs.109,500/- \text{ per month}$$

2. The annualized value of increased sales was

$$Rs.109,500 \times 12 = Rs.1,314,000/-$$

3. The value of increased subscription recharge is

$$Rs.787,315.00/- \text{ per month}$$

4. The annualized value of increase in recharge is

$$Rs.787,315 \times 12 = Rs.9,447,780.09 = Rs.9,447,780/-$$

The total benefit is the sum of increased sales and recharge value. Therefore, the total benefit is

$$Rs.1,314,000 + Rs.9,447,780 = Rs.10,761,780/-$$

Program Costs

As described earlier, a fully loaded cost profile was used to ensure all program costs were captured. Table 14.7 presents the costs incurred for the Winning Every Walk-in training program.

Return on Investment and Benefit/Cost Ratio (BCR) Calculations

$$ROI = \frac{\text{Net Program Benefits}}{\text{Training Costs}} \times 100$$

Net Program Benefits = Rs. Total Benefits − Total Costs

Net Program Benefits = Rs.10,761,780 − Rs.2,621,600 = Rs.8,140,180

Total Program Costs = Rs.2,621,600

Return on Investment (%) = (Rs.8,140,180/Rs.2,621,600) × 100 = 310.50%

Return on Investment (%) = 310%

This means that for every rupee invested, TataSky received Rs.3.10 /– in return after the cost of the program had been recovered.

BCR compares the annual economic benefits of the program with the costs of the program. This method compares the benefits of the program with the costs using a simple ratio. In formula form, the ratio is

BCR = Program Benefits/Program Costs

BCR = 10,761,780/2,621,600

BCR = 4.10:1

This means that for every rupee spent on the program, Rs.4.10 are returned in benefits.

TABLE 14.7 Total Costs Incurred

Ser. No	The Cost Category	Value (in Indian Rupees)
1.	Facilitation fees for the master trainer	200,000
2.	The cost for the content	1,200,000
3.	The cost for the market survey	25,000
4.	Participants' salaries (as per managerial grades):	
	M1: 2 participants (@ Rs.10,000 per day)	40,000
	M2; 2 participants (@ Rs.7,000 per day)	28,000
	M3: 2 participants (@ Rs.4,000 per day)	16,000
	M4: 10 participants (@ Rs.2,800 per day)	56,000
	M5: 22 participants (@ Rs.1,400 per day)	61,600
5.	Cost of internal venue for the six batches done for the company staff (ROIs and the ROMs). This included rent of venue and food.	150,000
6.	Cost of the 25 training batches for the Experience Zone employees (@ Rs.25,000 per batch). This included rent of venue and food.	625,000
7.	Cost of planning, collection, analyzing, and reporting the evaluation	70,000
8.	Cost of six refresher batches—required to tackle the employee churn (@ Rs.25,000 per batch)	150,000
Total costs for the training program		**2,621,600**

Note: ROM = retail operations manager; ROI = retail operations incharge.

Intangible Benefits

The following were the other benefits. These benefits were documented in the action planning sheet and the Winning Every Walk-in training ROI survey.

- The confidence of the Experience Zone employees increased due to the training. This was reflected in all the activities of the store. The morale of the Experience Zone employees as well as that of the owners increased. The effect was noticeable, but since we could not measure the difference in confidence pre- and post-training, this was reported as an intangible benefit.

- The skills learned were applied in other activities as well. The outdoor demonstration effectiveness increased. The Experience Zone started doing more mini-dish demonstrations. We could not establish a method to monetize this benefit and hence kept it as an intangible benefit.

- Better customer management at the stores reduced the incoming call load at the contact center. As we could not use any method to isolate the effect, we decided to keep it as an intangible benefit.

- Better handling of customers during the time of sale also ensured that they recharged for the first month more regularly. This reduced the casual churn of customers due to not recharging their accounts in time. Here again, since we could not find a way to isolate this particular effect of training, we decided to list it as an intangible benefit.

In addition, the ROIs received skilled on-the-job coaching. This will help in better channel management.

Issues and Barriers Regarding Feedback Responses

As with all evaluations, there are often challenges with data collection. Some of the issues regarding feedback response are as follows.

- The Level 1 feedback was to be obtained at the end of each workshop. All the facilitators ensured that this was done.

- Action planning was not intended to be done at the end of the workshop. The action planning was intended only for company staff. The managers were to compile it for their respective territories. The target was to get a 40 percent response rate. Managers were to report how many stores had been covered by their ROIs. Approximately 70 percent of the managers responded. The trend reported from across India showed that the Experience Zone employees had started using the skills learned at the store. This was being facilitated by on-the-job coaching done by the ROIs during their visits to the stores. Some challenges were reported:
  - an initial hesitancy on the part of employees to follow the script and the process
  - employee churn.

These issues were overcome by the sheer persistence of the ROIs. Also, once the employees started following the script and their initial hesitancy was gone, they started becoming more and more comfortable. By the first week of February, approximately 60 percent of the stores were showing usage of skills.

- Operational challenge: In January, another challenge arose when management decided to add another 100 stores. As the ROMs and ROIs became busy with opening the stores, they could not devote the requisite time to coaching the Experience Zone employees to become more consistent in using the skills. But the experience gained by the ROIs in on-the-job coaching enabled them to take on these additional stores. One additional month was given to ROIs to bring them to a level at which the Experience Zone employees started using the skills at their workplace.

- Implementation and impact: This was planned to be done through the Winning Every Walk-in training ROI survey. The ROIs and ROMs were to provide the responses, and the target was a 95 percent response rate. The response rate was 95 percent, and no major challenge was faced in collecting the responses. The active involvement of the vertical leadership, that is, the regional managers and the vertical head, was responsible for getting the responses.

COMMUNICATION STRATEGY

All the important stakeholders were kept informed of the results at various stages; they were closely involved and hence understood the chain of impact. That is why all the data from the field (the action planning sheet and the Winning Every Walk-in training ROI survey were documented and received from the field in time. The training team was constantly keeping a close watch on the chain of impact (Table 14.8).

As part of the communication strategy, the following events deserve mention:

- The learning during the training was to happen through role plays. Although the facilitators did a good job, there was no standardized document to capture the learning. There could have been a Role Play Observation Sheet, which would have brought standardization to the learning process.

TABLE 14.8   Chain of Impact

Level	Measurement Focus	Measures
1—Reaction	Participants had a positive reaction to the program.	Average reaction of the feedback
2—Learning	The participants acquired the three skills.	Facilitator's observation
	The ROIs also acquired the coaching skills.	
3—Application	The participants applied the skills at their workplace.	The activities done in the field were captured on the action plan sheet.
	The ROIs observed the employees using the new skills and coached the employees whenever they were not displaying the learned skills.	
4—Impact	The two business objectives were impacted in the desired manner. There was an increase in sales as well as subscription recharges. There were other intangible benefits as well.	Business data for the parameters were observed for three months.
5—ROI	The benefits of the program exceeded the total costs incurred.	ROI and BCR calculated as per the ROI model

Note: ROI = retail operations incharge; BCR = benefit/cost ratio.

- During the implementation phase, management decided to add approximately 100 more stores. This posed a challenge to on-the-job coaching. The training team brought this to the notice of the client. The implementation phase was increased by a month.

- During the implementation phase, the details of the walk-ins at the stores were not captured. Hence, the training team and the client agreed that walk-in conversion data would not be reported; only sales and subscription data would be reported for the impact.

- As the chain of impact was understood by all concerned stakeholders, the chain of impact from reaction objectives to learning objectives to implementation objectives to impact objectives and lastly to return-on-investment objectives was achieved. Although in one or two instances the chain was put to the test, timely action by the concerned stakeholders kept the chain of impact intact.

The above calculations are based on the ROI model and the 12 Guiding Principles.

- All the direct as well as indirect costs were loaded.
- The method of isolation used was estimation by the participants and their managers, as the other available methods could not be used.
  - The training was to be rolled out for all regions; the control group method could not be used.
  - There were other factors that impacted the targeted parameters such as the incentive scheme and wavering of the installation charges. Hence trend analysis could not be used.
  - Participants' and their managers' estimate methods were used to isolate the effects of training (Guiding Principle 5).
  - The estimates of improvement were adjusted for the potential error of estimate (Guiding Principle 7).
- The most credible source of data was used for data collection. The life term value of one customer (after accounting for all subsidies and expenses) was taken from the finance department and agreed to by the retail department (for whom the training was being organized). Similarly, the net profit percentage for the EPRS (subscription recharge) value was also taken from the finance department (Guiding Principle 3).
- The business data were taken from the retail department (Guiding Principle 3).
- While analyzing data, the most conservative estimate was taken (Guiding Principle 4).
- Only the first year of benefits (annual) was used in the ROI analysis (Guiding Principle 9).
- All the benefits that could not be converted into monetary values were reported as intangible benefits; examples include increased franchisee commitment and increased customer satisfaction (Guiding Principle 11).
- The results were shared with all the key stakeholders (Guiding Principle 12).

The Winning Every Walk-in program was a success, as all the objectives of the program were met. It received positive reactions from the participants when they attended the program. The participants learned the skills they needed. The skills were implemented at the workplace by the Experience Zone employees. They were duly assisted in this by the ROIs who observed them, gave them relevant feedback, and encouraged them to practice the skills at the workplace. When applied at the workplace, the skills impacted the business by way of increased sales and an increase in subscription recharges. There were other intangible benefits, such as increased confidence of the employees, use of the skills in other activities, and better life cycle management of the customers at the Experience Zone itself. This reduced the load at the customer contact centers and affected the cost of managing the customers in a positive way.

The following were the target percentages for the various levels and the results achieved:

1. Reaction: The target for the reaction questionnaire was to get responses from 100 percent of the participants. The expectation was to receive an overall average feedback of more than 4 on a scale of 1 to 5. It included all the Experience Zone employees who attended the program, all the ROIs, and all the ROMs. This was achieved for all the workshops. The average feedback received was 4.53 for all the workshops.

2. Action planning: The target was to receive responses from 40 percent of the ROIs and ROMs. Responses were received from approximately 70 percent of the population for ROIs and ROMs. They reported that the skills were being displayed at approximately 60 percent of the stores. This was achieved within 50 to 60 days after the training.

3. Application and impact sheet: Approximately 95 percent of the population of ROIs, ROMs, and regional managers responded. They reported the following:

■ The ROIs were able to visit more than 80 percent of the stores for coaching.

■ The ROIs were able to give feedback to approximately 80 percent of the stores.

■ The ROIs were able to get appropriate action plans after coaching from approximately 70 percent of the store employees.

4. Impact: Monthly sales increased by 16 percent; out of this, 37 percent was attributable to training. The monthly subscription recharge increased by 14 percent, out of which 36 percent was attributable to training.

5. Return on investment: A return on investment of 310 percent was achieved. This means that for every rupee invested, TataSky received Rs.3.10/- in return after the cost of the program had been recovered.

The BCR for the program was 4.10:1.This means that for every rupee spent on the program, Rs.4.10 were returned in benefits.

There were benefits that could not be converted into monetary values. They were important benefits, though, and hence were reported as intangible benefits:

- The confidence of the Experience Zone employees increased due to training.
- The skills learned were applied to other activities as well, such as outdoor sales and mini-dish demonstrations.
- The better customer management at the stores reduced the incoming call load at the contact center.
- The ROIs have been trained in on-the-job coaching skills. They will be able to better manage their channels. Also, when new stores are added in the future, they will be able to coach the newly inducted employees on the job.
- The casual churn of customers was reduced.

LESSONS LEARNED

The following are the recommendations for the future based on the findings of the present project:

1. For Level 1 evaluation: The questions should have been more focused on the relevance of the program, willingness to implement what had been taught and what could keep the participants from using the knowledge and skills used, and the participants' recommendation of the program to colleagues.

2. For Level 2 evaluation: Although participants learned the skills through role playing, there was no documentation of the observations of the facilitators. There should be a document to capture the comments of the facilitators. It could also capture the participants who were not up to the mark or weak in displaying the skills so that they could be supported by on- the-job coaching. This was a weak link in the chain of impact.

3. For Level 3 evaluation: Action planning should have been done in consultation with the participants' supervisors. This would have ensured more support for the implementation.

   Refresher training could also be planned for the weak participants who did not display the skills at the workplace.

4. For Level 4 evaluation: The data for this level were captured. The objectives were output focused. The walk-in conversion ratio also should have been captured so that all three parameters agreed upon at the time of objective settings could have been tracked.

Although there was good coordination between the training and retail operations teams, more coordination during and after the training was implemented should have been there. Also, the addition of approximately 100 stores made it difficult for the ROIs to coach the Experience Zone employees. Such things could be avoided in the future. Enough time should be given to the implementation phase. This was a weak link in the chain of impact.

RESOURCES

The following resources were referred to during various stages of the project.

Phillips, J.J. and Phillips, P.P., 2007. *The Value of Learning—How Organizations Capture Value and ROI and Translate into Support, Improvements and Funds*. San Francisco, CA: Pfeiffer.

Phillips, J.J., 2006. *Handbook of Training Evaluation and Measurement Methods*, 3rd edition. Delhi, India: Jayco Publishing House.

Phillips, J.J., and Drew Stone, Ron, 2002. *How to Measure Training Results—A Practical Guide to Tracking the Six Key Indicators*. New York: McGraw-Hill.

Phillips, J.J and Phillips, P.P., 2008. ROI fundamentals: Why and when to measure ROI. *Measurement and Evaluation Series, Volume One*. San Francisco, CA: Pfeiffer.

Phillips, J.J and Friedman Tush, Wendi, MBA., 2008. Communication and Implementation, Sustaining the practice. *Measurement and Evaluation Series, Volume Six*. San Francisco, CA: Pfeiffer.

QUESTIONS FOR DISCUSSION

1. Please enumerate the strengths and weaknesses of the case study.

2. The ROI model provides for flexibility. Please comment in the context of the case study.

3. Can you identify major external and internal operational and other challenges that left their impact? Relate it to your industry.

4. What are the cultural issues that impacted the study? Does your region or country have certain beliefs or practices that can have an impact?

5. Kindly comment on the role of the business function during the intervention.

ABOUT THE AUTHOR

Captain Charanjit S. Lehal is a management and organization development (OD) professional dedicated to helping individuals, teams, and organizations with change. Charanjit has 20 years of work experience in business, civil services, and the military. He applies this varied experience to co-create value for individuals and teams through learning and development interventions. He is a certified facilitator for Influencer Training, Crucial Conversations, Crucial Confrontations, Precision Questioning and Answering & Situation Leadership, and 4 Disciplines of Execution.

Captain Charanjit is a certified executive coach. His specialties include aligning training with business (Certified ROI practitioner), engaging high performers (executive coaching), and learning and development in the field of communication, leadership, culture, and change management in organizations.

Captain Charanjit can be reached at **captlehal@gmail.com** and +91 1 9971617111. He is based in New Delhi, India.

15

Measuring ROI in a Sales Force Coaching Program

A Brazilian Beverage Company: BBC
Brazil

João Solér, André Meira, and Valéria Blanco

This case was prepared to serve as a basis for discussion rather than an illustration of either effective or ineffective administrative and management practices. All names, dates, places, and data may have been disguised at the request of the author or organization.

Abstract

This study was developed to demonstrate the value of a coaching program designed to improve sales competences in a group of 42 outstanding team leaders from a Brazilian beverage company (BBC). The ROI Methodology was applied to its ultimate level, and all five levels of data collection and data analysis were performed following the 10-step ROI Model and its 12 Guiding Principles. The results found were used to validate the coaching program as a good investment for participants and for the company. The study was also very relevant to introduce evaluation as a strategic management and decision-making tool for BBC representatives.

PROGRAM BACKGROUND

Instituto Mazini, a Brazilian Business T&D company, was hired by a known Brazilian beverage company (BBC) to perform a result-oriented coaching program for a group of sales force leaders. The main objective of the coaching program was to improve sales management behavioral skills and attitudes in order to positively impact the company's sales performance.

The program was elaborated to understand individuals' characteristics, strengths, and possible weaknesses. Based on the group's assessments and unveiled needs, a set of relevant competences was compiled to serve as a professional development guideline covering the basics, but also emphasizing how superior performers achieve. Moreover, during the coaching program, the coaches were oriented to gather information about any possible technical and knowledge gaps so the company could plan future additional development activities for all members of its sales force.

The program was conducted with 42 sales leaders, each one having participated in at least 10 one-on-one sessions during 2009–2010. This was the first coaching program hired by the company. The contractor's HR team was confident with the solution supplied and the competences developed; however, they wanted to make sure executives would also perceive the benefits and results achieved. Consequently, Instituto Mazini decided to conduct an evaluation case study to demonstrate the value of coaching in a structured and systematic way that would suit and exceed executives' expectations. By doing so, Instituto Mazini also anticipated that the impact study could be used as a marketing tool for new business opportunities within BBC and other local organizations.

EVALUATION METHODOLOGY

The impact study was conducted by Sirdar Instituto, a company specializing in measurement and evaluation, applying the Phillips ROI Methodology as the evaluation method. This approach was selected for its comprehensive and standardized model. The ROI process produces six types of data: reaction and satisfaction, learning, application and implementation, business impact, return-on-investment (ROI), and intangible measures. It is a 10-step process that follows a set of 12 Guiding Principles.

Evaluation Planning

The coaching program evaluation project was designed just after the coaching sessions began. Since it was the first coaching program the company was going through and also the first experience methodologically evaluating an HR program, the list of objectives defined was general, and no goals were specific. Any findings would be welcome to prove the value of the program. Even having been advised that a more focused approach would facilitate the generation and evaluation of results, BBC chose to wait and see how the process would develop.

All data were captured and analyzed according to the ROI Process Templates as shown in Figures 15.1 and 15.2. It is important to highlight

FIGURE 15.1 Collection Plan

Level	Objectives	Measures	Data Collection Method	Data Sources	Timing	Responsibilities
1 – Reaction and Satisfaction	Participants should react positively to • Coaches' performance • Coaching environment. Participants should be satisfied with relevance and effectiveness of coaching. • If satisfied, participants should recommend coaching to other coworkers.	Likert scale	Electronic questionnaire	Participants (coachees)	Sometime after the fourth and before the eighth round of coaching sessions	Evaluation team
2 – Learning	Participants should develop awareness and understanding abilities to identify • Weak and strong competences • Behavior change and improvement.	Likert scale	Electronic questionnaire	Participants (coachees)	Sometime after the fourth and before the eighth round of coaching sessions	Evaluation team
3 – Application	Participants should frequently and well perform specific tasks evidencing sales force's behavioral competence development.	Accordance scale	Follow-up questionnaire	Participants (coachees)	Six months after program conclusion	Evaluation team
4 – Business Impact	Increase sales force teams' motivation and commitment. Improve processes that give support and stimulate challenges and achievement of goals. Increase sales.	• Motivation and commitment increase (%) • Processes improvement (%) • Sales increased (%)	Follow-up questionnaire Monitoring records	Participants (coachees) Company's records	Six months after program conclusion	Evaluation team
5 – ROI	Achieve a positive ROI.	Comments:				

393

Figure 15.2 ROI Plan Analysis

Measures	Isolation Methods	Data Conversion Methods	Cost Categories	Intangible Benefits	Other Influences	Communication Targets
Sales increased (%)	• Management's estimate of impact (%) • Separation of other possible impact factors	• Linked to the net profit result	• Coaching services • HR planning and supporting hours • Sales force team (coachees) hours (sessions + extra tasks) • Management hours (meetings) • Sales force team (coachees) hours (sessions + extra tasks) • Management hours (meetings) • ROI impact study	• Motivation and commitment increase (%) • Processes improvement (%)	• Two other relevant commercial programs directed to sales improvements • A new business process model being implemented	• HR manager and director • Sales director

that Instituto Mazini and BBC did not have any contact with the data collection process in order to guarantee data independence.

Data Collection and Data Analysis

Both companies were invited to analyze the information gathered and to help define the communication strategy and reports styles to be presented to HR and sales directors.

Level 1 and 2 data were individually and electronically collected by the end of the coaching process, and a follow-up questionnaire was submitted to all coachees six months after that. BBC's sales performance records were made available during and after the program.

The results were analyzed, and to isolate the effects of the coaching program, the evaluation team, supported by Instituto Mazini and BBC, decided to use participants' estimate of the impact after a sales trend line analysis was presented by the sales department.

In order to convert data to monetary values, the evaluation team estimated the profit considering financial global records provided by the company. An external expert was also consulted to support the final value and the estimation process. All costs were provided by the BBC HR team.

EVALUATION RESULTS

Level 1: Reaction and Satisfaction

The evaluation plan was previously set to perform an ROI Level 5 study. For that reason, the data collected for Levels 1 and 2 were not too comprehensive.[1] All information gathered during the coaching process was analyzed and used to adjust any necessary course of action in order to make sure better bottom-line results could be reached by the implementation of the program. Table 15.1 presents the overall reaction to the process.

Checking the reaction and satisfaction with coaches and the environment was considered relevant because any possible problems could be quickly solved. However, it was even more important to understand the acceptance of the program as a valid and effective development tool. These results are show in Table 15.2.

---

[1] Guiding Principle 2: When an evaluation is planned for a higher level, the previous level of evaluation does not have to be comprehensive.

TABLE 15.1   Level 1 Results: General Reaction

	Excellent	Very Good	Good	Regular	Weak	Not Applicable
Coaches' performance	66,7%	28,6%	2,4%	2,4%	0%	0%
Environment conducive to personal development	14,3%	45,3%	35,7%	4,8%	0%	0%
					Total respondents: 42	

Level 2: Learning and Confidence

The basis of a coaching program is stimulating behavior change by coachees' reflection and inner motivation. Therefore, it was important to determine whether coachees were aware of their responsibilities. This was a core factor for the program's success. Table 15.3 presents results of the Level 2 evaluation in terms of participants' developing awareness of the need to improve.

TABLE 15.2   Level 1 Results: Professional Development Satisfaction

	Strongly Agree	Agree	Neutral	Disagree	Strongly Disagree	Not Applicable
Relevance to professional development	70,7%	24,4%	4,9%	0%	0%	0%
Effective tool to develop skills, competence, and confidence	58,5%	39,1%	2,4%	0%	0%	0%
Recommend to others	63,4%	29,3%	2,4%	0%	0%	4,9%
					Total respondents: 42	

TABLE 15.3   Level 2 Results: Learning and Confidence Improvement

	Strongly Agree	Agree	Neutral	Disagree	Strongly Disagree	Not Applicable
Developed awareness of what needs to be done or improved in order to achieve personal and professional goals	51,2%	48,8%	0%	0%	0%	0%
Developed ability to identify what needs to be improved or done differently in order to achieve performance goals	45,2%	52,4%	2,4%	0%	0%	0%
						Total respondents: 42

Level 3: Application and Implementation Results

After checking that the program was well accepted and coachees were aware of the importance of their role in the process, the next step was verifying if and how the developed and improved competences were being applied on the job.

During the follow-up data collection, all coachees indicated being able to develop or improve one or two macro-competences (improvement greater than 75 percent) and to frequently apply them in their work routine. The top eight competences developed during the coaching program are listed in Table 15.4.

Barriers and Enablers

Most of the participants reported they expected to have greater executive management support. Another problem was the frequent lack of time due to the work load and challenging goals.

On the other hand, all participants appreciated the initiative of BBC in investing in their professional growth in a different way. They considered the coaching process a very good investment of their time, and it was a change from the traditional training programs they were used to.

TABLE 15.4   Level 3 Results: Competences Developed or Improved

Major Behavioral Competences (Developed or Improved)	Number of Respondents		
	> 90–100%	> 75–90%	Respondents per Item
Set objectives and goals	24	15	39
Be responsible for my professional development	23	16	39
Positive influence on coworkers	19	20	39
Deal with problems and difficulties in a resilient manner	17	22	39
Be open to changes	23	15	38
Give and receive feedback	20	18	38
Develop and stimulate members of my team	21	17	38
Plan result-oriented actions	17	21	38
Total respondents: 42			

Level 4: Business Impact

Some business impacts not previously anticipated were perceived and indicated by the participants (coachees) when they considered the period from June 2009 to May 2010. The time frame selected set the month before the administration of the follow-up questionnaire as the ending period. Since the coaching process commenced in February 2009, the evaluation team considered it viable to start collecting data in June 2009. During the process, coaches asked coachees to observe any performance improvements to be reported later. As shown in Table 15.5, coaches reported improvement in measures such as motivation and commitment. These measures are typically left as intangible[2] rather than converted to monetary values for use in the ROI calculation.

---

[2] Guiding Principle 11: Intangible measures are defined as measures that are purposely not converted to monetary values.

TABLE 15.5 Level 4 Results: Intangibles

Business Impact Perceived (Intangibles)	Number of Respondents		
	> 90–100%	> 75–90%	Respondents per Item
Motivational actions and monitoring process improvement for achieving goals	24	15	39
Team commitment increase (reaching group results, not only personal results, was also stimulated)	23	16	39
Sales teams showed an increase in motivation	19	20	39
			Total respondents: 42

The BBC HR department also reported a significant increase in market share during the evaluation period; however, they decided to leave it too as an intangible benefit.

Looking for tangible measures, the BBC HR team asked the sales department to calculate the average sales improvement of the coachees comparing the periods of June 2008 to May 2009 and June 2009 to May 2010. There was an average 12 percent increase in sales from one period to the other. The data collected came from only 30 of the 42 coachees in the program, from seven different market niches, who had been working in the company since June 2008.

Isolating the Effects of the Program

In keeping with Guiding Principle 5 (at least one method must be used to isolate the effects of the solution/program), steps were taken to isolate the effects of the coaching from other factors. In order to accomplish this, a group of sales directors identified three primary factors that contributed to the increase in sales in addition to the coaching. These factors were two commercial programs and a new business process model. A comparison of sales increase using trend data showed that a total increase in sales of 12 percent occurred, 3 percent of which was due to unknown factors. This left a 9 percent increase in sales associated with the coaching.

To ensure a more conservative estimate of contribution due to the coaching, estimates were taken by a group of sales directors. These directors considered the three additional primary factors (two commerical programs and a business process model). They then estimated how much of the 9 percent was due to the coaching. This source of data was selected to provide the estimate because it was deemed they were the most credible source, in keeping with Guiding Principle 3 (when collecting and analyzing data, only the most credible sources should be used).

Estimates indicated that 15 percent (after adjusting for error[3]) of the 9 percent increase in sales was due to the coaching. The final impact factor to be considered as the impact of the coaching program was calculated as 1,4 percent:

Impact Factor = 9% sales increase × 15% estimated contribution =
1,4% contribution due to coaching

Converting Data to Monetary Values

Converting measures to monetary values was an easy task for this specific impact study, because the database sales and financial records were available for the HR team analysis. Taking into consideration the increase in sales linked to the net profit result of the company during the 12-month time frame selected, the full monetary value calculated for the 9 percent sales increase was R$19.400,00 (19,4 million reals). (R$ is the Brazilian currency, the real.) Yet, the contribution of the coaching program was isolated to only 1,4 percent, which means a benefit of R$261.900,00.

Program Costs

According to ROI Methodology Guiding Principle 10, costs of a solution, project, or program should be fully loaded for ROI analysis. An estimate for the fully loaded cost profile of the coaching program for the 12-month period includes the direct and indirect expenses and costs listed in Table 15.6, which totals a monetary value of R$180.000,00.

---

[3] Guiding Principle 7: Estimates of improvements should be adjusted for the potential error of the estimate.

TABLE 15.6   Fully Loaded Costs

Coaching services
HR planning and supporting hours
Sales force team (coachees) hours (sessions + extra tasks)   Management hours (meetings)
ROI impact study
Total: R$180.000,00

ROI Calculation

As soon as the fully loaded costs and the isolated benefits were determined, it was possible to calculate the BCR (benefits/costs ratio) and the ROI.

$$RBC = \frac{\text{Benefits}}{\text{Costs}} = \frac{R\$261.900,00}{R\$180.000,00} = 1,45$$

and

$$ROI = \frac{\text{Benefits} - \text{Costs}}{\text{Costs}} \times 100\% =$$

$$ROI = \frac{R\$261.900,00 - R\$180.000,00}{R\$180.000,00} \times 100\% = 45,5\%$$

Therefore, for each R$1 invested, there was R$1,45 in return, representing an ROI of 45,5 percent. Since there were no previous financial expectations, we can consider the coaching program as a very good investment of BBC's resources, a gain superior to market margins at the time of this study.

COMMUNICATION STRATEGY

The results were compiled in two different presentations: a detailed slide show to be presented to the HR manager and director of BBC and an executive summary to be presented to the sales director.

The HR manager and director of BBC spent two hours with the HR and evaluation teams going through details and data, considering the information available for all five levels. They were pleased with the program results and with the evaluation process. They were very excited, too, and also concerned about communicating the results to the sales director, and they wanted to guarantee that he would be pleased with the evaluation process as well as with the results. The HR director wanted to use the evidence collected to justify having more employees engaged in a new coaching program in 2011.

The HR director decided to present the results to the sales director, and a focused communication strategy was designed. The evaluation team gave the HR director some tips to guarantee a better impact, such as never to unveil the ROI before presenting the other evaluation levels, or the conversation would never leave the ROI figures.

The second presentation was well received; however, the HR director did not prepare the sales director for the evaluation process. They weren't aware that an impact study had been conducted, and this caused some discomfort and extra need of explanation and justification. However, despite all the questioning, the sales director was pleased to see the results of the coaching process. Even better, after a few months, he was the one to sell the idea of a new coaching program to another BBC branch, and this time, he explained the possible results based on the previous case study.

LESSONS LEARNED

As this was the first ROI and impact study conducted by the HR department of BBC, a meeting to discuss lessons learned and points for improvement for future studies was done after all reports were delivered and presented. These were some of the main topics discussed during the meeting:

- The most important steps to guarantee the quality and efficiency of data collection and analysis are planning the evaluation and defining/revising the objectives of the program.
- Specific objectives and detailed goals reduce data collection efforts.
- Well-designed instruments facilitate data consolidation and analysis.
- Preparing the audience and the stakeholders for the impact study is a must.
- Celebrating results and instigating new studies after the first is a good strategy to keep evaluation as an important business tool.

RESOURCES

Phillips, J.J., and P.P. Phillips. (2007). *Show Me the Money: How to Determine ROI in People, Projects, and Programs*. San Francisco, CA: Berrett-Koehler.

Phillips, J.J., and P.P. Phillips. (2010a). *Measuring for Success: What CEOs Really Think About Learning Investments.* Alexandria, VA: ASTD.

Phillips, J.J., and P.P. Phillips. (2010b). *Proving the Value of HR: ROI Case Studies*, Second Edition. Birmingham, AL: ROI Institute.

QUESTIONS FOR DISCUSSION

1. Was this program a good first opportunity to conduct an ROI and impact study? Please explain.

2. What other collection methods could be used to keep track of Level 3 and 4 results?

3. How could this ROI impact study be made more credible or effective for business directors?

4. If a new coaching program is conducted by BBC, should another impact study be conducted? What level should it reach the next time? Please explain.

5. How should the BBC HR department use this case study from now on?

6. What are the next steps to sustain the ROI practice?

ABOUT THE AUTHORS

Valéria Blanco, MSc, is an executive coach, knowledge management and business consultant, CRP (certified ROI practitioner), and director of Sirdar Instituto. She represents the ROI Institute in Brazil, training, disseminating, and conducting ROI and impact studies. Her past 20-year business experience involves organizational and professional development; strategic planning; people, project, and knowledge management; and information technology in private and government organizations around Brazil. She is a member of ICF (International Coach Federation), PMI (Project Management Institute), and SBGC (Brazilian Knowledge Management Society), holding a volunteer position on the board of directors of the ICF Brasilia chapter. She can be reached by email at **vb@sirdar.com.br**.

André Meira, MSc, is a psychologist, knowledge management consultant, CRP—certified ROI practitioner (Phillips ROI Methodology specialist in results planning, evaluation, and measurement), and certified coach (ICF member). He is director of solutions and evaluations at Sirdar Instituto.

André has extensive experience with people management, knowledge management, talent management, psychology, and coaching within private and government organizations. He is an articulator and mediator with experience in conflict resolution and conversation, as well as a lecturer and author of several articles in measurement and evaluation, organizational development, and knowledge management fields. André can be contacted by email at **andre.meira@sirdar.com.br**.

João H. M. Solér is a psychologist, career counselor, T&D specialist, and executive coach. He has more than 30 years of professional experience. The first half of his professional life was dedicated to IT and telecommunication sales force management in major multinational companies. The second half has been dedicated to T&D as CEO of Instituto Mazini, training, orienting, and coaching executives and entrepreneurs. He is an accredited EMPRETEC trainer in SEBRAE and a member of ICF (International Coach Federation), having a position on the board of directors of the ICF Brasilia chapter. Solér can be contacted by email at **mazini@mazini.com.br**.

About the Editors

Patricia Pulliam Phillips, PhD, is an internationally recognized author, consultant, and president and CEO of the ROI Institute, Inc. Phillips provides consulting services to organizations worldwide. She helps organizations build capacity in the ROI Methodology by facilitating the ROI Certification process and teaching the ROI Methodology through workshops and graduate level courses. Phillips has a PhD in International Development and a master's degree in Public and Private Management. She is certified in ROI evaluation and has been awarded the designations of Certified Professional in Learning and Performance and Certified Performance Technologist.

Jack J. Phillips, PhD, is chairman of the ROI Institute and a world-renowned expert on measurement and evaluation. Phillips provides consulting services for Fortune 500 companies and workshops for major conference providers worldwide. Phillips is also the author or editor of more than 75 books and more than 100 articles. His work has been featured in the *Wall Street Journal, Bloomberg Businessweek, Fortune*, and on CNN.

 The Phillips serve as authors and editors for a variety of publications. Their most recent publications include: *Measuring the Success of Coaching* (ASTD, 2012), *10 Steps to Successful Business Alignment* (ASTD, 2012), and *Measuring Leadership Development: Quantify Your Program's Impact and ROI on Organizational Performance* (McGraw-Hill, 2012). Other books recently authored by the Phillips include *The Green Scorecard: Measuring the ROI in Sustainability Initiatives* (Nicholas Brealey, 2011); *Return on Investment in Meetings and Events: Tools and Techniques to Measure the Success of All Types of Meetings and Events* (Elsevier, 2008); *Show Me the Money: How to Determine ROI in People, Projects, and Programs* (Berrett-Koehler, 2007); *The Value of Learning* (Pfeiffer, 2007); *Return on Investment Basics* (ASTD, 2005); and *Proving the Value of HR: How and Why to Measure ROI* (SHRM, 2005), among many others.

About the ROI Institute

The ROI Institute, Inc. is the leading resource on research, training, and networking for practitioners of the Phillips ROI Methodology.

With a combined 50 years experience in measuring and evaluating training, human resources, technology, and quality programs and initiatives, founders and owners Jack J. Phillips, PhD, and Patti P. Phillips, PhD, are the leading experts in return-on-investment (ROI).

The ROI Institute, founded in 1992, is a service-driven organization that strives to assist professionals in improving their programs and processes through the use of the ROI Methodology. Developed by Jack Phillips, this methodology is a critical tool for measuring and evaluating programs in 18 different applications in more than 40 countries.

The ROI Institute offers a variety of consulting services, learning opportunities, and publications. In addition, it conducts internal research activities for the organization, other enterprises, public sector entities, industries, and interest groups. Together with their team, Jack and Patti Phillips serve private and public sector organizations globally.

BUILD CAPABILITY IN THE ROI METHODOLOGY

The ROI Institute offers a variety of workshops to help you build capability in the ROI Methodology. Among the many workshops offered through the ROI Institute are:

- One-day *Bottomline on ROI* Workshop—provides the perfect introduction to all levels of measurement, including the most sophisticated level, ROI. Learn the key principles of the Phillips ROI Methodology and determine whether your organization is ready to implement the process.

- Two-day *ROI Competency Building* Workshop—the standard ROI Workshop on measurement and evaluation, this two-day program involves discussion of the ROI Methodology process, including data collection, isolation methods, data conversion, and more.

ROI CERTIFICATION™

The ROI Institute is the only organization offering certification in the ROI Methodology. Through the ROI Certification process, you can build expertise in implementing ROI evaluation and sustaining the measurement and evaluation process in your organization. Receive personalized coaching while conducting an impact study. When competencies in the ROI Methodology have been demonstrated, certification is awarded. There is not another process that provides access to the same level of expertise as our ROI Certification. To date, over 5,000 individuals have participated in this process.

For more information on these and other workshops, learning opportunities, consulting, and research, please visit us on the web at www.roiinstitute.net, or call us at 205.678.8101.